ARMOR
OF
SUCCESS

A True Story

By Fred Hughes
Veteran radio broadcaster,
newspaper publisher, and
investigative journalist

First Edition -- December 2019

Published by:
Mountain Sleeper, LLC
All rights reserved
Printed in the USA

Copyright © 2019

The publisher welcomes the use of excerpts by reviewers, published authors, bloggers and websites who wish to quote brief passages and credit the book title and author for inclusion in a printed or online book, magazine, newspaper, periodical, internet website or blog, or radio and TV broadcast on cable, internet or public airwaves.

Front and Back Covers designed by:
Chelbie Samuel Designs, Sylva, North Carolina
Chelbie Samuel has that rare ability to see an idea in her head and convert it into a creative design. Aside from book covers, her passion is designing logos and airbrushing. "I like taking a blank canvas and turning it into a masterpiece. Most of the airbrushing I do is on wood of all types." And she does Business Cards, Vinyl Decals and Signs, Postcards, Brochures, T-Shirt Designs and Letterheads.

Photographs by:
Fred Hughes, Polacek Family albums, public domain, JWF Industries

Printed by:
Advanced Print & Finishing, Roswell, Georgia

Library of Congress Control Number: 2019916890
ISBN 978-0-578-59487-3

Web addresses contained in this book may have changed since publication and may no longer be valid.

CONTENTS

For the curious who want to sample the contents with minimal effort, glance over the chapter headings, sub-headings, and bold type in each of the 82 chapters, and walk away with a wealth of wisdom in just a few minutes of your time.

Even the book's BACK COVER is a micro-course on becoming an entrepreneur.

Foreword 9
Introduction 12
Chapter 1. **Hunt For World's Deadliest Terrorist** 16
    Can't find a job? Create one!
Keys to Understanding "Armor of Success" 21
Chapter 2. **The 'Rocky' Mentality** 23
    Are you willing to get your hands dirty?
Dedication 27
Chapter 3. **U.S. Troops Were Being Killed** 29
    Learn to say "I don't know"
Chapter 4. **Mission Was To Save Lives** 34
    You can depend on Yankee ingenuity
Chapter 5. **Fight One, Fight All** 38
    Innovation in manufacturing has no limits
Chapter 6. **All Of A Sudden, Boom** 42
    Expect the unexpected
Chapter 7. **Work Ethic Developed At Early Age** 46
    You have to want it to get it

Chapter 8. **Grandma Eva's Secret Influence** 51
　　Work hard, do the job right, the first time
Chapter 9. **Know What You're Talking About** 56
　　Follow your heart, do the right thing
Chapter 10. **Family's First Entrepreneur: Female** 61
　　Pay your bills, protect your reputation
Chapter 11. **Know What You're Good At** 67
　　It's okay that you don't know everything
Chapter 12. **Keeping Both Feet On The Ground** 72
　　Overcome fear, follow your dream
Chapter 13. **Little House, Battered Doors** 76
　　To succeed, you need a sense of who you are
Chapter 14. **Big John's Cancer Diagnosis** 79
　　Ask questions, talk less, listen more
Chapter 15. **Building Something From Nothing** 83
　　Offer compelling value
Chapter 16. **Please Weld My Broken Ironing Board** ...87
　　Risks come with the territory
Chapter 17. **The Accidental Entrepreneur** 90
　　Be responsible even if you can't spell it
Chapter 18. **How To Be A Father** 95
　　Stick to what you do best
Chapter 19. **Disappointments Will Happen** 101
　　It's your choice to never give up
Chapter 20. **Culture Of 'Can Do' Attitude** 104
　　Leaders, don't subcontract your thinking
Chapter 21. **Lucky I'm Breathing Today** 109
　　Strive for worker safety, zero accidents
Chapter 22. **Uncle Ray, Diamond In The Rough** 113
　　Keep workplace clean, organized
Chapter 23. **Safe Work Practices, Zero Accidents** ..117
　　If something can go wrong, it will
Chapter 24. **Never, Never, Never Give Up** 121
　　Where there's a will, there's a way
Chapter 25. **Job Creation Is A Priority** 126
　　Don't be afraid to try something new

Chapter 26.	**What Really Runs In His Veins?** 129
	Timing, timing, and timing
Chapter 27.	**The Man Was A Hero** 132
	Be humble enough to ask questions
Chapter 28.	**Bill's Decision To Reinvent Himself** 138
	God has a plan for your life
Chapter 29.	**All Leaders Are Readers** 144
	Get over the fear of trying to start a business
Chapter 30.	**Protect Your Mind From Critics** 148
	Get the job done, and get it done right
Chapter 31.	**Union Organizes Against JWF** 152
	Learn art of disagreeing
Chapter 32.	**Kill Them With Kindness** 158
	Zero defects. No exceptions. No excuses.
Chapter 33.	**Seriously, What's In A Name?** 162
	Don't put all your eggs in one basket
Chapter 34.	**Laying Off Workers Is Never Easy** 168
	Leadership is a decision made in bad times
Chapter 35.	**It All Started With A Lie** 172
	Team work, cross-training are critical
Chapter 36.	**Blue Collar Workers, Intelligent People** ...177
	Test for skill, hire for attitude, character
Chapter 37.	**Leaders Can Make Employees Better** 182
	Don't be afraid to take some risks
Chapter 38.	**Sally And John's Christmas Train** 186
	Selfless acts are hallmarks of great leaders
Chapter 39.	**Fired Up But Fair** 191
	Obstacles are teaching situations
Chapter 40.	**An Imagination In Overdrive** 194
	If you don't show up, expect to fail
Chapter 41.	**Risking Everything To Grow A Business** 197
	Do quality work at prices that can't be beat
Chapter 42.	**Can One Man Make A Difference?** 200
	Build your business on a solid foundation
Chapter 43.	**Anyone Know How To Kill Dracula?** ..203
	Have a plan, make people part of solution

Chapter 44. **Embrace True Meaning Of Success** **206**
Strategies may involve fighting the system

Chapter 45. **Humble Polacek Humor Factory** **211**
Being foolishly funny can be good business

Chapter 46. **Giggles What Doctor Ordered** **215**
Workplace laughter increases job satisfaction

Chapter 47. **Take This Job And You Know What** ..**221**
Don't under-value your time and expertise

Chapter 48. **If First Impressions Matter** **227**
Find customers' needs, provide solutions

Chapter 49. **Not A Gold Mine, But A Gold Field** **232**
Recycle abandoned property

Chapter 50. **"I Decided To Sink Or Swim"** **237**
Stop talking and try listening!

Chapter 51. **The Boy Born On Christmas Day** **242**
Quick response a hallmark of service

Chapter 52. **Laying Off A Family, Not A Person** **245**
Use siblings as sounding boards

Chapter 53. **"I'll Never Forgive Myself"** **250**
Employee morale comes down to leadership

Chapter 54. **Steel Mill Closes, Panic Grips Town** **255**
Don't be hobbled by doom-and-gloom

Chapter 55. **Vision, Determination Get It Done** **258**
You're not a loser unless you quit trying

Chapter 56. **I'm Not Going To Keep You Very Long** ...**264**
Always make time for family

Chapter 57. **Who's Next American Entrepreneur?** **269**
Making something out of nothing

Chapter 58. **Exercise Leadership With Civic Pride** ...**273**
Enthusiasm gets people focused

Chapter 59. **The Work Fighters Are Battle Ready** ..**277**
You can't teach character and pride

Chapter 60. **Some Things Cannot Be Changed** **282**
Focus on solutions, not problems

Chapter 61. **Time With Family Is Priority** **286**
To beat the clock, delegate effectively

Chapter 62. **Find Purpose, Passion, Not Perfection** ...290
In midst of bad news, control attitude

Chapter 63. **Expect To Deal With Jealousy** 294
No dissatisfied customer, not a single one

Chapter 64. **That's Not How We Do It Here!** 298
Trust your customers

Chapter 65. **Customers Help Develop New Products** ...304
Give people more than they expect

Chapter 66. **Finding The Right People** 311
Lack of college degree does not prevent success

Chapter 67. **Peers Have Big Say In New Workers** 316
Do nothing, and nothing is going to change

Chapter 68. **Focus On Fixing Problem** 320
Gotta know your customer's first name

Chapter 69. **Dumb Young Kid Got Last Laugh** 326
It's okay to make mistakes

Chapter 70. **Marine Corps Hero Led By Example** ..330
Focusing on others will serve leaders well

Chapter 71. **Promote Culture Of No Excuses** 335
Quality and on-time delivery do matter

Chapter 72. **Are We There Yet?** 339
World is full of people doing average jobs

Chapter 73. **You Must Have Leverage And Options** 343
Find a mentor for wise and trusted counsel

Chapter 74. **Lessons Of Digging Well With A Shovel** ...347
Ideas must create real value for customers

Chapter 75. **We Hire A Family, Not A Person** 351
Will your business survive you?

Chapter 76. **Evaluate Complaints, Create Solutions** 354
Is project well thought out and practical?

Chapter 77. **Hometown Hero** 357
Rooting for the local boy

Chapter 78. **As Entrepreneur, Have Bold Dreams** 359
Don't forget to be grateful

Chapter 79. **That's My Suit, And My Car** **364**
    Never be willing to accept defeat

Chapter 80. **Put Employees In Jobs That Suit Them** **369**
    Show up, always give more than 100 percent

Epilogue 373

Chapter 81. **Leaders Believe In Making Difference** **378**
    Hire the best people, let them do their jobs

Chapter 82. **America's Biggest Natural Disaster** **381**
    Is your dream rooted in reality?

Bonus Chapter 384

FOREWORD

By Richard F. Natonski
Lieutenant General U. S. Marine Corps (Retired)

In 2010 I retired from the United States Marine Corps after 37 years of service. The business world was a bit foreign to me after all my years in uniform. Fortunately, I was invited by Bill Polacek, the chief executive officer for JWF Industries, to be a member of his Advisory Board.

(Note: There's a chapter in this book that sheds light on the name of Bill's business. It's called, "Seriously, What's In A Name?" If you can't wait to see what JWF Industries means, go ahead and flip over to Chapter 33. Otherwise, keep reading.)

Bill proved to be a mentor for me from the start as I transitioned to life in the civilian world. I quickly learned that JWF had been instrumental in armoring vehicles which helped to save the lives of numerous Marines and soldiers in Iraq and Afghanistan but was also involved in a myriad of other projects outside the Defense industry as well.

Having commanded Task Force Tarawa during the invasion of Iraq, we never faced the threat of IEDs (Improvised Explosive Devices).

However, when I returned in 2004 as the Commanding General of the 1st Marine Division, the situation was different regarding IEDs. Marines were resorting to many ad hoc solutions to protect themselves from stationary IEDs and vehicle-borne IEDs driven by suicide bombers.

One of the success stories of Operation Iraqi Freedom was how the Department of Defense and American industry stepped up to the plate and circumvented the acquisition process to expeditiously manufacture armored vehicles and get them in the hands of the War Fighters, which in turn saved lives. JWF was part of this very successful effort.

Armor of Success tells the story of how Bill Polacek took a business founded by his father in a two-car garage and built it into a multi-million dollar company with hundreds of employees and along the way, helped the city of Johnstown, Pennsylvania, survive while so many other cities and towns withered on the vine due to an economic slowdown.

The decline of these cities and towns was the result of business failures which closed their doors leaving behind scores of unemployed, living in depressed areas, and with little hope to find new jobs.

Fred Hughes, a former radio broadcaster, newspaper publisher, and the brother-in-law of Bill Polacek, has had a front row seat to the challenges and tribulations faced by Bill and JWF and the successful company that JWF has grown into today.

In the Marine Corps, accomplishing the mission and taking care of your Marines was always foremost in our minds.

Fred has illustrated the difference that leadership, faith, and doing the right thing can make in the corporate world.

Bill is a personable individual who truly cares for his employees, but he is also a visionary who can lay down goals but is flexible enough to modify them to reflect reality. He is also focused on his customers, identifying their needs and providing a quality product on time and at a fair price.

He believes in diversification within JWF which proved critical during hard economic times when one sector of JWF picked up the slack when business in other sectors of JWF was faltering.

This book should be required reading for all those in leadership positions or who aspire to those positions in the business world.

Fred gives us an insight on how hard work, enthusiasm, perseverance, caring for your people, and working to meet your customers' needs lead to success in the business place. It is a template for those who want to succeed in our challenging economy today.

I personally have benefited from my close observations of Bill and JWF through the years, and *Armor of Success* can help you as well.

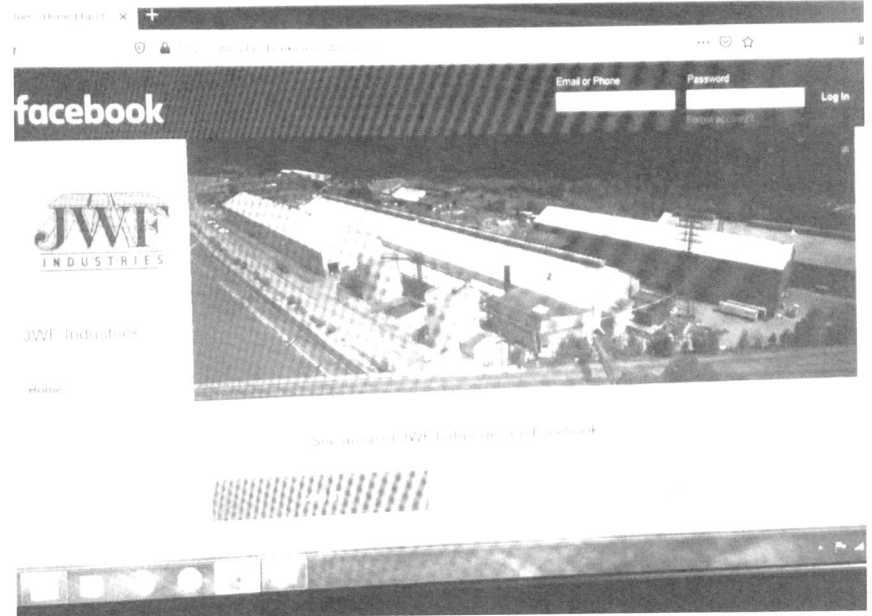

Shot of JWF's Facebook page on computer monitor with huge buildings in foreground and background

INTRODUCTION
*Believe in yourself
and you'll be unstoppable*
Truth is more entertaining than fiction

Do you know what was happening in America on the day you were born?

On the day that William Charles "Bill" Polacek (pronounced pole-ah'-check) took his first breath, on July 29, 1961, Americans were still reveling in NASA's successful launch and safe return the previous May of Alan Shepard, one of the original Mercury Seven astronauts, in a spacecraft he named Freedom 7. Shepard was the first American to travel in space.

Whether as a concept of choice, independence, or self-determination, the word "freedom" would become an important part of Bill's vocabulary and, in fact, his very being.

In mid-1961, "pop" deejays across America were spinning a single that started with the lyrics, "I couldn't sleep at all last night." *Tossin' and Turnin'* by Bobby Lewis was the number one song on Billboard's Hot 100. As a high school disc jockey, I played that vinyl 45-RPM record until the grooves wore out (AM 1230 WMAF, Madison, Florida).

Kitty Wells was number one in the country music world with *Heartbreak U.S.A.*

Bill's mother's labor was almost as dramatic as the opening dialogue of the radio drama "Dragnet."

Even if you never enjoyed the Dragnet experience that hit the airways in 1949 or watched the police drama when it premiered on television a couple of years later, you and nearly every other adult in America have heard the show's opening narration.

"The story you are about to hear is true; only the names have been changed to protect the innocent."

It was novelist, inventor and entrepreneur Mark Twain, of Tom Sawyer and Huckleberry Finn fame, who said, **"Truth is stranger than fiction."** Let this be a warning; truth is often more entertaining, too.

At the ripe young age of 25, Bill took over his father's home-based welding business in the family's detached two-car garage on April 1, 1987.

To date, Bill has created a conglomerate which currently employs approximately 600 workers, utilizes one million square feet of manufacturing space and operates seven subsidiary companies in Johnstown, Pennsylvania, Baltimore, Maryland and a Texas operation with combined sales as high as $125 million.

Combining his early career, plus years as the CEO of JWF Industries and JWF Defense Systems, Bill has amassed over 40 years experience in the metals manufacturing industry. But his journey has not always been a bed of roses.

Like retired Pro Football Hall of Fame quarterback Brett Favre, Bill's parents taught him to do his best, and when he failed, try again and try even harder.

And that's what he did.

This is Bill's true story, complete with the pain of his grassroots rebellion, humble beginnings, sibling rivalries, heartaches, sacrifices and disappointments, business successes and failures, character lessons, public accolades, and civic contributions. For better or worse, the names in this book have NOT been changed to protect the innocent.

By the time Bill charged into his twenties, he had earned a two-year post-secondary certificate in welding technology and began his lifetime on-the-job training that led to numerous seminars and classes on everything from continuous flow production methods all the way to leadership and finance instruction. In 2010, he received an Honorary Doctor of Humane Letters from St. Francis College.

Oh, it's a respectable recognition, that honorary doctorate, but a thousand such doctorates can't use an acetylene torch, weld a steel staircase, make a weekly payroll or teach an employee the absolute necessity for teamwork.

Bill became an early advocate for vocational education which offers many of the technical skills needed in a global workplace. And he has opposed the biases against vocational education, putting collegiate and vocational education on a level playing field.

There's another equally famous business-like catch phrase spoken by Dragnet's Sgt. Joe Friday: "Just the facts, ma'am."

As the facts unfold, the stories may ignite your journey into the world of entrepreneurship; they will definitely cause you to laugh, maybe cry, be happy and sad, and make you a better leader.

Bill's most recent honors and awards include receiving The Chapel of the Four Chaplains "Humanitarian Award" of the Legion of Honor in 2005, the Smart Business "Smart 50" Honoree in 2015, *Pittsburgh Business Times* "Family Business Award" in 2016, and Northeast Manufacturer of the Year 2018 presented by the Oil and Gas Industry.

Honors and awards are not the stuff of compelling true crime stories or compelling how-to and leadership books. For riveting crime, you should read the blow-by-blow account of John Wilkes Booth's escape after shooting Lincoln, and the 12-day chase that brought him to justice. James L. Swanson did a masterful job in his book, *Manhunt.*

Like Lincoln's assassination, real history can mesmerize a reader, and so can true rags-to-riches stories like this one.

Bill's companies were founded on a commitment to family values -- his family, his employees' families, and his community, better known as his family-at-large. Bill's enterprises have partnerships with the U.S. military, Lockheed Martin, GE, BAE, JLG and other major national and international corporations.

Bill is generous to a fault. "This is the most giving person I've ever met," says his wife. "He would give you anything. He would give you the shirt off his back. Extremely generous." But you can't put a value on what Bill is giving in this book.

The Lord's Prayer is 66 words, the Gettysburg Address is 286 words, and there are 1,322 words in the Declaration of Independence. These facts were found in the October 1995 issue of *National Review*. But government regulations on the sale of cabbage total 26,911 words. **Yep, it takes a man with vision leading a dedicated team to face the modern business world.**

In a way, this book *IS* about a manhunt, a hunt by one man to find his way out of a depressing and dying steel city, and then to come back to invent his own job, provide work for hundreds of families, and save the lives of thousands of U.S. servicemen by building innovative protective armor for military vehicles (Humvees).

Bill coined an endearing term for his employees -- The Work Fighters Supporting the War Fighters® -- because of their combined abilities to design and build specialized armor for the U.S. military, and support the men and women who find themselves in peacekeeping roles as well as combat.

The message is so critical to the philosophy of Bill's company that JWF Defense Systems registered the slogan.

This is *NOT* a book that explores in detail all the nuts and bolts of building a business.

It *IS* a book, nearly five years in the making, about an immigrant family, and one man with an almost-magical drive and motivation to help his employees succeed.

If you're genuinely interested, you'll understand how it happened, and you can do it, too, because this passionate story *IS* filled with page after page of encouragement.

Fred Hughes
Christmas 2018

(While the Introduction was written in December 2018, the finished book was not completed until Veterans Day, November 11, 2019)

Can't find a job? Create one!
CHAPTER 1
Hunt For World's Deadliest Terrorist

The idea for this book first surfaced in the back of my mind about five years ago when I heard someone mention a possible connection between Seal Team Six and the 2011 mission to capture Osama bin Laden, the founder and head of the Islamist group Al-Qaeda.

My wife (Bill's oldest sister Barbara) and I were at a family function and someone remarked that the Seals at some point rode in Humvees up-armored by JWF Industries, her brother's company.

Initially, I was stunned. "Wow," I said to myself. "I'm impressed." My mind immediately started spinning. I could not get this idea out of my head. Then the subtle thought became a killer idea, sort of a Eureka moment.

Eureka what? The Greek mathematician named Archimedes is often credited with the expression which is usually associated with a moment of inspiration. Was I having such a moment?

I still wasn't sure.

"Eureka moments are the stuff of legend," says freelance journalist Virginia Hughes (no relation to the author), who writes about neuroscience, genetics, behavior and medicine on an Internet blog (phenomena.nationalgeographic.com).

"According to historians who specialize in the development of inventions and the thought processes of inventors, innovation is often a slow and iterative process."

And wrapping one's brain around a good idea can happen the same way -- slowly and with much repetition. That's how this book began. It was a process, not an instant revelation.

Bill literally had to invent his own job in order to have a livelihood in his hometown.

His decision was definitely a Eureka moment for him. The outcome -- a massive company known as JWF Industries -- is certainly the stuff legends are made of.

Weeks later, the killer idea was still rattling around in my head. The idea played involuntarily over and over again like a silly lyric in a catchy song you can't shake. It was as infectious as the theme songs to Gilligan's Island and the Beverly Hillbillies. Finally, I put some words on paper.

Bin Laden, the mastermind of the four coordinated September 11, 2001, attacks on America, had been on the FBI's Most Wanted Terrorist List for a decade.

Imagine, a school boy from a little borough next to Johnstown, who has eight siblings and immigrant grandparents in his family tree, growing up to develop a hometown factory that builds armor for military vehicles, and some of them played a role in the successful international manhunt for the world's most deadly terrorist!

Well, as it turns out, the Seals on this mission may not have ridden in Humvees up-armored by Bill's company, not even from their command post to an airfield to board helicopters, at least we can't prove that they did.

However, the record speaks for itself; lives of countless U.S. soldiers have been saved by up-armored vehicles painstakingly manufactured to ultra-precise specifications at Bill's plant in Johnstown, Pennsylvania. That we can prove.

We know that soldiers in Iraq employed all sorts of tricks to protect themselves in un-armored Humvees, like laying sand bags on the floor and duct taping old flak jackets to the exterior sides, welding scraps of plate steel at strategic points, and even fastening partially shattered bullet-proof glass over windows, products that were pilfered from junk piles.

Unfortunately, far too many soldiers were either killed or maimed by homemade roadside bombs made with steel pipe or pressure cookers -- better known as IEDs (Improvised

Explosive Devices) -- that tore through early Humvee models, whether they were fitted with sand bags, recycled flak jackets and bullet-proof glass or not.

The injuries were greatly reduced and countless lives were saved with the arrival of up-armored vehicles. This is one role that JWF Industries played in saving lives.

But this life-saving miracle in a tough, gritty but dying steel town almost didn't happen.

In 1976, more than a decade before Bill's journey in manufacturing began, Paul Newman starred as an aging player-coach in the film *Slap Shot*. The movie, which wasn't released until 1977, depicted a minor league hockey team that resorted to violent play to create drama and excitement and fill arena seats in a declining factory town.

You guessed it! The movie was largely filmed in Bill's hometown, which lives and breathes hockey, and there are hundreds of hockey relics around to prove it.

Even overnight visitors who know nothing of the town's history are treated to a large framed movie poster featuring Paul Newman in the lobby of the downtown Holiday Inn.

Bill's hometown attracted other films as well. *All the Right Moves* with Tom Cruise and parts of the Mark Wahlberg movie *Rock Star* found Johnstown a suitable film location, too.

It's a good thing that *Slap*

Shot executives didn't delay filming in 1976, because a severe thunderstorm dropped 11 inches of rain in eight hours on the watershed above Johnstown on the night of July 19, 1977.

The city was flooded by dawn; in the surrounding area, dozens of residents were killed, and tens of thousands were rendered homeless.

Some people say this 1977 flood was the beginning of the end for Johnstown's steel industry. The city was devastated, both physically and economically, prompting a mass exodus of residents. Good jobs began disappearing. By the mid-1980s, good jobs were scarce.

"It's not a town that dies easily," Johnstown police Capt. Chad Miller told ESPN writer Joe McDonald on the movie's 40th anniversary. "It's definitely a fighting town. People here love it and have their heels dug in and won't let the town die."

Miller, who is now captain of police, moved to Johnstown from Pittsburgh. He attributes the town's "fighting mentality" to its love of hockey. The town gets its lumps, he says, and "keeps on going."

Bill's journey can best be put into perspective by examining some headlines in 1987, the year he started his business.

- Ten years after *Slap Shot* was filmed in Johnstown, Paul Newman was back in the news. He played the role of a pool hustler in *The Color of Money* and won an Academy Award for Best Actor.
- Wayne Gretzky won his 7th straight National Hockey League scoring title.
- On the global stage in 1987, Ronald Reagan challenged Soviet General Secretary Mikhail Gorbachev to "tear down" the Berlin Wall.
- The year 1987 brought a sad day for professional baseball and Cal Ripken, Jr. His streak of 8,243 consecutive innings (908 games) was broken.
- And the first contemporary global financial crisis unfolded on October 19, 1987, a day infamously known

as "Black Monday" when the Dow Jones Industrial Average dropped 22.6 percent.

The year 1987 marks the primary event upon which this book is based. On April 1, Bill dug in his heels, signed the papers and bought his dad's business from his mother, and started his own journey to help save Johnstown. And, yes, how he did it is the stuff legends are made of.

Bill desperately tried to find a job in Johnstown; a good job, a dependable job. But no jobs were available for him as someone's employee, so my brother-in-law grabbed hold of an idea and made history. He took his father's welding business located next to the family home and created his own company and his own job.

Although he literally made work for himself, he had higher aspirations. **He didn't want to be a one-man band.** Even though he was a skilled welder, Bill soon realized that he couldn't make a living in the repair business, and he turned his attention to an entirely new pursuit: manufacturing.

From the outset, even while working in a 30- by 30-foot garage, Bill was determined that his company would do its part to keep the town alive and make it thrive.

How exactly did Bill, an accidental entrepreneur, do this?

Well, for one thing, **he had to overcome his fear of failing.** In fact, Bill had to overcome many different fears. Today, he's a successful businessman, an effective leader, and an owner who treats his hundreds of employees like family members.

Not that long ago, in one of the greatest compliments Bill could ever be given, his employees overwhelmingly rejected an outside movement to unionize.

This didn't happen by accident! It was the result of an enviable workplace culture, where employees take pride in their accomplishments and behave like a family because they are treated like family.

If work can be pleasure, this is it.

KEYS TO UNDERSTANDING
ARMOR OF SUCCESS

*Either write something worth reading
or do something worth writing.
-- Benjamin Franklin*

Life Events Shape Our Thinking

"If you can't explain an idea or a concept to a third grader, either you don't understand the idea, or it's not a good idea."

This quote is attributed to former Minnesota Vikings and Baltimore Ravens center Matt Birk, a Super Bowl champion who received the Walter Payton Man of the Year Award in 2011 for his commitment to improving literacy among at-risk youth.

Maybe this TRUE STORY about businessman and community leader Bill Polacek and the Miracle on the Conemaugh River, an hour-plus east of Pittsburgh, Pennsylvania, is a little beyond the comprehension of a nine-year-old.

However, a middle school student with moderate reading skills and a touch of intellectual curiosity should comprehend the basic message because it is not complicated and the storytelling does not use elaborate language.

There's nothing formal, literary or intellectual about the way this story is told. The captivating, personal, serious, and funny reflections are related in informal, everyday, EASY-TO-READ conversation.

Bill is the principal character in this book, but he's NOT the only character. Most of the stories that relate to Bill are NOT in chronological order, but every story has a purpose.

Whoever heard of an author including a chapter about how to understand the other chapters? Even the Dedication is NOT at the beginning where it's supposed to be. Neither is it just a sentence; it's a true story with a real application for daily living. The Epilogue is NOT the last chapter in the book, where it's expected to be, either. But there are reasons for this madness.

Bill was an average student in school, but in the workplace, he became the hardest worker in the room, patterning himself after Thomas Jefferson, Founding Father, principal author of the Declaration of Independence, and third American president.

Said Jefferson: "I'm a greater believer in luck, and I find the harder I work the more I have of it."

This book uses real-life events from Bill and his siblings, parents, and ancestors, as well as the author and his parents and grandparents, to illustrate practical and useful ideas as well as basic business principles that anyone can IMMEDIATELY utilize in starting, growing, or improving their business or leadership skills.

Inspirational and educational quotes and illustrations are pulled from more than a hundred different authors.

The ideas and principles involve faith, character, business and personal ethics, honesty, integrity, hard work, long hours, exhaustion, rejection, doubt and fear, and, yes, success.

There are dozens of them. Each one is exploited to educate and encourage anyone who reads this book to have the faith and determination to apply its examples.

Bill could have failed a hundred times because of ignorance, lack of experience, lack of capital, or dozens of other reasons beyond his control, but he never thought of himself as being a victim. "When you think you're a victim," he says, "you'll become one."

Armor of Success relies on Bill's personal story and family background to demonstrate how to manage people and build a successful business on a foundation of ethics and faith.

In that sense, it's a "how to" book, and can be used by any aspiring entrepreneur, businessman, manager, an employee seeking a better future, or any leader in any field, from private industry to public service.

Are you willing to get your hands dirty?
CHAPTER 2
The 'Rocky' Mentality

Mention Philadelphia and most people typically think of Independence Hall, the Liberty Bell, and the Declaration of Independence. Bill thinks of a blockbuster movie filmed there.

The fifth most populous city in the United States is or was home to many famous people: anthropologist Margaret Mead, American Bandstand leader Dick Clark, pro basketball player Wilt Chamberlain, Civil War general George B. McClellan, sports analyst Mike Golic, founding father Benjamin Franklin, boxer Joe Frazier, political commentator Mark Levin, singers Frankie Avalon, Pearl Bailey and Patti LaBelle, and actors Kevin Bacon, Michael Landon and Will Smith.

In the world of movies, "National Treasure" (Nicholas Cage) and "Trading Places" (Eddie Murphy and Dan Aykroyd) were filmed in Philadelphia.

Ever wonder how many movies have been made throughout the history of film beginning in the 1890s? Including major Hollywood studios, independent films, documentaries, made-for-TV movies, as well as films from countries other than the U.S., some wild estimates are from two to six million.

As I said, these are "wild" estimates. I suspect the real number is much lower, as in hundreds of thousands, not millions.

As for movies made by big Hollywood producers, the realistic number is probably no more than 40,000 over the past 120 years. Allowing for different tastes and objective analysis, the number of "good movies" is likely less than 5,000.

However, there are far fewer movies that are remembered largely for their *inspiration*, and ***inspiration* is a key word in the vocabulary of any entrepreneur, including Bill Polacek.**

"Miracle on 34th Street" in 1947 *inspired* us with the holiday comedy-drama about a department store Santa Claus who claimed to be the real Santa. "To Kill a Mockingbird" in 1962 *inspired* us with warmth and humor while dealing with rape and racial inequality. "Schindler's List" in 1993 *inspired* us as we watched a group of faith-hardened Jews survive the horror of the Holocaust.

Then came the blockbuster film starring Sylvester Stallone, who was an unknown underdog actor/writer with 32 previously-rejected scripts. *Rocky*, albeit fictional, is about another famous Pennsylvania success story.

"I've always said, if you were to do a movie about my life, it would emulate the *Rocky* theme -- the least likely person with raw talent that just needed a shot," says Bill.

Rocky was the phenomenally successful, uplifting, *inspiring,* highest-grossing film of 1976, and the winner of three Oscars, including Best Picture.

It tells the rags-to-riches story of Rocky Balboa, a hard-living, uneducated but kind-hearted working class Italian-American boxer working as a debt collector and enforcer for a loan shark in the slums of Philadelphia.

Ironically, even the movie's theme song, "Gonna Fly," received lofty accolades, topping *Billboard's* charts in 1977. Most aspects of *Rocky,* the movie, can be applied to the life of Bill Polacek.

Rocky Balboa started out as a small-time club fighter, who later got a shot at the world heavyweight championship. The movie is ranked as one of the greatest sports films ever made. After the final bell, the ring announcer called the fight "the greatest exhibition of guts and stamina in the history of the ring."

Like Rocky, **Bill accepted the risk of failure and took the shot.** Companies that he would be competing against ignored him. One man "literally laughed at me," Bill remembers. Another competitor said Bill's new venture "wouldn't go anywhere."

Meanwhile, Bill applied a lot of hard work and intestinal fortitude which his competition "took lightly," he acknowledges.

He was driven to success, and he was willing to get his hands dirty to have it. His mantra was "never quit." Do these things -- work hard and be persistent -- "and you can succeed," he says.

And Bill's success quickly spilled over to his employees. **"The purpose of this company is for the employees to succeed as they are the ones that truly are the reason for celebrating our success."**

Bill even used the *Rocky* theme to inspire his mother, Sally, in his role as her encourager.

He escorted her to the exercise room in the building where she lived and filmed her on his smart phone as she rode the exercise bike. All the while Bill was humming the *Rocky* theme and emailing short video clips to his siblings.

Bill regularly shares his Rocky encouragement speech with high school students. **"If you're going to go into business for yourself, you have to have that 'Rocky' mentality. You're going to get knocked down, no matter how well you've planned. The key is you've got to keep getting up and fighting if you want to be successful."**

But you must be willing to sacrifice!

In 1900 American railroad hero Casey Jones refused to abandon his post in the engineer's seat of a speeding steam engine in order to ensure the safety of his passengers from an inevitable high-speed, nighttime collision in Mississippi.

Casey's locomotive crashed into the rear cars of a freight train that was unexpectedly stopped on the track. The engineer only had a few seconds to react.

Moments before impact, he ordered his fireman to stop shoveling coal and leap to safety as Jones pulled on the whistle cord, locked down the brakes, and attempted to slow the train.

Terrible fatalities were prevented by the engineer's loyalty to duty, proclaimed newspaper headlines. He was the only fatality.

The engineer was immortalized in the song, "The Ballad of Casey Jones," recorded by a variety of artists, including The Grateful Dead, Pete Seeger and Johnny Cash.

In peacetime, Casey Jones made the ultimate sacrifice.

There's hardly a family in America that hasn't grieved the loss of someone in their family tree who paid the ultimate sacrifice in war or while maintaining peace.

In business, there are different levels of sacrifice. When Bill's journey began, he lived paycheck to paycheck, "sometimes not receiving one so I could pay my employees first."

Partly because that commitment established the ethical framework for JWF Industries, today the company employs numerous second generation family members.

And they share in the profits, more than $5,000,000 so far. "They inspire me with their energy and quality-minded and caring gestures." In fact, JWF employees started their own non-profit, JWF Cares, to help the less fortunate.

Rocky is not totally about guts and glory. The movie script nurtured a relationship between Balboa and Adrian, a clerk at the local pet store, played by Talia Shire. Balboa gains the shy Adrian's trust, culminating in a kiss, and eventually marriage.

"And, yes, I have an Adrian," says Bill. "Her name is Shari."

DEDICATION
To the memory of a law enforcement officer fondly known as the

"Sheriff of Florida"

Unless you were a student in my teacher's history classes or a resident of her hometown, you've never heard the name, Opal Argenbright. She was *the* high school teacher who left an indelible imprint on my life. I don't need a chapter or even a page to explain what she accomplished. A single word will do. She *inspired* me.

Most of us have people in our past who were inspirational, so much so that we'd like to roll back the calendar and say thanks.

In 1967 my half-century journey as a radio broadcaster and community newspaper publisher took me to a rural North Florida town to work at the local radio station (AM 1250 WNER, later to become WQHL). I was about to encounter another inspirational person who greatly impacted my life.

One of my tasks was to create an aggressive local news department. This was years before "talk radio" and "all-news-all-the-time" formats became popular. The plan was to maintain the station's music identity but creatively spice it up with intense local news coverage.

I was befriended by a young, soft-spoken sheriff's deputy. A former U.S. Army Military Police officer and a recent graduate of the FBI National Academy, he often invited me to ride with him on patrol at night. I was single and sometimes his wife invited me over for dinner.

Getting the exclusive scoop on a midnight robbery, a murder investigation, arson fire, or a bridge collapse were all benefits of my after-dark exploits while accompanying the officer. But it was the minutes of quiet time between calls from his dispatcher, that paid the greatest dividends. Too bad I didn't know it at the time.

Sometimes blessings will stare us in the face and the moment goes unnoticed, at least until much later, maybe many years.

Even with the background of static, and chatter from other officers on the car radio's police bands, two guys can do a lot of talking about careers, life, love, one's purpose on earth, faith, happiness and success. Our conversation was like peering into a man's soul.

I quickly learned that J. M. "Buddy" Phillips, Jr. was a natural leader who put God and family first, in that order. A year later, as a resident of Live Oak, he was elected sheriff of Suwannee County, Florida.

His illustrious career took him to the Florida Department of Law Enforcement where two different governors tapped him to be an interim sheriff in times of sadness and turmoil. Buddy became the only person in Florida's history to serve as sheriff in seven counties.

After 45-years in law enforcement, Buddy retired as executive director of the Florida Sheriff's Association in 2002. He died in 2008.

While this book largely focuses on leadership qualities, overcoming one's fears, and maintaining faith and ethics in the course of building and operating a business, the principles are also true for private life, public service, and even ministry.

Day in, day out, I watched Buddy demonstrate passion for his work as well as compassion for the people he served.

He never compromised on his priorities. I like to believe that some of his admirable character traits rubbed off on me.

Fred Hughes

Learn to say "I don't know"
CHAPTER 3
U.S. Troops Were Being Killed

Few things in life cause my blood to boil more than paying good money for a product, only to discover it's a piece of junk, or for a service that isn't done right.

You buy a three-horse gas-powered lawnmower, and you expect the engine to start easily and be powerful enough to cut grass. You buy a freezer, and you expect it to keep your food frozen. You buy a pair of shoes, and it's perfectly normal to expect the soles not to fall off the second time you wear them. You buy a hairdryer, and you expect it to dry your hair, not burn it.

Even if a product is covered by a warranty, it's a nuisance to have it replaced when it fails to perform because of poor materials, poor workmanship or poor quality control processes.

Most people with a complaint "never come back to the business where they were wronged," says Tom Borg, a business consultant writing on an Internet blog (entrepreneur.com). "They opt for the easy way out." He's talking about me. I'm notorious for not returning to such businesses. Ever!

JWF Industries solved this irritation for its customers in the beginning when the company's roots were taking hold. **Everything is built right the first time because the quality-control process is also a culture, and the culture does not accept building junk.**

"In our business, quality counts," says Bill. "We achieve and maintain our customers' expectations through a relentless emphasis on reliable and consistent processes that provide consistent results."

Quality requires both diligence and a visionary work ethic.

These are companywide traits that filter down from Bill and his family, and they're as old as the human race.

"God values diligence in His people," writes Margaret Garner of the Worldwide Discipleship Association, as evidenced by the numerous biblical references to diligence.

Garner points to the last chapter of Proverbs where a godly woman is described as one (discipleshipbuilding.org) whose life is characterized by diligence.

Many of the descriptors refer directly to the investment of her time and energies; she selects wool and flax and works with eager hands, gets up while it is still dark, sets about her work vigorously; her arms are strong for her tasks. She watches over the affairs of her household and does not eat the bread of idleness.

In 1942, future entrepreneur and businessman Ross Perot earned his Eagle Scout badge, scouting's highest achievement.

Seven years later he was appointed to the U.S. Naval Academy and helped establish its honor system. He left a sales position at IBM in 1962 to found Electronic Data Systems in Dallas, Texas, and was refused 77 times as he courted large corporations before getting his first contract, and becoming wealthy.

After only 20 years of hard work at Electronic Data Systems, Perot sold the company for $2.4 billion. He clearly possessed a worthy work ethic, in addition to a worthy value system.

Perot possessed something else, too: **insight and awareness**.

"Without self-awareness, you cannot understand your strengths and weakness," says Anthony Tjan, writing in the online Harvard Business review (hbr.org). He's CEO, managing partner and founder of the venture capital firm Cue Ball, and co-author of the book, *Heart, Smarts, Guts, and Luck*.

Tjan makes an astute observation: The marketplace is filled with people and methods that "profess to lead you by the hand to the promised land of business success." Tjan doubles down on the thought to know thyself.

Writing in *Poor Richard's Almanack* in 1750, Benjamin Franklin said: "There are three things extremely hard: steel, a diamond, and to know one's self." In spite of the obstacles, Bill sensed that he was on the right track.

Remember the "giant sucking sound" from the 1992 presidential elections?

It was the phrase that same guy, Ross Perot, used as a presidential candidate to describe jobs heading south to Mexico -- mimicking the negative effects of the North American Free Trade Agreement (NAFTA) that he feared would follow. Time proved him right.

Perot is the source of another profound statement: "Most new jobs won't come from our biggest employers. They will come from our smallest. We've got to do everything we can to make entrepreneurial dreams a reality."

"When you start your own company, you're the salesman, project manager, supply chain, chief financial officer, and you're in charge of Human Resources," says Bill. "So when the company started growing, I recognized that I can't be all things to everyone. I needed a sort of divide and conquer mentality."

JWF was still feeling its way forward about 1989 when Bill hired a part-time employee to work in HR. Within a couple of years, the job became a full-time position, but HR ultimately was going to be a different animal at JWF Industries.

A lot of decisions hinge on the integrity and effectiveness of a company's Human Resources department. These are the guys and gals who deal with employee benefits, recruitment, training and development, industrial relations and performance appraisals, and keep all of this stuff in line with a company's strategic objectives.

Many people understand HR to be exclusively the purveyor of benefits and employment law. Not Bill.

"I wanted HR to be service-oriented, where the customers are the employees. It's a different mindset."

Bill set out to find the best way to empower his workers. "They're my eyes and ears to the rhythm of morale and what's fair to employees." So the focus in HR, from the outset, was on employees.

At JWF Industries, U.S. Marine Corps Retired Colonel John Skelley, a veteran of the Gulf Conflict, was hired as vice president of HR. He said that joining forces with JWF was his "best career move," although he didn't realize the implications of that until December 2004.

That's when former Secretary of Defense Donald Rumsfeld was speaking to a group of soldiers in Iraq, and one of them stood up and point-blank pinned him down: "Sir, why is it that we have to scrounge in landfills to get armor for our vehicles and also scrounge to find compromised ballistic glass so that we can up-armor our own vehicles?"

U.S. troops were being killed in alarming numbers as they rode in Humvees whose armor was no match for the enemy's firepower.

Rumsfeld was known as a straight shooter, especially when answering to the president.

Early in his political career as a U.S. congressman from Illinois, he was a proponent of the Freedom of Information Act, and he had business experience as CEO of several major corporations.

Rumsfeld famously said: **"Learn to say 'I don't know.' If used when appropriate, it will be often."**

But Rumsfeld's response to the soldier's question didn't sit well with the troops who essentially started to boo him out of the room, according to published media reports.

Bill had occasion to repeat Rumsfeld's clever line -- I don't know -- many times, but the admission didn't hinder his progress in growing his business.

When he faced a question or situation and he didn't know the answer, he always found someone who did. This is an incredibly important distinction from the manner in which many business people operate.

Col. Skelley was in the Operation Desert Shield and Desert Storm conflicts. He took 230 local Marines from the western Pennsylvania area over, and brought 230 back. But death and injuries to America's servicemen began to increase.

It wasn't quite the same for Operation Iraqi Freedom because the tactics had changed. "The enemy learned, as they will do, and they knew that if they established a new tactic and came after us in a new way, maybe we'd give up the fight."

"We never did [give up the fight]," Skelley declared, "and that's where you come into the picture," he told employees at JWF Industries in 2012.

"Twelve years after I came back from that war, my son went into the Marine Corps, and 15 years after I came back, he found himself crossing the same Saudi sands that I did."

Unlike Skelley's flimsy Humvee, his son was driving an MRAP (Mine-Resistant, Ambush-Protected vehicle), "and guess where the armor came from?"

It was another Eureka moment. Skelley's son was driving an up-armored Humvee manufactured by his father's employer, JWF Defense Systems in Johnstown, Pennsylvania!

You can depend on Yankee ingenuity
CHAPTER 4
Mission Was To Save Lives

When Col. Skelley arrived in the Middle East, his vehicles had less armor than a bootlegger's souped-up 1940 Ford powered by a flathead V-8 and used to out-run revenue officers and G-men when hauling moonshine in Appalachia.

At least, the customized Coupes had a sheet metal roof, fenders and doors; the canvas-skinned Humvees had nothing to stop a rock, much less a bullet!

"When we crossed the breach into Kuwait, our Humvees had plastic doors and plastic windshields. There was canvas all over those vehicles. Trucks that I took over had canvas all over. Nothing was up-armored. Nothing was prepared for the conflict that came after that."

Years later, when Skelley's son went over with the 3rd Battalion, 3rd Marine Regiment, "everything changed," said the colonel.

Addressing every member of JWF's team, from general welders to laser operators, Col. Skelley declared, "There are a lot of people who are alive today who would not have been as a result of the work that you did!"

The process started with un-armored vehicles being shipped from Humvee, the Detroit-based builder in Michigan, directly to JWF's plant in Johnstown. When JWF's anticipated production schedule shifted by three weeks, the deadline to finish the total conversions didn't change.

But the race to meet the deadline was on.

It was time for JWF's work force to overcome the odds, even in the face of personal sacrifices, and get the job done. This was the catalyst for the descriptive term "work fighters." It characterizes everyone at JWF that had a role in producing up-armored Humvees.

Although the workers were stationed in Pennsylvania and not the Saudi desert, they were all critical to the war effort.

So a finished Humvee arrives at Bill's plant in Johnstown. How do you make a fully-built vehicle safe for American troops and not alter its performance?

"We had to literally take the Humvee apart," explained Bill, "the roof, doors, windshield, the back, even remove the air-conditioning."

The remanufactured up-armored vehicles had to be in port to get to the Middle East. "If we missed that date, that's 30 more days that troops would be in harm's way."

"Not one of us could live with ourselves if we didn't get those Humvees to the port on time," says Bill.

"Thirty days is a long time for troops to wait for protection. And we did it, and lives were saved. **We put all hands on deck. Everybody got involved in helping.** The mission wasn't to build up-armored Humvees. The mission was to save our troops' lives."

"What we're doing with defense work is very personal to me," Col. Skelley told workers. "So that's why it's a great honor for me to stand in front of you. I was here. I watched you manufacture them. I didn't realize that the vehicles that would come from here [Johnstown, PA] would someday be supporting my son."

How did JWF employees get proficient in meeting and exceeding the military's stringent requirements?

The answer is quite simple.

"We were a commercial business long before we were a defense contractor and the work that we did on the commercial side established the work ethic that we all emulate in order to bring our products and services to our customers that just happen to be people in harm's way," said Skelley.

Even the commander of the 1st Marine Division in 2004, then Major General Richard F. Natonski, rode in the canvas-skinned Humvees.

Air Force One was photographed on the tarmac in the Middle East. The Humvee in the foreground was up-armored by JWF's Work Fighters in Johnstown, Pennsylvania.

Natonski retired as a lieutenant general in 2010, but he well remembers those dangerous maneuvers in unprotected vehicles.

"America has a global military force," he says. "No one vehicle is suited for every war zone." In 2004, the insurgency had started and troops, exercising their Yankee ingenuity, were waiting for the arrival of up-armored vehicles.

But it wasn't idle waiting.

Troops were busy doing "hillbilly welding for protection," he remembers. "That's when the insurgency was big time. It's when we needed those up-armored Humvees."

"The work that JWF did literally saved lives," says Natonski, known by many as one of the battle heroes of the Iraqi city of Fallujah, "but then the insurgents started building bigger IEDs. They even used around Baghdad what we called explosively formed projectiles (EFPs), which would literally go through one side of an armored Humvee and out the other side and through any flesh it met in between."

The tit for tat with insurgents wasn't unexpected. "You can armor a vehicle, but the enemy is always going to try and get one up on you," says Lt. Gen. Natonski. "When you armor something, they're going to figure out how to get around it."

As long as armored vehicles have been on the battlefield, soldiers have improvised ways to better protect themselves.

Before JWF Industries emerged with its innovative armor designs, there were basically three levels of protection for soldiers -- homebrew or makeshift, lightweight retro kits, and full armor with heavy steel plate.

The original canvas- and plastic-covered Humvees were up-armored in the field with sandbags and scrap steel plates, often scavenged from transportation containers and discarded vehicles, and even plywood and boards to protect against small arms fire. It was jokingly called "hillbilly armor," "redneck ironclads," and even "farmer armor."

Then the **U.S. Army deployed up-armored kits and the U.S. Marines developed bolt-on protection** for crew compartments, even suspension upgrades.

Fully armored Humvees, outfitted with ballistic glass and steel plate reinforcement around the sides and under the crew compartments, appeared in 2006.

The Mine Resistant Ambush Protected family of vehicles (MRAP), which was designed to provide protection against underbody mines, improvised explosive devices, rocket-propelled grenades and small arms fire, has now been saving lives for more than a dozen years.

And the military's brass are on the record about the effectiveness of up-armored Humvees.

Insurgents had to "increase the size of their explosive devices to have any effect on these more survivable vehicles," explained retired Marine Corps Brig. Gen. Michael Brogan. "No recent program has had the impact that MRAP had on the survivability of the force."

Said Paul Mann, joint MRAP program manager from 2006 to 2010, "Originally, we did not know if we could create the vehicles in the numbers we needed. However, we had permission from Congress to take the risk and at least try."

The reward was great.

Innovation in manufacturing has no limits
CHAPTER 5
Fight One, Fight All

The neighborhood where Bill grew up was quiet on the one hand, and rough and tumble on the other, a typical small community with worthy values and cantankerous kids.

There was a different atmosphere 600 miles to the west in Chicago involving the legendary feud between Prohibition-era gangsters Al Capone and Bugs Moran. Both men operated in the underworld with little fear of retaliation from police.

What both men did fear, was each other. John, Marty, Jim, Bill and Tom operated in much the same way.

The five Polacek brothers made up their "own little gang," Bill says. They weren't gangsters, murderers, thieves, or thugs, and they didn't go looking for trouble. But they didn't run from it, either. They feared no one, not even another sibling.

These boys were taught to stand up for each other. In other words, if anybody came after one of them, the aggressor better be prepared to fight all of them.

Bill doesn't remember what started it, but he spotted his two older brothers against three other guys.

"I'll never forget this one kid was hitting my older brother. I grabbed him by the hair and I yanked as hard as I could. I looked, I literally saw the roots of his hair, him screaming and blood coming down the side of his head."

When it came to preserving their family honor, the Polacek boys stuck together.

"To be prepared for war," said George Washington, the first president of the United States, "is one of the most effective means of preserving peace."

Cherokee citizen and humorist Will Rogers of Oklahoma seemed to agree. Speaking about the world heavyweight boxing champion (1919-1926), Rogers once remarked, "I've never seen anyone insult Jack Dempsey."

Here is Bill's take on lessons learned about peacekeeping: "When we have a disaster or we're in a war, what has always made America successful is, just like my mother said, **you fight one of us, you gotta fight us all."**

That's a message that should resonate among all American manufacturers of military hardware and supplies, and it rings loud and clear at JWF Industries.

The "fight-one-fight-us-all" mentality has sparked many innovations at JWF, no one more important than up-armoring Humvees for U.S. Army Special Forces and U.S. Navy Seals.

"Our troops have the support of every contractor that does anything for the military because we're not just building products, we're protecting our troops and our country. Defense manufacturing is a very different mindset," says Bill.

"If your product is not exceeding the mission, someone's son or daughter, mother or father, brother or sister may not be coming home." Bill says no American Work Fighter -- the men and women who plan, design and build military hardware -- wants to live with that.

There will always be a day of reckoning.

In Iraq, the familiar Humvee suddenly proved extremely vulnerable to roadside bombs; in the first four months of 2006, at least 67 U.S. troops died in Humvees.

The race was on to stop the carnage.

In the war zones, there were "unnecessary casualties," explained U.S. Army Lt. Col. Josh Bowes, 44, a Green Beret who served seven tours, mostly in Afghanistan, beginning with the 10th Mountain Division, and later the 7th Special Forces Group, Eglin AFB, Florida. "An evolution of equipment" was necessary.

Back at JWF Industries and JWF Defense Systems, the innovation evolution was on. New design ideas surfaced.

Decision Time

This view of JWF Industries suggests the size of the building. But notice the steel staircase on the side of the building. It's a critical component in Bill's decision to reinvent himself. You will read more in Chapter 28, Page 138.

"The latest up-armor was ineffective in many ways," Bill explains. "It may have stopped bullets, but it also stopped the vehicle." The weight load of the armor plating led to reduced speeds and shorter-range missions. In a roll-over, guys couldn't get out because the doors weighed 400 pounds."

Military commanders wanted something that was lightweight yet afforded the protection. JWF's workforce delivered.

"We had 90 percent of the protection with 30 percent of the weight. Now they could perform their mission to the fullest; they could go as fast as they want, and they could go off road a lot easier," Bill explained.

"At the end of the day, it gave them more protection because they didn't have to be a sitting duck because of speed and weight limitations."

But even the heavily armored, overweight vehicles still saved lives, as did the lighter and innovative JWF-manufactured armor.

Scott Mallard, an Orlando, Florida native, was stationed with the 1st Marine Division at Camp Fallujah, Iraq. He now lives in the mountains of North Carolina.

Scott and I worship at the same church. My friend stands as the unofficial spokesperson for thousands of American servicemen who returned to their wives, children, and families in the past dozen years because of up-armored Humvees.

Even with the beefed up protection, some of these heroes sustained life-threatening injuries, loss of limbs, loss of hearing, or mental and emotional scars.

But they came home!

They came home because up-armored Humvees saved lives! "I'm a huge fan of that statement," declared Lt. Col. Bowes. "The evolution of that Humvee, I guarantee it has saved hundreds, if not thousands, of lives."

Expect the unexpected
CHAPTER 6
All Of A Sudden, Boom

It was after dark on November 21, 2006, as Scott Mallard's up-armored Humvee approached the infamous Abu Ghraib prison in Iraq where he and four other Marines would turn around and head back down the road they were patrolling.

Mallard, a sergeant in charge of five Humvees and 25 Marines, who was as physically fit as he's ever been in his life, was sitting behind the gun in the vehicle's turret wearing night vision goggles.

As they neared a small village, the Marines spotted a suspicious trash pile on the driver's side of the road, probably a hundred yards away. Was it a hiding place for a roadside bomb?

The Humvee, with its beefed up armor-plating and bulletproof glass, "slowly, slowly crept up on it, got closer, closer, closer until finally we were pretty much side by side." The questionable pile of debris was at the road's shoulder.

"I was looking at it. I had my head out of the turret, which was a stupid move. I was trying to get as close as I possibly could to see if I could see any wires or artillery shells," which were often used to build IEDs (Improvised Explosive Devices).

All of a sudden. Boom.

"I dropped into the turret." As Mallard's 6-foot 230-pound body fell into the bowels of the two-axle, four-wheel vehicle, his face slammed against cold steel, injuring his jaw, shattering a dental bridge in his upper left mouth, and leaving him temporarily deaf.

"I knew what just happened but my brain was rattled and I couldn't think straight." Mallard was sidelined for a week with a severe concussion.

"By God's wonderful grace I was not hit with shrapnel. I didn't get hit by anything but the blast, resulting in a Blast TBI (Traumatic Brain Injury). Nobody else was injured." TBIs were common in Iraq because of concussions.

Mallard completed 221 missions in Humvees and was awarded the Purple Heart.

An investigation revealed that the IED was made from four 155mm artillery shells, but one of them did not detonate. It landed, unexploded, on the Humvee's hood.

There were shrapnel marks all over the side of the vehicle. A front tire was destroyed, but the Humvee handled the explosion.

Mallard's primary job was to control the main supply route, the six-lane highway between Baghdad and Syria, in addition to patrol smaller roads in the area. "Literally, our mission was to bait and kill."

The Marines would drive up and down the highway, all day, all night, "hoping to get attacked by the insurgents so that the convoys don't get attacked when they come through."

Soldiers wore as much extra body armor as they could, and they packed the floorboards with flexible blankets of Kevlar, the registered synthetic fiber that can perform stronger than steel. Battlefield adjustments are as old as war itself.

Mallard and his Marines were always anticipating a roadside explosion or a sudden attack.

They were prepared for their exposure to the enemy.

They planned for it.

But many businesses are not ready for something bad that happens because they haven't prepared.

Waiting for disaster to strike is not the time to begin planning. Planning may not prevent, but can usually lessen, the impact of the unexpected.

There are many lessons businessmen and entrepreneurs can learn from the military. Being prepared for the unexpected is just one of them.

Mallard witnessed the aftermath of other roadside bombs when up-armored Humvees were hit by an IED; one explosion blew off the entire front engine compartment, where there was nothing left, not even the axle or engine block. In front of the firewall, "Everything was gone."

"And everybody in the Humvee walked away."

Mallard's roommate was in an early morning patrol that headed out to a stretch of road that had not been patrolled in forever. "We knew going into this that vehicles were going to get hit with an IED," Mallard said.

As soon as the sun came up, it happened. His roommate's patrol got hit by two IEDs that disabled two of their trucks, so now they were combat ineffective." Mallard was in the QRF (Quick Reaction Force) and headed out to relieve them. "They had a couple of guys that got concussions from those two separate blasts."

It was mid-morning. Mallard was point vehicle. "That's usually the vehicle that gets hit by the IED. The enemy's intention was to hit the point vehicle, that stops the patrol, so now they have targets to shoot at. Usually, the first vehicle is catastrophically destroyed."

Mallard chose to be in the lead vehicle in an attempt to protect most of his men. "My Marines that were in my truck, they knew that. I told them when I decided we were going to be point vehicle."

On this day, it was the middle Humvee that set off a blast aimed at the driver's side door. "It blew the door off the hinges." A piece of this "humongous plate steel hinge" struck the driver and "destroyed his ankle."

The investigation revealed that the blast came from a jug filled with a hundred pounds of homemade explosive (HME). Thanks to their up-armored Humvee, the Marines lived.

Thousands of Humvees were produced for the U.S. military beginning in the mid-1980s. Variations, manufactured by different companies, were used in the invasion of Panama, the Gulf War, Afghanistan and Iraq. The vehicle's design and capabilities evolved with battlefield experience. The U.S. Army owns the bulk of them -- more than 100,000. The U.S. Marine Corps operates more than 24,000.

Mallard, age 43, is a relatively recent newlywed. War-related events continue to haunt him, but his faith is strong and he married a godly woman with an angelic singing voice who helps him deal with his physical disability, anxiety issues and mental health challenges.

Thirteen years later, after his explosive experiences, Mallard suffers with traumatic brain injury "so my memory isn't very good anymore," and he's a bit hard of hearing in his left ear (perforated ear drum from the blast).

He often thinks about the men and women who built his Humvee. Given the opportunity, he would thank each Work Fighter personally. "You should sleep well at night knowing that your hard work saved the lives of countless Marines, Soldiers, Sailors and Airmen."

Mallard actually experienced double jeopardy while in Iraq. "I was blown up twice. That was the enemy's mission, to kill us."

Written on a Humvee that was up-armored at JWF Industries in Johnstown, PA, this message says it all: This truck saved my life as well as five others on April 2, 2008.

You have to want it to get it
CHAPTER 7
Work Ethic Developed At Early Age

The roots of JWF Industries run deep, extending all the way across the Atlantic Ocean.

Martin and Eva Polacek, Bill's grandparents, were wed on April 16, 1907, in St. Martin's Roman Catholic Church, Czechoslovakia.

It wasn't a shotgun wedding like one might have suspected if the fabled Hatfields and McCoys of moonshine and Appalachian Mountains fame were involved, but it was an arranged marriage, nevertheless, and not a bit unusual in early 1900s Europe.

The same year in America, the Chicago Cubs won the World Series, Oklahoma became the 46th state admitted to the Union, and Ford Motor Company produced its first Model R with extra fancy trim, full front fenders and attached running boards.

Martin and Eva eventually celebrated their 50th wedding anniversary as citizens in their adopted country on Easter Sunday 1957. He retired on pension 10 years earlier.

Their story is the foundation of the Polacek family's journey from Europe to Johnstown, Pennsylvania. In many ways, it is the inspiring and challenging story of JWF Industries.

After all, few men could hold a candle to Martin's work ethic, not to mention his grit and determination to do better by his new wife and child. He tossed and turned many sleepless nights for sure before settling on a plan to abandon his European roots.

The decision was finally made. He and Eva would relocate to America, Martin traveling first and Eva coming later with their baby boy, the first of three sons.

It's amazing what men and women can accomplish when they develop a work ethic at an early age.

Take Jim Rohn, for example. Like Martin and Eva, Rohn had a work ethic instilled in him, too.

He was an only child born to an Idaho farm family in 1930. He became an entrepreneur, author and motivational speaker, and helped people all over the world sculpt life strategies that expanded their imagination of *what is possible.*

Martin and Eva Polacek on their 50th wedding anniversary.

Rohn has authored many books including, *The Keys to Success.* "When you know what you want, and want it bad enough, you will find a way to get it," he once said.

It's in this manner that Martin and Eva's story is also the story of their grandson, Bill, who turned a home welding business into a major U.S.-based manufacturing company with clients around the world.

Bill wanted it. Bill found a way to get it!

Like Jim Rohn, Martin was also born into a farm family. He cut hay with a scythe and did mostly hand work. Formal education for boys stopped at third or fourth grade in Europe. Girls were schooled to the fifth or sixth grade. It was an era when people took pride in their vocational skills.

Martin's fancy was to learn blacksmithing, an old craft with a long tradition, but his father couldn't afford to pay for a five-year apprenticeship. So Martin started learning the skill on his own and became quite competent.

He obviously passed a gene or two to his grandson.

Learning by doing has a long history.

Martin was soon serving a mandatory three-year enlistment in the Austrian-Hungarian Army assigned to artillery where he pulled heavy cannons and cared for the animals. "A lot of times I just ate oats with the horses. They took care of the horses better than the men," Martin told his grandson, Joe Polacek (Bill's cousin), years later as he displayed a tattoo.

Joe, who has a memory like an elephant, became the unofficial family historian. The tattoo "looked almost like a Civil War cannon, wooden wheels on it, pulled by horses."

Eva Polacek had a brother who worked in the coal mines in Windber, Pennsylvania, near Johnstown, and he invited Martin to come to America, offering to help him get a job.

Martin was a strong, healthy man when he stepped off a steamer at Ellis Island, the nation's busiest immigrant inspection station, on March 12, 1912. Martin's wife, one of 14 children, remained in the Old Country as he left to seek employment 4,100 miles across the Atlantic.

Ellis Island was the gateway for over 12 million LEGAL IMMIGRANTS. Today, over 100 million Americans -- more than one-third of the U.S. population -- can trace their ancestry to the immigrants who first arrived at Ellis Island.

Eva followed her husband four months later, accompanied by their nine-month-old son, Joseph. She stepped off the ship carrying a big hemp bag which she crafted herself on a loom. She didn't know at the time she'd never return to her homeland.

Standing on a street corner in New York City, Martin was drawn to commotion nearby. He observed a man being referred to as "Boss" pointing his finger at various people in the crowd. "You, you, you, come here." Martin caught the Boss's eye and was directed to show up at a paint factory for the night shift.

"My grandfather left early to see if he could get the job. Didn't want to be late," explained Joe, who heard this story directly from his grandfather's lips.

Martin was unable to find the address. So he headed to Johnstown knowing there was work in the "mines" although he had no mining experience, and no understanding about the dangerous, underground challenges.

Martin, a stout man, noticed a fellow shoveling a large pile of coal at the potential jobsite. "I can do that all day," he muttered under his breath.

Then he was told he'd have to "go down in the hole." Going into the bowels of the earth was not Martin's bag. "I'll spend enough time down there when I'm dead. I am not doing it now. I'll go back to Europe before I go in a hole like that."

He refused the job and walked back to downtown Johnstown where a guard at Cambria Iron (later the Gautier Division of Bethlehem Steel) nodded to the stranger dressed in foreign-looking attire. The guard called him over and spoke German.

"My grandfather spoke German pretty good, and so did the watchman, who did not speak Slovak," Joe says. Martin actually spoke five languages, including Polish, Hungarian, and Slovenian.

"I said to him, 'Pap, how'd you know all these languages?'"

"He said, 'When I was in the military over there, if you had a Hungarian commander, the regiment spoke Hungarian regardless. Same way with Polish, if you had a Polish commander, they had to speak Polish. Not only that, I had to learn all the names of the parts of the harnesses, the buckles, and everything on the horse in those languages. Cause when you went to get something, you had to say what you needed.'"

Although Martin's language skills gave him an immediate leg up in his frantic job search, a lot of immigrant men were searching for jobs, and the competition was stiff.

The guard took Martin over to the watchman's shanty and notified a foreman that an immigrant was at the plant entrance and willing to work. "They took him from right there, and put him right on the job," and began paying him in gold coins. "I said, 'Pap, if you had that gold today it'd be worth more than what you worked for. He was laughing at that.'"

Martin Polacek and his immigrant friends were known as "hunkies," unskilled eastern Europeans who stoked Bethlehem blast furnaces six days a week for 10 cents an hour.

"Hunky" was an ethnic slur that originated in the coal mines of Pennsylvania and West Virginia. Most Americans lumped men like Martin into the category of Slavic immigrants, regardless of their country of origin.

After Martin took work in Johnstown, he received a draft notice from the Czech government in 1912, two years before World War I started in Europe.

Joe Polacek recalls his grandfather's defiant reaction. "He said to me, 'Who the hell is going to support my wife and kids over here, who's going to pay my way over there, and who's going to take them if something happens to me?'

He shrugged his shoulders and said, 'To hell with it.'

So he didn't go back."

Martin had a brother who came to America later and took a job in the same steel plant. But he got homesick and soon returned to Europe. Then World War I started and the brother was never able to return. His fate is not known.

Martin and Eva bought a farm and raised plenty of food, but no one could afford to buy it during the Depression. In spite of their enterprising spirit, they lost the land to bankruptcy.

Originally, Martin planned to stay a couple of years, save up some money, and then go back home. But the war in Europe ended those plans. Martin and Eva never saw their families again.

As the grandson of these Czechoslovakian immigrants and the son of a steelworker, Bill Polacek now owns the very plant where his grandfather, Martin Polacek, and father, John Polacek, worked and helped build America.

Work hard, do the job right, the first time
CHAPTER 8
Grandma Eva's Secret Influence

The work ethic at JWF Industries has grown in fertile ground, starting with Martin Polacek, and his wife, Eva, the family's first entrepreneur **(you'll be amused later when you read about Eva's business skills).**

JWF's work ethic is much like the value system that former presidential candidate and entrepreneur Ross Perot acquired during his time in scouting:

The Boy Scout Oath says in part:
- To do my duty to God and country.
- To help other people at all times.
- To keep myself physically strong, mentally awake and morally straight.

To anyone with even a scant knowledge of how JWF operates, the Boy Scout Oath has JWF Industries written all over it.

Bill's mother grew up in a racially diverse community. However, even with life's ups and downs, she "never saw color." She knew what it was like to be looked down upon, so *she treated everyone as an equal*, and looked for ways to help the less fortunate.

The concept of hard work and doing the job right was embraced by Bill's immigrant grandparents.

It didn't change in the 1940s either, when the massive conscription of men in World War II, including Bill's father, led to a shortage of available male workers and resulted in a demand for labor which could only be met by employing women.

A typical government advertisement asked women: "Can you use an electric mixer? If so, you can learn to operate a drill."

Thousands of women responded to produce munitions, planes and war supplies, and they inspired the cultural icon, Rosie the Riveter. "Rosie" also inspired a social movement.

More importantly, however, women proved that they could do a "man's job" and "could do it well."

Today, women are a key component of JWF's workforce, possibly because of Grandma Eva Polacek's secret influence.

The work ethic in Johnstown can be traced back to the city's founding in 1800 by a Swiss German immigrant.

The English novelist Charles Dickens visited Johnstown in 1842 via the Pennsylvania Main Line Canal, the year before he published *A Christmas Carol*, featuring the old miser Ebenezer Scrooge and the ghost of his former business partner, Jacob Marley.

Iron, coal and steel were already synonymous with Johnstown when John (Big John) Polacek -- Martin's son and Bill's father -- returned from overseas service in World War II and took a job with Johnstown Welding.

Chilling wartime experiences were fresh on his mind.

Big John was on duty below deck in the boiler room of the USS San Francisco when the cruiser was taking on enemy fire.

John stepped on deck and spotted an antiaircraft gun idle because the sailor firing it had been killed. Instinctively, he pointed the gun in the enemy's direction and pulled the trigger.

John learned underwater welding in the United States Navy and spent a lot of his time both below deck and below the water as he repaired holes in the hull, boilers and anything else made of steel.

When he was stationed on a South Pacific island, John befriended a little boy who followed him around like a puppy dog. To Bill, his father's wartime friendship made sense. "He had natural father-instincts back then when he was 19 years old."

It wasn't long before John hired on at the steel plant and continued to work part-time at Johnstown Welding until that company went out of business.

John bought some of their used equipment and started acetylene welding, especially repairing cars and fixing various metal items for chicken farmers on the side (the two-car, concrete block garage, future home of Johnny's Welding, was not built yet).

And he began to weld on smaller projects in his basement. When he needed an electric welder for special projects, he borrowed one. At night, he attended a trade school.

As time passed, he seemed to become more claustrophobic and may have had a little PTSD (post-traumatic stress disorder), both remnants of the war.

John's almost feverish pace to provide for his growing family continued the work ethic that Martin and Eva Polacek fostered.

After all, "There is no excellence without labor," said Liberty Hyde Bailey, American horticulturist and botanist who was instrumental in starting 4-H and rural electrification as a means to help preserve rural civilization. The author of many books, including *The Holy Earth,* he wrote, **"One cannot dream oneself into either usefulness or happiness."**

Frankly, there are different kinds of labor, and all are worthy. In America the terms "blue collar" and "white collar" are occupational classifications that generally distinguish workers who perform manual labor from workers who perform professional jobs. It takes both kinds to build excellence. And you will find both kinds at JWF Industries.

Entrepreneurs come from all walks of life. Grandma Eva Polacek may have been surprised to discover her hidden business talent. I know I was, once I recognized that I had such a thing.

After recording a public service announcement for Boy Scout Week in February 1960, I was shocked to get a phone call from the manager of the local radio station offering me a job. "You have a natural radio voice," he informed me. I was 15. Over the years I utilized my voice in a number of entrepreneurial ways.

Conservative radio talk show host Rush Limbaugh, who has millions of listeners, also began his broadcasting career as a teenage disc jockey. His flair for business followed. A few years later he pioneered his talk show career and labeled his nationally syndicated program as the Excellence in Broadcasting (EIB) network.

His entrepreneurial talents emerged over time as he marketed personalized merchandise, authored several books, including *See, I Told You So,* and a series of Rush Revere action books for kids written with his wife Kathryn Adams Limbaugh.

It's apparent that Limbaugh appreciates the concepts of honesty and integrity. He once said: Character matters; leadership descends from character.

It was Ronald Reagan who said, "Excellence does not begin in Washington." The former president was correct, of course. Excellence begins in businesses and factories all over America, no different than the ones in Johnstown.

My brother-in-law constantly praises his workforce. "These men and women never perform less than excellent," says Bill. He points out that a blue collar heart is a patriotic one, and that is reflected by the attitude of JWF's workers, where men and women on the floor, who actually build things, strive for excellence by exceeding all specifications for every job.

John Joslyn's 1987 expedition to recover images and artifacts from the sunken luxury liner Titanic, a venture that cost over $6 million, eventually led to the creation of the Titanic Museum attractions in Branson, Missouri, and Pigeon Forge, Tennessee, where Titanic artifacts, history and photographs are preserved.

Preserving history is important for many reasons.

Christopher McAfee, posting an Internet blog at FamilySearch (familysearch.org), says a good reason for studying history is that it "promotes nostalgia." Thoughts of the past can be "an antidote to the stresses of today," he says.

My wife was washing dishes when I solicited her help identifying a nostalgic event that brought up pleasant, stress-relieving childhood memories. She immediately referenced two well used bicycles that her father devoted many hours to refurbishing as Christmas gifts for the two eldest girls.

Bingo!

A flood of good memories came rushing back for me, too. I had the same experience. My grandfather gave me my first bicycle in the early 1950s, a hefty junker he had picked up for practically nothing. It had tread-bare "fat" tires, as we used to call them. The only thing new was the bright red paint. But it ran like a top.

My grandfather and my wife's father, Big John, both managed to preserve pieces of Americana. Decades later, mere mention of the bicycles triggered happy memories.

Bill and his brothers and sisters are big on nostalgia. Get them together and there is no shortage of family stories because pieces of Americana are alive and well in their memories.

Martin Polacek walked down a gangplank in New York City a month before more than 1,500 passengers and crew perished on the ill-fated maiden cruise of the Titanic (April 15, 1912).

In a section of the Titanic Museum devoted to the expedition that recovered images and artifacts, John Joslyn poses a question: How do you pay respect to those who gave their lives?

For that matter, how do you pay respect to one's parents and grandparents? Joslyn offers an answer to his question: It's simply by telling their story!

And my answer is the same -- by simply telling their story.

Follow your heart, do the right thing
CHAPTER 9
Know What You're Talking About

When Bill Polacek's parents, John and Sally, began having children in 1948, the number of kids in the average U.S. household was about 3.5. Early on, there was nothing average about their home.

The household was eventually 11 people -- two adults and nine children -- crammed into a space a little larger than a modern-day Tiny House.

Managing such a large family in an equally small space is even more impressive when considering the time frame between the oldest and youngest sibling was less than 15 years.

Sally lost two babies; she had 11 pregnancies.

There was one point when she had three children in diapers -- cloth diapers, mind you, the kind that had to be washed and dried. The three children in diapers were all boys, I might add. There was no indoor clothes dryer; she hung diapers on an outdoor clothes line, regardless of the heat or cold.

Jokes about large families are a dime a dozen, but Sally never adjusted to the humor. She and her only sister, 15 years her junior, often went shopping together.

One day a sales lady in a department store made the mistake of suggesting that Sally should buy a certain hat for her daughter. "That's my sister!" Sally shot back, totally insulted.

And the same thing happened when the oldest girl was in public with the youngest sibling. I mean, how does one weasel out of a compliment about the mother's baby only to discover the 'mother' is the oldest sister?

Even though quarters were cramped, there were no excuses because of the family's size, not any legitimate excuses anyway. John Polacek didn't want anything done half-way. He frequently said, "Don't do it half-ass."

And his wife pushed their children to make the right choices and be the best they could be in everything they did. The children were also allowed to face the consequences of their actions.

Sally was fond of saying, **"Everything in life has its price."**

Listening to John and Sally encourage and correct their children was sort of like listening to legendary coach John Wooden telling his players, "If you're not making mistakes, then you're not doing anything. I'm positive that a doer makes mistakes." This tidbit of wisdom should not go unnoticed by businessmen and entrepreneurs.

As a 12-year-old, I played Youth League baseball one summer and my father was the coach.

Kids learn more about life while participating in sports, arts, band, and other extracurricular activities than we often give them credit for. On the way home after a game I bragged about not making any errors. My father quickly poured cold water on the claim. "You must not have been playing very hard."

My father wasn't ugly. He did not raise his voice. He didn't smirk. He made an observation and uttered an eight-word statement, and he never mentioned it again. But the message stuck with me like glue to this day.

John Wooden won 10 NCAA championships in a 12-year period as head basketball coach at UCLA. He published more than a dozen books on leadership. My brother-in-law relates to Wooden's concept of playing hard, playing smart, and having fun.

Whether a championship coach or a blue-ribbon businessman, **it's okay to fail, to make mistakes**. This was a life principle that was drilled into the nine Polacek children.

Maybe coming from a large family really can instill in children the concepts of preparedness and inspiration.

It did for Barbara Corcoran whose book, *Shark Tales,* earned her a review by *People Magazine* which revealed her "dizzying rise from dyslexic D-student growing up with nine siblings" in New Jersey, to a real estate queen in Manhattan.

The big lesson here is to **know your subject matter**. "Knowing what you're talking about is imperative to your success," says blog manager and planning expert Ben Sailer of CoSchedule (coschedule.com).

As for Corcoran, by her own admission, she flunked the tryouts for her high school cheerleader squad because she didn't bother to learn the cheers. She swore she'd never again be caught unprepared, noting that really smart people over-prepare. Not only does Corcoran know her subject matter, but she's always prepared.

At the online ThinkAdvisor site (thinkadvisor.com), Chelsey Emmelhainz uses a dentist, doctor and lawyer for illustration purposes.

A dentist reviews your chart, she says, before pulling out the picks and drills. "Can you imagine any of these professionals going about their daily routines *without* being prepared?"

Both of Bill's parents had to experience on-the-job training as they learned from the infamous School of Hard Knocks. After all, they were practically kids when they got married, even though John had served honorably in World War II.

Yet, neither John nor Sally pushed career paths on their children. They did challenge them to find something meaningful to do with their lives.

While the parents didn't dictate their children's career choices, John did put an obstacle in the path of Bill's oldest sister, Barbara, who was in high school and already planning her career.

She wanted to be a family practice physician. But her father's friend, a foreman at Bethlehem Steel, told John that he had wasted his money by sending his daughter to college to be a teacher. The co-worker said his daughter graduated, got married and never taught a single day.

John was adamant; he wasn't going to waste his money. To Barbara, he said, "You can be a secretary or a nurse."

Betsy Myers, who had leadership roles in Barack Obama's first presidential campaign and the Clinton administration, speaks about fear and courage in her book, *Take The Lead.* She says fear can turn opportunity into stumbling blocks.

According to Myers, courage is required "to live our convictions, to persevere, to take risks, to tell the truth, to apologize and admit mistakes."

Myers is a proponent of following one's heart and doing the right thing, "even if it isn't popular." That's the greatest act of courage, she notes.

Ironically, Barbara was determined to follow her heart. She became an RN (registered nurse), graduated from anesthesia school as a nurse anesthetist, and lived to hear her father apologize "for not allowing me to go to college and follow my dream." Although her career followed a different path, she never considered herself a victim.

Give John and Sally credit. They always encouraged their children to find their purpose. And all of them did just that, all nine of them.

Myles Munroe, internationally renowned business coach, preacher, and founder of Bahamas Faith Ministries International Fellowship, left his mark on history with a profound statement uttered 11 years before he and his wife, Ruth Ann, died in a tragic plane crash at the height of their ministry in 2014.

"The greatest tragedy in life is not death," Munroe observed. "You weren't born just to live a life and to die, **you were born to accomplish something specifically."**

We should never lose sight of the fact that many people in America still practice what they preach in their personal lives and businesses. They have an abiding faith, genuine concern about their neighbors, and are as honest as the day is long. Their lives and businesses are operated according to the dictates of the Ten Commandments and the Golden Rule.

That's how Bill Polacek operates. He controlled his own destiny. His honesty, faith and concern for others came naturally, thanks to his parents and grandparents. **"I'm setting a tone. I need to look in the mirror first,"** Bill says.

It's easy for me to relate to Bill's business ethics because my parents shared the same values.

My grandfather was a station agent and telegraph operator for the L&N Railroad for nearly half a century, and he helped six children graduate from four-year colleges, borrowing money from the only bank in a town of about 1,200 people, on a handshake and his signature. He repaid every penny on time.

In other words, my grandfather gave his word, and his word was his bond.

I have a friend in New York state whose family LEGALLY IMMIGRATED to America in 1959 after his father obtained a "special means" based on his exceptional artisan skills in Old World cabinetry.

The family stepped off a plane with no coats -- parents, three brothers and a baby sister -- in the dead of winter.

My friend tells a similar story about his father who worked in an impoverished town in southern Italy after World War II. "He was a fine expert cabinet maker who never charged enough money to his compatriots for his superb custom cabinet work and paid all his workers first."

When his father needed to buy a lathe for his shop, he was asked about collateral. "You see my face, this is my collateral as a man of my word."

He, too, paid his debt, on time, in full.

This attitude of responsibility runs deep in Bill's family as well as mine, and it goes back many generations.

Pay your bills, protect your reputation
CHAPTER 10
Family's First Entrepreneur: Female

"The story of steel begins long before bridges, I-beams, and skyscrapers," Jonathan Schifman wrote in *Popular Mechanics* in July 2018. It began in the stars, he said, when a "glistening meteorite" composed of iron and nickel fell from the sky.

Nearly a century ago, British archaeologist Howard Carter discovered a dagger made of iron in King Tut's tomb. The source of the iron is ironic; it was a heavenly body.

When Martin Polacek arrived in Johnstown in 1912, the place was already well-populated by immigrants, and steel was king.

Wolf Leib, aka Louis Glosser, had arrived at Ellis Island in 1903, onboard a German ship with less than $10 in his possession. Like Martin, Louis came from the Old Country. His native home had a dirt floor and thatched roof. Cossacks roamed the streets, and the threat of ethnic massacre was always present.

Louis Glosser and his family set about doing something historic; they built America's first supermarket in downtown Johnstown.

In his book, *Long Live Glosser's,* Robert Jeschonek says by 1927 the store advertised five floors, three modern elevators, 71 departments, 200 employees and a grocery store whose phenomenal success was attributed to the "best prices around, plain and simple."

The founder of Chick-fil-A, one of America's largest fast food chains, was a man of faith. The company's corporate purpose says the business exists to "glorify God by being a faithful steward of all that is entrusted to us."

Glosser's founders were also men of faith.

Jeschonek wrote: Even when struggling financially themselves, Louis and Nathan Glosser provided financial support for victims of pogroms in Russia. (Pogroms is a Russian word designating destruction, looting of property, murder, and rape, perpetrated by one section of the population against another.)

Like most of his neighbors, Martin had some farm animals -- a cow, pigs and chickens. Cows were pastured in back yards. Some neighbors had sheep and goats. There was a lot of pasture around Daisytown (Bill's childhood neighborhood) in the early 1900s.

Although Martin's wife, Eva, was a stay-at-home mom with children, that was no excuse for her not to bring more than hard work to the table. Money was tight, and life could suck if she allowed it.

Eva Polacek's solution was to become the first female entrepreneur in the Polacek family. In fact, she may have been the first entrepreneur in the family, period, male or female.

Eva devised an ingenious three-for-one plan using a single spare bedroom in the family home.

Her boarders all worked at the steel plant, but had different schedules. She had three boarders all sleeping in different eight-hour shifts in one room, on one bed, and Eva changed the bed linens and fed her guests, besides doing all her other housework and taking care of her own growing family.

As the years passed, Eva often utilized the manpower of her 15 grandchildren.

She cooked and baked on a coal stove in the kitchen. Cleaning the soot out when Eva was ready to bake was a task assigned to her grandson, Joe, on Saturdays, who used the wings from a goose as a brush.

The summer temperatures in Johnstown were always in the high 90s, and sometimes made it to three digits: 103 on August 7, 1918, 100 on August 9, 1930, and 104 on September 3, 1953.

"She'd bake bread in the summer and never complain about the stifling heat," Joe remembers.

Grandma Polacek made butter from milk. Some neighbors even milked sheep.

And she made "hobo" coffee, says Joe. "You had your coffee pot filled with water and you'd dump the coffee in there and when they cooked it, they had to wait for it to settle down. She said you pour it easy because it has all the grinds in it. They still make it over in Europe like that."

Almost the entire yard was a garden. No trees took up valuable space, unless they produced fruit. "At one time a yard was for profit, today it's an expense," muses Joe, noting that Grandpap Martin "would have never bought lawn fertilizers."

What grass there was got cut with a push mower. "We were little and it took two of us to push it." Martin followed with a scythe and whacked the dandelion stems and other tall weeds the mower missed.

If a stern face conveys meaning, Martin and Eva were serious about life. But they were not affectionate, not even to each other. Eva once remarked that she had never kissed her husband. Love was demonstrated by providing food and essentials.

The closest thing they might have done for fun was to sip a variety of homemade wines: elderberry, blackberry, grape and peach. Even this didn't always produce a smile.

Once when the insurance man stopped by to pick up a payment, he accepted Martin's offer of a glass of homemade elderberry wine and sipped slowly. Only after he left did Martin discover the wine had turned to vinegar, but his guest was too polite to say anything.

Another time, Martin put his foot down when Eva wanted to install carpet over the wooden floors. He refused to walk on his hard-earned money.

In spite of his quirks, Martin was neighborly and more than a little superstitious, but not in a tragic, bad luck sort of way, not like breaking a mirror, encountering a black cat, or fearing the number 13.

He followed his own set of rules to make sure that life went the way he wanted.

Martin had some odd beliefs.

He avoided leaving a spoon in a cup because he associated that with not sleeping. He never slept with his hand behind his head. He associated that with bad dreams. He was full of old wives' tales.

Martin and Eva went to church all the time. "That's why we have these ethnic churches in Johnstown," Joe says. "Every language had their own church almost -- Hungarians, Polish, Slovaks, Croatians. We had four Slovak churches, so that gives you an idea of how many churches there were at that time."

But the language is all gone today. "I only know one guy that I could speak Slovak to. He's close to 90. One man."

In school, Joe's teacher would tell his mother, "This boy's got to learn how to talk English." In turn, Joe encourages learning more than one language. He tells his grandson that he must "learn the names of tools, and what you're doing, in two languages, because he (Grandpap Martin) never talked English to me, neither did my grandmother."

Even though they were limited in their English skills, Martin and Eva gave priority to paying their bills. Although they didn't operate a store front business, **they protected their good name.** "That ain't like today," says Joe.

Paying debts promptly is a time-honored tradition that helps protect a good reputation, says Beth Laurence, J.D., on the legal website of Nolo (nolo.com). "To survive," she says, "your business will eventually have to pay its debts." Delaying payments raises the risk of losing one's good reputation, and there's nothing gained.

Martin and Eva paid their bills on time and earned every penny they spent or saved. As immigrants, they knew they were not entitled to anything other than an opportunity.

Grandpap Martin told Joe, "If you didn't work, you didn't have money, you didn't eat, you couldn't support your family. How you going to do this? You had to go to work. You got along the best you could. People coming from Europe today, they get a chance to go to school, learn English, learn the language."

In the wintertime, Martin bundled up in an old sheepskin coat for his walk to the mill. He carried a lunch bucket with homemade bread and homemade bacon. "He loved bacon," Joe says.

"If a doctor seen what he'd eat, he'd have a heart attack himself. We used to make it. We'd go to the slaughter house and order 300 pounds of bacon slabs. We went and cured that all out in wooden tubs we had in the basement. Lot of salt went into that. That's a salt brine. That was an old-time cure. You could keep that outside all the time and it wouldn't spoil. Same way with kielbasa. They didn't have refrigeration."

Martin used a portion of his yard to grow tobacco for his personal use. "I used to cut the core out of that and roll that thing up and make a cigar and walk down to school through the woods and we'd smoke that cigar," says Joe.

His grandfather rigged up a machine to shred the tobacco. "He was a genius at that kind of stuff." Then he packed it in cans on humid days so the leaves wouldn't break apart. Martin chewed and smoked a pipe, but not cigarettes.

If he needed a ladder, he'd walk into the woods, cut a tree, bring it home, and make one. Martin once split his arm on a circular saw while cutting firewood and lost feeling in a finger as a result.

Martin got up and went to work every day, always dependable, never complaining. He never owned a bicycle. He walked to work, rain, sleet, snow or shine to earn about 10 cents an hour. He had a reputation as a strongman for using his bare hands to straighten a horse shoe.

Martin never took on side jobs. He worked at the mill and then worked his garden. If he helped somebody, it was for free. Nobody got paid. "As long as you got something to drink, something to eat, that was it," says Joe.

Martin was a horseman in the Old Country and had only one encounter with an automobile. Somebody had one of the few cars in the Daisytown area -- a Model T -- and Martin attempted to drive it to a nearby ball field. Rounding third base, a wheel came off, "and that was the end of that," says Joe. No more cars, ever.

Joe's father, Joe Polacek, Sr., made armor-piercing, .50-caliber machine gun bullets at the Johnstown mill. During the war, the whole plant was utilized for the war effort.

"When I was a kid, my uncles all talked about rolling bullet cores and armor plates," says Joe. "When you'd see the trains going through Johnstown, they were all loaded with artillery, cannons, tanks, Jeeps, trucks, all that kind of thing."

Bill took over his father's business less than four years after this 1983 family photo: (L-R, front) Barbara, Debbie, Sally Ann, Vicki, (second) John, Sally, Big John, (third) Jim, Tom, Bill and Marty.

It's okay that you don't know everything
CHAPTER 11
Know What You're Good At

Most children grow up into adults who don't know how to save, spend or budget. Why?

Far too few parents teach the value of money, perhaps because they were never taught. Furthermore, it's a rare school that teaches children about money, whether budgeting, spending or saving.

In Bill's home, money was a precious commodity. He and his siblings understood that simply by listening and observing their parents.

"A penny saved is a penny earned" is a saying attributed to Benjamin Franklin, although he never said it. The inventor of bifocals, the odometer, the lightning rod, and swimming fins did say, "A penny saved is a penny got."

In an age of instant gratification, few children in modern America are taught that they might have to wait to buy something they want.

Steve Siebold, a self-made millionaire, interviewed over 1,200 wealthy people and compiled his research -- thoughts, habits and philosophies -- into the book, *How Rich People Think*.

When it comes to money, he found that most average Americans teach their children to survive, whereas rich people teach their kids smart money habits, and also teach it's okay to want to be rich, and that **wealth is possible for anyone who thinks big enough.**

Siebold's simple strategy boils down to this: Learn how rich people think, copy them, take action and get rich.

Bill was about eight years old when he heard a customer ask his father how much was owed for welding a broken shovel. "Oh, no, nothing," Big John replied as he turned and walked away. John had a reputation for generosity, and often that included not charging for a small job. The customer, apparently feeling guilty for not paying something, handed Bill a dollar bill. "That works for me," said Bill.

Maybe the incident with the dollar bill was the start of Bill's entrepreneurship. "I don't know," he admits. Either way, Bill's father found out later about the dollar and "took it off of me."

For whatever reason, Bill experienced a time in his childhood when he had a thing about money, and it led to some serious trouble. However, there was an upside to his short-lived bad behavior, just like the upside to the bad behavior of a well-known celebrity.

Some years ago a famous Hollywood actress was caught red-handed stealing over $5,000 worth of designer clothing and accessories from Saks Fifth Avenue.

Now there's no direct comparison between an adult stealing merchandise valued at thousands of dollars and a child stealing $1.75. But there's a valuable life lesson in both stories.

The actress would say later that getting caught was the best thing that ever happened to her because she was already on a downward spiral, and she had a new opportunity to change her life. A similar thing happened to Bill.

Controlling impulses can be hard for young kids, especially when their parents already have well defined rules about lying and stealing. Bill's parents were not about to allow one of their children to have the misguided impression that crime pays.

One day Bill eyed some loose change on his father's dresser. He figured it was fair game; his dad wouldn't miss it. Bill grabbed the coins. He got caught. He was punished. The heist was less than two bucks, not a few thousand, but it was the principle that got him into real hot water with his father, his hero.

Let's face it, every kid has at least one ugly, dumb story to tell.

Bill didn't know the loose coins in the bedroom were for 50/50 tickets his father was selling for the church. He didn't think his dad would even miss it. Boy, was he wrong!

Bill took the change and made a beeline for the neighborhood store a quarter mile away. Before he returned with some penny candy and other specialty sweets, he thought of his siblings. "I'll bring enough home for my brothers to have some, too." His siblings say this was an early signal of his generous spirit.

As he began chewing, Bill thought the "candy" tasted funny, but he ate it anyway. It turns out he had picked up prunes thinking they were big raisins, which he and his brothers loved.

"The good news is I had prunes to share; the bad news is that I couldn't stay out of the bathroom." But the greater punishment was yet to come.

Bill knew he was in trouble when his father spotted him with the paper bag filled with goodies.

With the theft discovered, Big John gave Bill a whipping, had him pack some clothes in a brown paper bag, drove out of town, dropped the youngster off on the roadside, pointed the direction to an alleged reform school -- a scary looking building surrounded by a black wrought-iron fence that resembled something from the 18th Century -- and told him to start walking to his new home.

Run that picture through your mind for a minute!

At first Bill was determined to accept his fate. "I'll show him," he thought as he walked slowly away from the car, accepting the consequences of his "crime." Bill periodically looked back at his father who had seen the glistening tears flowing out of the youngster's big, brown eyes.

Suddenly, Bill turned around and ran back to the car, promising never again to take anything he hadn't earned. Years after Big John's passing, Sally reminisced with her son and related that his father was only a heartbeat away from going after Bill and bringing him home. The child's tears broke Big John's heart.

Bill was fortunate that his parents were determined to teach their children right from wrong, and to make amends immediately, even if the lessons required a dose of tough love.

It was a lesson for Bill that never again needed repeating.

As the late radio broadcaster Paul Harvey would say, now here's the rest of the story. Bill actually had a candy fetish, not so much a money fetish. But he needed the pocket change to appease his sweet tooth.

The bigger lesson for Bill, no matter what, was to earn his way. The incident prompted him to start *earning* money by mowing grass and shoveling snow.

As for the incident when Bill took a dollar from his father's customer, "Why wouldn't you take the money when they're paying you for something you did?" he wondered. And rightfully so; his father was the one that earned it.

Prior to the stealing episode, Bill's primary chore as a child was to empty the garbage, a task he frequently failed to do. He acquired the nickname, Gman (for garbage man). He sauntered around like everything was an effort; his siblings described him as a very mopey child.

"Ironically, my siblings teased me. When I was younger, I was lazy. We called each other out, but none of us accepted being a victim." His mother thought of him as lacking ambition.

Although Gman wasn't intended as a compliment, it may have served a purpose. Bill developed a thing for nicknames.

None of his brothers and sisters dreamed he'd be a successful businessman, although they considered him to be cute, soft-hearted and beyond funny.

Bill may have been born with a rare sense of humor. The latter trait has served him well as a businessman, but it sent his parents and siblings into stitches when he began slapping a nickname on everybody, based on their personality traits.

Remember the fictional Chewbacca character who was the loyal friend and first mate of Han Solo in the *Star Wars* franchise? "My brother Jim was so hairy, he looked like Chewbacca," says Bill.

Maybe that's where the creative names all started. If Bill noticed that one fellow was hairy, and the other one was heavy, he quickly used name association and called them "Chunky Hunkie" and "Hairy Hunkie" (the name he gave his brother Jim).

"I think my sisters would laugh at anything. They have a great sense of humor. It started with that, and just making light of people," says Bill. "Laughter lightens the mood, allows us to be more introspective of ourselves. I'm not a comedian but I seem to have a knack."

"Laughing about our imperfections allows us to have humility and not take things too seriously. It helps us to realize that none of us are perfect. It's okay that you don't know everything. It's okay that you're not perfect."

"Because of growing up in a family like mine, it taught me to be more thoughtful, **to know what I'm good at** and what I'm not," says Bill.

"If I'm not good at something, I really don't want to do it. If I don't want to do it, I'm not going to do it very well. I may do it the best I can, but when you recognize what you're weak at, and you hire people who are strong at it, that creates a great eco-system and balance and growth in your organization."

"A lot of mistakes that some small entrepreneurs make, the reason they don't grow is that they try to control everything. In their minds, if they don't know it, then there's not a solution," Bill says.

Laughter has always been therapeutic for Bill; he can laugh at himself as well as others, and he uses laughter to help identify his assets and liabilities.

Overcome fear, follow your dream
CHAPTER 12
Keeping Both Feet On The Ground

So how did lessons learned from Bill Polacek's siblings, parents and immigrant grandparents help turn an upside down steel town right side up?

Although only two of Bill's siblings are fully involved in JWF Industries in management, the roles they, their parents and remaining siblings played in Bill's support network can't be ignored.

Good people in any profession have the ability to push those around them to greater achievements. And while Bill was climbing the ladder of success, his wife, children, brothers and sisters were also pushing him and helping to keep him grounded.

The author's father, Al Hughes, always had men and women working under him as he managed thousands of acres of timberland, supervised wildfire suppression and pine tree planting crews, and drew a closet full of maps for his employer, International Paper Company.

He was not an entrepreneur, not by any stretch of the imagination, but he was a disciplined detail man and a man of faith.

He was humble, but carried an air of confidence about him. After all, he was a U.S. Navy pilot in World War II whose radio operator and turret gunner put their lives in his hands each time they lifted off the deck of the aircraft carrier USS Yorktown in an 18,000-pound Grumman TBM torpedo bomber.

Bill's father was much more of an entrepreneur than my father, but men put their lives in Big John's hands, too. The American fable about the little Dutch boy who discovered a leak in a dike, and jammed his finger in the hole and prevented his whole country from being flooded, reminds me of Big John.

There were times when Bill's father had to be lowered into the deep blue sea with his heavy underwater welding gear to patch a hole in the USS San Francisco's hull. The 900 men aboard the World War II cruiser were surely grateful for his bravery, selflessness and willingness to act in the defense of their ship and the nation.

The always-present smile worn by the author's father may have betrayed his hard work ethic. The same could be said of Bill's father.

I remember that my dad's positive mind-set was contagious and I like to believe I caught a large dose of it. My father's paper company employees, like his Navy crew members, loved and respected him, not just for his professional competence, but because they knew he genuinely cared about them and their families; he had their backs.

He was a Bill Polacek-like fellow long before Bill Polacek was born. I find a lot of similarities between my father and Bill and Bill's dad.

My father taught me to make **a sincere effort in every undertaking, large or small.** He helped cultivate my tireless work ethic, not so much with words, but by examples, and he believed that **anything worth doing was worth doing well.**

Judge Andrew Napolitano, a Fox News analyst, lost his father in recent years and paid homage to the 92-year-old son of Italian immigrants.

"He taught tough lessons to his boys at home -- lessons about honesty, humility, self-reliance and teamwork. His favorite one-liner was, 'Anything worth doing is worth doing well.'"

In the early 1950s, although my father had no training as an architect, he took his familiarity with drafting instruments and coupled that with months of painstaking research and planning, and then drove 300 miles from south Alabama to Jacksonville, Florida to keep an appointment with the Veterans Administration.

He was seeking approval of his blueprints for a compact 1,150 square foot, 3-BR, 2-bath home.

The plans were approved and the VA official in the Jacksonville office told him it was the only perfect set of plans they'd ever been presented.

Daddy never coddled me for minor accomplishments, but he encouraged me to **have confidence.** I have no doubt that my father headed off to Jacksonville *expecting* full approval of the first set of house plans he'd ever drawn.

I have no doubt that Bill Polacek did the same thing. **He *expected* to be a success.**

Although Daddy took drafting courses in college, he had to do a lot of reading on home construction and materials before creating a perfect set of blueprints. Frankly, I was surprised to learn there's a contrary yet legitimate variation of the thesis which contends that "anything worth doing is worth doing *well*."

In his book, *Before You Quit Your Day Job*, Robert T. Kiyosaki says his father had a different take. Kiyosaki's dad replaced the word well with the word poorly -- anything worth doing is worth doing *poorly*.

In other words, **if a product has merit, making it will only lead to improving it.** This was the thinking of one of America's industrial giants. Henry Ford, founder of the auto company that bears his name, said: "Thank God for my customers. They buy my products before they are perfected."

Whether it's flying a plane on a bombing mission, welding a ship's hull in dark, murky waters, or starting a business, there's the fear factor to consider, and it is likely to be lurking nearby.

Kiyosaki points out the major reason many folks do not become entrepreneurs is that they're afraid of failing, a point made by many successful entrepreneurs.

And there's another reason: Some would-be entrepreneurs will not start their dream unless everything is perfect. "That is why many of them never start."

A few days after the November 2016 presidential election, Frank Tanner, a blogger and investigative journalist, was thinking politically when he asked the question, "Do you believe in miracles?"

He wrote: "Of course Donald Trump is not perfect and he is not going to be a perfect president. But this is about as perfect a moment as you are going to get in American politics. Donald Trump took on the entire American political universe and he won."

It was the same question famously posed 39 years ago by ABC sportscaster Al Michaels when the U.S. hockey team, which was the youngest team in the tournament and in U.S. national team history, came from behind in 1980 in the final seconds and upset heavily favored Cold War rival and defending gold medalist Soviet Union 4-3 at the Winter Olympics in Lake Placid, New York.

The "Miracle on Ice" became one of the most iconic moments in American sports history and sent an entire nation into a patriotic frenzy.

I suspect there are literally thousands of men and women in the Johnstown, Pennsylvania area who are grateful that Bill Polacek followed his dream, overcame his fear, and worked tirelessly for his family *and* his hometown.

As I think of Bill's meteoric rise as an American manufacturer, he had as much to overcome as Donald Trump and the United States hockey team combined. Yet, he continues to be a second set of eyes offering unconditional support to both family, employees and community.

Make no mistake about it; Bill has their back.

To succeed, you need a sense of who you are
CHAPTER 13
Little House, Battered Doors

"The homestead was right here!"

Bill's youngest brother, Tom, executive vice-president of JWF Industries, was pointing to the small home which had experienced modest remodeling and small additions in its lifetime, and the generous yard that surrounded it.

"This spot used to be a chicken coop. This is where we all grew up, all nine of us in this little house. So the job my mother and father had to do raising us and trying to keep us all sane in a little house was quite an undertaking."

The average American home is a little more than 2,300 square feet. Elle Decor, the lifestyle and design group that's part of Hearst Communications, reports that homes in China average just over 500 square feet.

Even though Big John added more space as more children arrived, the structure remained a little house considering that 11 people eventually called it home.

How did the parents and nine children remain sane? To say that remaining sane in an undersized house was "quite an undertaking" may be an understatement.

To save money, John and Sally installed hollow-core doors. By 1964, the doors looked like they'd been in a war zone, full of dents and holes because the girls and boys were always fighting.

Maybe it wasn't fighting in the typical sense. Depending on which sibling you talk to, it was zealous horseplay, or the kids were rambunctious, rowdy, unruly, or boisterous. The end result was the same: the doors could have been authentic props in a war movie.

Some walls served as message boards. For example, one of the girls would write MYOB (Mind Your Own Business) and add the name of a sibling near a light switch. Couldn't miss that!

It's fair to say that John and Sally had zero parenting skills when they got married. It was 1947 and she was 17, he was 22.

"We were very poor when we got married," said Sally. Despite living first with John's parents, and then with Sally's parents, the newlyweds didn't have a pot to pee in. That's when they got the idea to build three little rooms.

No one is absolutely sure how this construction project came about, but there's ample speculation. The thick, all-purpose Sears Roebuck and Company general catalog, known as the Big Book, was a fixture in virtually every home in America. In 1958, for example, the catalog was 440 pages.

Way back in the late 1800s, Sears recognized the potential for mail-order merchandise, and over the years the company published specialty catalogs, too, including the famous Sears Christmas Wish Book.

More than 70,000 mail-order home kits had been sold through the catalog by the American retailer between 1908 and 1940. Maybe the neat pictures and floor plans sparked an idea. However, instead of choosing Sears, John and Sally purchased a shell package from Liberty Homes Co., in Pittsburgh.

Their decision to build was made more than 50 years before small houses started to become fashionable.

Tiny Homes did not become a social revolution until around the year 2000 when more people were trying to escape the maintenance and debt associated with a typical American home of 1,800-2,300 square feet or more.

By comparison, the average size of an American prison cell is 50-80 square feet, and a typical Tiny Home on wheels averages 65-140 square feet. Modern-day Tiny Apartments are even available in some cities with 300-400 square feet.

A home that measured less than 400 square feet is how the newlyweds started out.

John and Sally's home package was delivered on May 2, 1949, and included materials for a 384-square foot, four-room plan -- living room, bedroom, kitchen and bath -- for $1,495. They paid $40 extra for a picture window.

They got extra space for a washing machine, storage and small workshop area for John by digging a basement by hand. Of course, the newlyweds needed materials for cabinets and flooring. But John was resourceful.

John welded more boilers than he could count, but the only train locomotive boiler that John worked on during his entire welding career was the steam engine used in the lumber yard at Boswell Lumber Company, and that job became critical to finishing their new house.

The locomotive boiler refurbishing project allowed John to repurpose the waste cut-offs of milled, tongue and grooved oak flooring from Boswell. He carried an arm load of pieces home after work every day in his car and stored them in the garage at his father's house.

Those little scraps of wood formed an attractive and durable mosaic as he meticulously pieced them together to cover the living room's rough sub-floor.

The unique floor became a visible and lasting testimony to John's creativity, craftsmanship and devotion to his family.

Artist sketch of 16- by 24-foot house kit. Standard living room window was upgraded to a picture window.

Ask questions, talk less, listen more
CHAPTER 14
Big John's Cancer Diagnosis

The story of Bill Polacek and his siblings is one of great respect and admiration for their parents. It probably wasn't apparent when the kids were young, but they were watching and listening. All kids are watching their parents! Actions and words are making impressions!

"Do not underestimate that toddler in the house. He or she is extremely sharp, intelligent and observant," according to an Internet article compiled by Rahul Chandawarkar and posted on the news site DNA (dnaindia.com).

The story is told about a three-year-old who was asked, "What does your father do?" The young girl replied, "He watches television!"

In spite of the turmoil in their small home, John and Sally could be funny as well as serious. **And the children learned to smile. They also learned to refrain from talking about themselves all the time, and to listen to others.**

These just happen to be important pillars of a successful businessman. Like most youngsters, Bill had to mature some before he embraced these concepts. But **he quickly learned to pay undivided attention to everyone he met**.

This takes effort because we live in a world of distractions. In fact, there's even a name for this common childhood malady: ADHD (Attention Deficit Hyperactivity Disorder).

Most adults and children have heard about the Golden Rule: Do unto others as you would have them do unto you. In an adaptation, journalist and educator Frank Sesno advocates asking more questions and speaking less.

In his book, *Ask More*, Sesno says the golden rule in listening "is to listen to others as you would want others to listen to you."

As the Polacek children came along over the span of 15 years, all nine of them developed a strong faith and learned family values as exhibited by their parents.

They saw their father's humility as he kneeled to pray in his bedroom, and he taught the children to pray, kneeling by their beds each night.

Sally Ann, the youngest daughter, once saw her father hand a dollar to a stranger. They were at the iconic Coney Island, a downtown hotdog joint frequented by men from the steel mill after their shifts.

"We didn't have it," she remembers. But the message was clear, and no words of explanation were needed. The kids saw John sacrifice daily. Actions do speak louder than words.

At 6-1 and 270 pounds, John was a big eater, but around the dining table, he made sure his children were fed first. Bill remembers his mother serving pork chops. His father "would literally go around the table and individually ask each one of us if we wanted the last pork chop. He made sure that we were first."

Barbara was the first child to be cared for in the little Daisytown house. "We had Barbara, our oldest, and when I moved in I thought I died and went to heaven," remembered Sally.

"We had no lights, water, heat. Nothing." No indoor plumbing means no indoor bathroom! But an outhouse was nearby in the backyard.

"My husband would go out and weld for people and of course it was dirty in the car and I'd take Barbara over to my mother's and *bath* her (British usage) and bring her home. Well, by the time she got home she was dirty again because the car was always dirty."

"Then we had Debbie. Well it was tough with three little rooms. I remember when we brought Debbie home from the hospital, we had a potbelly stove in the middle of the living room, but I still thought I died and went to heaven because it was ours."

"I'd put Debbie in bed with us, a snowsuit on and a big blanket, didn't sleep very soundly because I didn't want anything to happen to her. I didn't want her to suffocate. As time went on, we had Vicki and Sally. I had the four girls first."

"The doctor told me I'd probably never have a boy because I lost two children in between. He said I'd probably lose every boy I went to carry."

"Well, the fifth baby was due on January 1. I went over my [expected due] dates with the second, third and fourth babies [to compare], and I thought I'd probably go over my date with this one. But I didn't," said Sally.

"He was due January 1. I prayed and prayed for a boy. I asked God, I didn't care if he gave me 12 girls, just give me one boy to carry on my husband's name, and he sent me that boy right after midnight on Christmas Day. So that was the answer to my prayers."

The "boy" carries his father's name, John, born December 25, 1956. Young John was special in many ways. In the U.S., about 170,000 babies have the unique distinction of being born on Christmas Day.

Many parents don't relish the idea of balancing a birthday party and Christmas gifts on the same day and purposely try to avoid a Christmas Day delivery date.

Nor has it been easy for these Christmas Day children, especially in their formative years.

John's attitude about his unique birthday is very sensible. "It's symbolic when you think about it. I just popped out on Christmas!" And he correlates the event to faith and God's delivering gifts.

"Then I had Martin, Jim, Bill and Tom. And that made our family complete. Then I had to have surgery." Having a hysterectomy was a medical necessity, but that didn't prevent Sally from agonizing over the decision, and even seeking some solace from her priest.

She could no longer have children after the procedure, but she loved children and wanted to have more babies. "I couldn't even go to see any of my friends in the hospital when they had a baby because I was so jealous. I wanted my babies, but God had other plans for me."

Partly out of necessity and partly to keep her mind occupied, Sally turned to higher education. "I went to school to be a practical nurse when I was 39, then I went to be a registered nurse when I was 47, then I went to be a teacher when I was 51."

Sally added, "I knew the children had to be educated and they couldn't be educated on what John made in Bethlehem Steel because they were always going out on strike and we had trouble just feeding the children, but God always took care of us."

The Bethlehem strikes took a toll on Sally. She wanted John to find more reliable work.

"When things were going well, Tom (the youngest child) was a senior in college, and John was diagnosed with mesothelioma (lung cancer). He didn't smoke but from being in the Navy and with welding rods and all the things that welders put up with, and from working at Bethlehem Steel, he was exposed to a lot."

Steam pipes were insulated with asbestos. Bill recalls his father saying the surface was not sealed, and light would hit the loose particles in the air, and it appeared to be snowing.

"I couldn't believe when the doctor told me he couldn't do anything for John," Sally said. "I couldn't believe that the love of my life was going to go. I knew I had to be brave for his sake and for the children."

John died February 14, 1987.

When Bill took over the business after his father's passing, Sally pushed him, too, to "move beyond" where he was, and to better himself.

Offer compelling value
CHAPTER 15
Building Something From Nothing

Bill's mother was 82 in June 2012, when she recounted the family's history at the 25th anniversary of JWF Industries at "the place where it all started," the original Johnny's Welding shop (two-car garage).

A sign painted on the front concrete block wall identifies the landmark, which is owned by one of Sally's daughters and is still used as a family garage. Sally shared a straight-from-the-heart story about love, family, triumphs and personal sacrifices.

"I was going to write something up that I wanted to say, but I thought, ahhhh heck, I don't like to do that. I'm going to tell you the real story about JWF. I hope it doesn't make anybody mad, but I gotta tell it like it is."

Ask anyone that knew her. That was vintage Sally talking! She always seemed comfortable in her roles, whether as matriarch of the Polacek family or as a stand-up comic.

Sally grew into her roles; she wasn't always a comic and practical jokester, unlike actor and comedian Walter Matthau.

He joked that his best review came in a play early in his career where he posed as a derelict. The other characters just looked like actors in make-up, a reviewer wrote, but Matthau "really looks like a skid row bum."

The characterization was a badge of honor for Matthau, the son of immigrants; his mother was a Lithuanian Jew and his father was a Russian Jewish peddler and electrician. He served in World War II as a radioman-gunner on a Consolidated B-24 Liberator.

Being an immigrant or direct descendant of immigrants and serving the United States in wartime is a common thread in many American success stories, even for Matthau, who was best known for his role as Oscar Madison in *The Odd Couple.*

"Every actor looks all his life for a part that will combine his talents with his personality," Matthau once said. "*The Odd Couple* was mine. That was the plutonium I needed. It all started happening after that."

Sadly, it wasn't until after Big John's passing that Bill found his plutonium.

A lot has been said about the history of Johnny's Welding, which dates back to 1957, and Big John's two-car garage. So what is there about garages?

There may not be a more important story to tell than a blog written by Michael Dunlop and posted on the Internet (retreat21.com). It's the heart of inspiration for anyone wanting to start their own business when they have limited space. It's why the history of Johnny's Welding and Big John's two-car garage is so significant!

Dunlop briefly outlines the roots of 10 world-famous companies that started in garages beginning with Amazon. The company's founder, Jeff Bezos, started operations in his family's garage in Seattle, and soon expanded into a nearby 2-bedroom house.

In their book, *Bold,* authors Peter Diamandis and Steven Kotler asserted that Bezos was determined to offer customers "compelling value."

Seven years *before* Amazon was founded, Bill concluded that offering "compelling value" must be part of his business plan. He recognized that he was the new kid on the block.

What could Bill offer a customer that would make him their first choice, or move the customer from a competitor?

Offering a "compelling value" meant having some specific answers to that question. John Locke, the chairman and president of the John Locke Foundation, wrote about getting more than you pay for. Although his comments were directed at the quality of public services, government, and politics, they also apply to private businesses.

"We all know that hiring 15 people to fix a pothole will not necessarily get it done 50 percent faster than hiring 10 for the job," said Locke.

There are plenty of forward-thinking companies that embrace efficiency, innovation and economies of scale, that could send a two-man crew to patch the pothole faster, permanently, and cheaper than any 15-man crew simply because the employees have pride, a work ethic, high-tech equipment at their disposal, and teamwork training.

Early on, Bill embraced new technologies, innovative management practices and other ways to boost the productivity of his new business. He also embraced the concepts of honesty and avoiding being trapped in a kickback scheme. "I'd close the door before I do that."

DeVon Franklin worked two decades in the extreme secular environment of Hollywood. **"You have to serve before you lead,"** he asserted on Fox & Friends in September 2017 as he was promoting his new book, *The Hollywood Commandments*. **"Make yourself an asset for whoever you work for and you'll never be without work."**

Franklin moonlights as a traveling preacher and inspirational speaker and contends that secular and spiritual success are not opposites.

Bill built his business on faith, and his customers became the beneficiaries of his honest dealings and work ethic.

Sam Ewing, the All-American from the University of Tennessee, who played pro ball for the Chicago White Sox and Toronto Blue Jays, hit home runs with some of his much-publicized quotes. "Hard work spotlights the character of people: some turn up their sleeves, some turn up their noses, and some don't turn up at all.

Thirty years later, Bill shows up and rolls up his sleeves. Customers, employees and his hometown continue to be the beneficiaries.

As Michael Dunlop continued his outline of businesses that started in garages, he listed Apple, Disney, Google, Harley Davidson, Hewlett-Packard, Lotus Cars, Maglite, Mattel, and Yankee Candle Company.

Technically, Harley Davidson, arguably the most recognized name in motorcycles, was started in a 10- by 15-foot wooden shed in Milwaukee in 1901 because William S. Harley, who drew the plans to create a small engine to power a bicycle, and his friend, Arthur Davidson, didn't own a car and had no garage.

Dunlop asks the question, What's the point?

The answer he provides is simple and yet profound: **Everything starts with nothing.**

Every business has humble beginnings. It may be a garage, a bedroom, a basement, or a dilapidated building on the wrong side of the tracks. A business idea may also blossom while someone is working in a high-tech laboratory for a Fortune 500 company. But that's still only an idea, and it still requires starting from nothing.

In every circumstance, there has to be an inspiration.

We've all heard the English proverb, "Necessity is the mother of invention," and need is the primary driving force for most new inventions. Not so fast, says Jared Diamond, writing in the *New York Times Magazine*, who contends the opposite.

Diamond is a prolific writer and researcher whose works include the book, *The World Until Yesterday: What Can We Learn From Traditional Societies?*

He cites penicillin and X-rays as modern wonders accidentally discovered -- "by tinkerers driven by curiosity."

JWF's birthplace.

Risks come with the territory
CHAPTER 16
Please Weld My Broken Ironing Board

Although he was extremely good at fixing things, John Polacek did not venture into the world of basic research and inventions. We see this in his wife's humor.

A couple of years before she died, Sally's wit got the best of her and she insisted on publicly setting the record straight.

Speaking of her husband's business, Johnny's Welding, **"It didn't start in that garage, it started in our basement!** We had the dirt floors and plasterboard walls. That's where John welded for people before he started a business."

Ventilation was poor in the basement. Head room up to the floor joists was less than the standard eight feet, and some weird smells drifted up to the main floor of the house above -- heat and fumes from burning arcs, dust, even the smell of burning hair occasionally. All were annoying.

John welded "any and everything" for other people, lamented Sally, and it was getting on her nerves. "I couldn't get him to weld an ironing board for me."

So she resorted to deception. "I took the cover off my ironing board and I put it where he could see it. I said, 'You know what, somebody brought this ironing board for you to fix.' He fixed it immediately!"

The Internet had not been invented when Sally sought incentives to get John to tackle the basic and needed repairs around their home, and there were many. But he put off and put off. Who knows why? For some men, it's the fear that they can't do it, and they're afraid to ask for help.

But that doesn't fully explain why the building contractor who's really good at making repairs fails to do so in his own castle.

One thing is for sure: "Life rewards action," says author and life coach Margie Warrell, in her book, *Stop Playing Safe*. "Nothing great is accomplished without it."

In Sally's eyes, John tried in every way to be a good provider and she gave him credit for his effort.

"He was a good man," she declared. "He was a hard worker, but he just didn't want to deal with all the confusion nine children can make. I remember the boys would fight and I'd cry and I'd say, 'John, they hate each other, they're supposed to love each other. We're teaching them to love each other.'"

John would console his wife, "Don't you understand, this is how brothers do."

Not only did the Internet not exist, but neither did Google. Today, if you Google the phrase, "How to motivate a husband to finish his DIY projects," you'll get thousands of responses, some dramatic, others thought-provoking, and many of them hilarious.

"My husband has Renovation ADD (Attention Deficit Disorder)," says one housewife. "He works really well with deadlines, but if he thinks he has an infinite amount of time, that's how long it takes to finish. That seems to be the common ground amongst all the DIY men I know."

"It's an all too familiar syndrome," says a second housewife. A third housewife decries, "My husband is an engineer (chemical), and like all engineers thinks he can do anything, and like most engineers I know, overcomplicates the job, then screws it up, leaving me to fix it."

To resolve the DIY stalemate, some housewives say they resort to withholding intimacy until the project is finished. Others stop cooking his meals. Or stop doing his laundry.

The ironing board repair was a fairly easy fix. However, it was a little more difficult for Sally to get her clothes posts built and installed in the back yard. She couldn't figure out a way to trick John into action.

Sally knew there was more than one way to shear a sheep because Mark Twain said so in *A Connecticut Yankee in King Arthur's Court* in 1889. Sally would find a way.

She introduced a novel approach to the problem; Sally sought a higher power! When her priest wanted John to build some metal railing for him in his basement, Sally finally put her foot down. Again, this was vintage Sally.

"No, Father, he doesn't get that done until I get my clothes posts to hang my clothes out." The priest had words with John. "That's how I got my clothes posts."

Sally often pushed her husband to better himself and leave Bethlehem Steel, but he resisted. Deep down in her heart, she understood his reluctance.

"We had nine children. He just couldn't go out on a limb and try to start something new."

Although she pushed John, her husband lacked a degree of self-confidence, but no one ever accused him of being lazy. Throughout their marriage, Sally saw in John a hardworking man and she reinforced her admiration frequently.

On the other hand, Sally grew to appreciate Bill's willingness to take risks. And Bill listed a few of them as he addressed his employees on JWF's 30th anniversary.

"There were many areas of risks," Bill said, including financial risks and people he hired.

"When I started this business, I worried about my family. Then, as it grew, I worried about your families. And then it grew bigger and I worried about the community."

The risk of a layoff was always present with Bethlehem Steel. "My father worked in the mill and I knew what that meant if he lost his job." And Bill cited the risks his grandparents took coming to this country, "giving up everything, traveling across an ocean."

Perhaps, the biggest risk of all was Bill's age. He was 25 when the official JWF journey started.

Be responsible even if you can't spell it
CHAPTER 17
The Accidental Entrepreneur

John and Sally Polacek's first two children were born in 1948 and 1949 as post-war parents were becoming more affluent and having children in unprecedented numbers. Seven children were born during the 1950s and early 1960s when cultural norms in America were being challenged, especially the role of women in the workplace.

During one period, Sally had three children in cloth diapers and the oldest children -- all girls and kids themselves -- were caring for kids.

Sally carried a lot of guilt because she had no choice but to ask the older girls to do so much to take care of the boys, all younger. Barbara, Debbie, Vicki and Sally Ann learned about responsibility before they could use the word in a sentence, much less spell it.

George Guilder, writing in the September 1986 issue of *The Atlantic*, noted that more than one-third of American families were engaged in agriculture 80 years ago. Today, the number of farm families has dropped to fewer than three percent. He says labor provided by women on farms, "in an array of arduous jobs beyond the hearth and crib," was "never monitored by statisticians."

Sally wasn't raised on a farm but the real point of Guilder's story is that "women have always worked," and they did more than cooking and raising children.

Anyone with some age on them remembers the outside-the-home disasters that Lucille Ball portrayed on her television show, *I Love Lucy*, which indicated "her discontent with remaining at home," suggested an article written by Dr. Michelle Getchell published on the website of the non-profit Kahn Academy (kahnacademy.org).

"Lucille Ball, while playing the role of a hapless housewife on TV," said Dr. Getchell, "was in reality a highly successful actress and producer, and thus challenged society's expectations of women."

John and Sally's daughters each became successful in their own right.

It was only natural that the Polacek girls could handle the responsibility of helping to raise their brothers; it was in their genes. Grandma Eva Polacek spoke frequently about the Old Country where she was one of 14 children working in the fields. Once, no one knew Eva was pregnant until a midwife walked in carrying the newborn baby. Talk about tough!

Big John developed a dependency on his wife; he had faith in Sally's ability to do the arduous household tasks of tending to children, cooking, washing, ironing, cleaning and, all the while, supporting his side business.

And Bill seems to have acquired the lion's share of his mother's ability to balance all the different demands of maintaining a home, raising a family, and working a job, all at the same time.

Between his day job in the steel mill and welding when not working at Bethlehem Steel, Big John didn't have a spare minute, much less a spare dime. He vacationed with his wife and children one week a year; the rest of his vacation time was spent working.

Running the business side of the venture known as Johnny's Welding fell to Sally, who served as secretary, treasurer, comptroller, bill payer or "whatever you want to call it," but she wasn't a paid employee. It was a role she accepted out of a sense of duty, responsibility and necessity.

After learning that he was terminally ill, John set the course for the future of his home-brew welding business. **He trusted his inner wisdom. He listened to the message from his heart.** Big John was as sincere about his scheme as the day is long.

I was flying to Boston on jetBlue when a video series (Women on the Fly) appeared on the monitor that was mounted on the rear of the seat in front of me. Anne Fulenwider, editor-in-chief of *Marie Claire*, an international monthly women's magazine, was offering some career tips. "Trust your gut." The times she failed to trust her gut, she regretted it, she added.

Bill had already expressed appreciation when his father taught him to weld. John said to Sally, "If anything happens to me, I want Bill to have the business for half of what it's worth because he's the only one interested in it."

When Sally first learned that John had cancer, she visited a friend, a "very religious person," who had recently lost a daughter. "Helen, I don't know how I'm going to get through this. Can you please help me?" The two women went for a walk. Sally's friend said, "This is the day the Lord hath made, let us rejoice and be glad in it."

Years later when she was in her 80s, Sally told her children she always remembered that special stroll with her friend. She repeated the comforting verse every day, "always thinking about the good things that happened and not the bad."

"It was tough," Sally admitted, "but I didn't want to dwell on the bad because we brought the children up to know that everything in life has a purpose. I always said, **everything in life has a price.**"

Although Bill had worked alongside his father during the summer months and learned many skills, he recognized that the repair business simply wasn't growing. Bill was literally coming of age in the age of throw-away.

"From disposable cameras to disposable diapers, few products marketed to consumers are made to last," wrote Lisa Smith in an online Investopedia article (investopedia.com).

"Creating products that aren't meant to last is a very viable business strategy as this means that consumers will need to buy replacement products," Smith wrote. Not so with our grandparents and great-grandparents.

Smith points to straight razors that were intended to be reused after sharpening on a leather strap. Cloth diapers were made at home and reused repeatedly and then recycled again as cleaning rags.

Let's face it. The age of throw-away isn't the ideal environment in which a repair business might thrive, welding or otherwise.

I had a friend in the 1960s whose father owned a TV repair shop located on a side street in a small town that boasted three traffic lights. The storefront facing the sidewalk might have been 10 feet wide. He did not sell electronics; he only repaired them.

Dozens of televisions, radios and record players were stacked on the floor and others filled his shelves and workbench. He was always busy. When the family TV stopped working, you hauled it to the repair shop. The repairman replaced a picture tube, vacuum tube, transformer, or some capacitors and resistors. The TV worked again. The repair cost a fraction of a new TV.

Nearly every town in America had one of these repair businesses.

Then one day the 'guts' of new televisions were solid state. And replacing a 'mother board' cost nearly as much as buying a new set. America's TV repair shops gradually went out of business.

Something similar happened to Johnny's Welding. "By the time I got involved," says Bill, "my father hardly did any business at all."

It was 1986 and Bill was planning to be a teacher, but a vision was beginning to take root in the back of his mind. Bill had taken welding technology for two years at Johnstown Vocational Technical School, although the course wasn't college accredited, when he realized he wasn't going to be satisfied with a teacher's salary.

A lot has been written about the Greatest Generation, the generation that Bill's self-reliant father belonged to, as did my father. Their attitudes involved more than repairing and repurposing their possessions. **Self-reliance was also a way of life.**

In an Internet article (askaprepper.com), writer Claude Davis drew some striking conclusions about men and women from the Greatest Generation:

- They looked for solutions instead of someone to blame.
- They accepted the consequences for their decisions.
- They made do or fixed it.
- They didn't stress over things they couldn't change.
- They didn't boast about their accomplishments.

"If you hadn't worked for something it wasn't truly yours," stated Davis, **"and if you couldn't afford something yourself you had no right to expect others to pay for it."** (*The Lost Book of Remedies* and *The Lost Ways* are self-reliance books by Claude Davis.)

Self-reliance. Every serious entrepreneur must possess this time-tested personal trait.

Bill had attended the University of Pittsburgh for teaching. He was offered an emergency teaching certificate with the stipulation that he go back and finish his degree.

But that's not how the story ended. He didn't get the teaching job he was promised. He was angry, in fact, "pissed" is the word he used. "The heck with them," he thought. "I'll get control of my own destiny. I'll give this a shot."

Up to this moment, Bill was present but not actively involved in his future. His growth and development as a young adult were in limbo.

In the twinkling of an eye, that changed. The loss of the teaching position fueled a fire within Bill, and the accidental entrepreneur was born.

Stick to what you do best
CHAPTER 18
How To Be A Father

Walt Disney, the famous creator of family theme parks, lived by a four-point success formula: dream, believe, dare, and do.

Bill Capodagli and Lynn Jackson, in their book, *The Disney Way,* noted that while all four principles are important, everything starts with the dream. And Walt Disney shared the spotlight with those who shared his dreams.

With no college degree and no real business experience under his belt, Bill had to literally educate himself. He was pushed to turn his dreams into reality. There was no time for specialized learning in an academic setting, no time for how-to courses in business, finance and public relations.

He needed to create an income stream, and quickly. Time was of the essence.

Bill's workplace literally became his classroom. On his own time, he sought out seminars, read books, and picked people's brains.

Bill latched onto author, pastor and leadership expert John C. Maxwell's book, *Good Leaders Ask Great Questions,* an on-the-ground-running playbook for leaders or anyone who wants to influence others. Here's one of many quotes attributed to Maxwell: "A man must be big enough to admit his mistakes, smart enough to profit from them, and strong enough to correct them."

Bill hated the details but had a knack for networking.

"If I met an attorney at a chamber of commerce event, I'd pick their brains. If I met an accountant, I'd pick their brain about taxes. I latched onto companies that were bigger than mine and asked them principles of leadership questions. They referred books to me to read. They were happy to give me ad

Outside the two-car garage, Bill welded on the six-ton challenge. Upon completion it was delivered to a Bethlehem Steel site where his dad worked during the day.

vice: how to deal with difficult employees and make tough decisions."

Aside from working long hours, Bill was having fun doing something he was good at.

It didn't take long before he was wishing he'd started this adventure sooner.

In his book, *Tools of Titans,* author Tim Ferris has some comments about Peter Thiel, the founder of PayPal and author of the book, *Zero to One.* Thiel was asked what he wished he'd known about business 20 years ago. He responded: "I wish I would have known that there was no need to wait ... to start something."

Armed with a dream, Bill began the journey that would define his existence. The two-car garage was well off the beaten path, but his father continued to help by going after supplies. "He was mentoring me." And Bill sought his dad's advice at the end of every workday.

Bill would often observe his father who was figuring out how to fabricate something.

"I remember sitting there in amazement and looking at him and thinking, wow, I'd love to have all that knowledge in my brain one day. I thought the best way to get there was to ask him a lot of questions."

"We'd talk about growing the business," Bill recalls. A special bond emerged.

Sometimes the learning experience was awkward. Circumstances forced Bill to be clever. Once he needed to move a six-ton manufactured piece. "I had a one-ton crane in the garage, and it wouldn't fit in the garage. I had to use a four-ton forklift to pick up one end and be able to weld it."

The shop's limited size caused problems other than space. "A lot of times metal needed to be pre-heated, and there was no way to do that in the wintertime." And it wasn't unusual to be outside welding under tarps to keep a project dry.

Although Big John was agreeable to increase the garage's size, Bill insisted the business needed to relocate to a main road with better visibility and enough room to maneuver tractor-trailers.

Big John resisted. "I don't want any part of that," he told his son. Bill was taken back. However, after John gave the idea some thought, he relented. "What I mean by that, I'll help you, but I can't risk my retirement," declared Big John. Bill now understood. "That told me all I needed to know about why my father never moved the business."

"I think because he never looked at it as a full-time business, is part of why he never charged what he should have, and I think in some ways if he made good money doing it, he probably figured he had cheated someone, and the other part is if it made money, he would have to do it full-time and take some risks."

"When you're a Depression baby, risk is something that's not in your DNA."

John's pain increased as the cancer took its toll. He told Bill his "biggest regret in life was not spending more time with his kids." Yet, the children don't see it that way. "He spent quality time with us. My dad worked a lot of hours, yet every year we went on vacation."

"My father showed me how to be a father by his actions," says Bill. **"He taught us how to work with our hands, how to support a family, he taught us humility, honesty, integrity, and how you put your family first."**

John died on Valentine's Day in 1987. Bill's brother, Martin, a CPA, was asked to inventory the business; he determined it was worth $11,000.

The inventory included welders, air compressor, drills, grinders, vices, anvil, sand blaster, chains, railroad jack, die and tap sets, miscellaneous hand tools, and a 1986 Dodge pickup.

Bill made sure the highest value was placed on all assets. "I probably gave her the equivalent of full value anyway."

His mother accepted a deal with payments and interest and rented the garage to Bill with the caveat that he had to make sure there was no snow on her car since she could no longer park in the garage.

Sally kept her word to Big John and fulfilled her husband's request.

When she explained the details a quarter century later, JWF Industries was already a multi-million dollar company. "So Bill got it for $5,500. My one son-in-law kept saying, 'Mom, you should have kept 10 percent of it. Look where you'd be today.'"

But Sally considered John's dying request sacred; honoring his request was one way to honor John's memory. "You know what, that's what Dad told me to do and I did what he wanted me to do."

Bill fully understood. He said to his mother, "I know why you didn't keep 10 percent. You did what you always wanted us to do, be our own person, be what we wanted to be, and be a hundred percent ours."

Sally had a sense or intuition that Bill would become tremendously successful; she had told him so on more than one occasion.

Writing on Procter & Gamble's website P&G Everyday, Laurie Sue Brockway described an incident involving her three-year-old son, an incident she could not rationally explain. "I came to understand that Mother's Intuition was not something out of the *Twilight Zone*."

"Mother's intuition is the deep intuitive blood bond a mother can have with her child," says psychiatrist Dr. Judith Orloff, author of *Guide to Intuitive Healing*. "It is a sixth sense mothers have that the child may be in danger or in need."

Dr. Victor Shamas, a psychologist at the University of Arizona, also firmly believes in the power of intuition. He was quoted as saying: "I describe intuition as knowing something without knowing how you know."

"Bill had foresight," said Sally. "I thought exactly [about Bill] what I had said to John all those years. Bill could take the chance because he didn't have nine children to support."

Bill needed more than foresight and vision. He needed what Warren Bennis, a pioneer in the field of leadership studies, described as "the capacity to translate vision into reality."

After Bill officially bought Johnny's Welding in 1987 and all the paperwork was finalized, he thought the climate was right for a quality welding company to prosper.

His dad's business started as a part-time endeavor 30 years earlier, and it always operated on a very small scale, a shoestring, to be sure.

Bill wanted to grow but he wasn't sure yet how to go about it.

What he knew for certain was that he couldn't make much of himself by attempting to grow a repair business in the age of throw-away.

People simply do not board a commercial airliner or a cross-country train and not know where it's headed. Shucks, most people wouldn't even board a big city bus without knowing its next stop. Can you imagine waving down a big city taxi and asking the driver to take you to your hotel? And you don't know the name of the hotel or its address.

Yet, how many business owners will show up for work tomorrow with no idea where their company is going, much less how it will get there?

"Lack of a clear vision is a problem because vision is the starting point of all leadership," according to the preface in the book, *Full Steam Ahead*, written by Ken Blanchard and Jesse Lyn Stoner. "After all, leadership is about going somewhere."

You can't give directions without a destination.

Two years later, Bill had expanded from the original two-car garage and was operating in a 54- by 90-foot metal building. Gross revenue increased from $5,000 with no employees to a million dollar business that employed 13 people, thanks in large part to contracts with large customers, like Bethlehem Steel and Sani-Dairy.

Bill was sticking to what he did best, and that's good business advice for any entrepreneur.

Outside 2-car garage, Bill was welding with his father on a sewage truck converted from an old fire truck.

It's your choice to never give up
CHAPTER 19
Disappointments Will Happen

Big John Polacek worked with steel every day. From an early age Bill understood its importance. It was everywhere. As a matter of fact, that's a promotional point emphasized by the World Steel Organization.

Bill saw the metal used in a clothes line pole, kitchen chair, pickup truck frame, bridges, buildings, manhole covers, electrical power stations and railroad tracks. A one-foot section of rail once used by the Pennsylvania Railroad weighed over 51 pounds. The military applications are tremendous. A single Abrams tank requires 22 tons of steel.

Bill didn't need a college course, think tank or brainstorming session with deep thinkers to understand steel's impact on the American economy. He observed it. Up close and personal.

"When I was 13, I couldn't wait to learn how to weld. My father was my hero. When I was 16, he took me in the shop, and I was so happy that he showed me how to weld."

Bill continued: "He put his hand on my shoulder and I walked away thinking that not only was I honored that my father did that, but that I think he was honored that his son cared enough to look up to him to be a welder just like him. I think it validated him."

Some fathers bond by throwing balls with their kids. Big John bonded with Bill by putting a welding rod in his hands.

Harmon Killebrew, the prolific power hitter for the Minnesota Twins, was second only to Babe Ruth in American League home runs at the time of his retirement.

His father played baseball with Harmon and his brother in the yard. It's reported that his mother would come outside and say, "You're tearing up the grass." Harmon's father would reply, "We're not raising grass, we're raising boys."

Speaking of grass, the Polacek boys often mowed it at the home of their grandparents, Martin and Eva Polacek. Mowing the grass for the first time became the very definition of disappointment for one of the children.

Bill's older brother, Jim, was hot and sweaty one afternoon as the last patch of greenery was cut and he raced to the house for the cool treat he had been promised. He got ice cream, all right, melted ice cream! His grandmother dipped the frozen treat into a bowl and made Jim wait until it completely melted.

In the Old Country, Grandma Eva was taught that eating cold food would make a person sick.

When there are nine kids in a family, there's plenty of room for unmet expectations.

A famous television personality and puppeteer was born in Latrobe, an hour away from Bill's home; he started his career in Pittsburgh. Before long, Fred Rogers was the host of *Mister Rogers' Neighborhood*, and he helped children deal with disappointments and frustrations.

"I don't remember being really disappointed," Bill recalls, "but I do remember that you sort of learn to depend on other people. We were poor and never knew we were poor."

But growing up, Bill may have needed a support network more than other kids his age. His father did not play sports in school and had no interest in sports as an adult. And for good reason.

Big John was never allowed by his parents, Martin and Eva, to participate in sports and had grown up thinking it was foolishness. John wasn't even allowed to ride a bicycle.

Nevertheless, he violated the rule on one occasion, apparently unaware that one's sins will find you out. The pedal came off the bike and he wrecked it and the pedal shaft went through his calf. "My grandmother beat him for riding a bicycle, and then took him to the hospital."

John rarely showed up for Bill's wrestling matches, but for one particular event, he led Bill to think he would get off work in time to be a spectator and cheer for his son.

"We were walking home from church one Sunday and I remember one of the parents said to my dad, 'Wow, your son's undefeated. He's 4-0. You must be pretty proud of him.'" But Bill's dad had no idea.

Bill ended up with a 9-3 record, losing one match because he dropped in weight. He had a college looking at him during the first round of District. Bill won the first match.

He had previously lost to his next opponent; in fact, Bill ended up with a cracked rib. It was time for payback.

"I thought I could beat this kid. I was pretty fired up. It was 2-1 going into the second period. "I was on a down position and all I did, I looked up and all I heard was this big crowd cheering for this kid. I asked my dad if he would come to the match, and he said he'd try to. I looked up and looked around and he wasn't there, and I gave up."

Bill was looking for approval and inspiration from his hero. The hero was nowhere to be found.

Bill lost the match, but learned two powerful lessons that day. **First, "You've got to do it yourself." Secondly, "I swore I'd never give up again.** You decide whether you're a victim or not. I made that decision. Whether my father was there or not had no bearing on winning or losing. I made that decision."

Mental toughness is something that a person develops from life's experiences.

As Bill built on his cache of life experiences, he often reflected on the events of that wrestling match, and came to realize the importance of the mental aspects of leading and managing.

Mental toughness involves psychology, bravery, knowledge, problem solving ability, and adaptability. Bill combined these traits with his fundamental optimism.

Leaders, don't subcontract your thinking
CHAPTER 20
Culture Of 'Can Do' Attitude

My wife laughs when she hears me respond to someone asking, "How are you?" I generally reply, "If I was any better, I couldn't stand it." I try not to say it unless I mean it.

Our attitude has everything to do with how we experience each day.

For example, if we have to look adversity in the eye, we can either be overcome with fear, which is a mind-killer, or we can just smile, and continue to take care of business.

It's a choice.

Bill learned a long time ago that he couldn't afford to allow outside circumstances and influences to negatively impact the work taking place at JWF Industries. To grow and operate a truly successful business, the idea of having "no excuses" has to become a way of life.

Some of JWF's "can do" attitude has spilled over into the community where Bill grew up and built his company. Fifteen years ago, an international business magazine headlined a story, "Open for Business," and described how Johnstown has survived by putting aside partisan politics.

"While it may have gone blue in 2000, it's the color of money that really counts here," wrote Thomas Kellner in the September 6, 2004, issue of *Forbes*. "People from opposite poles have had to find common cause, thanks to Johnstown's cursed history."

For many observers, killer floods -- major and minor -- coupled with the devastation of the steel industry presented insurmountable odds for Johnstown. Just look at some of the historical ugliness.

- The 1889 Flood killed 2,200 people, and all but wiped the town off the map.

- Less severe floods occurred in 1894, 1907, 1924 and 1936.
- In 1977, a "100-year flood" ripped up sewers and roads, causing $300 million in damage. Bethlehem Steel became a perpetual layoff machine.
- The city's largest employer was being strangled by cheap Japanese and Korean imports. Bethlehem Steel slashed its payroll of 13,000 workers by 40 percent and eventually shut down for good in 1992.
- Johnstown's jobless rate became the highest in the nation at 24 percent. That was the government percentage. Using a different calculation, the unemployment rate may have been closer to 50 percent.

But the devastation described by *Forbes* wasn't enough to keep the good people of Johnstown down. Along came Bill Polacek, the accidental entrepreneur, and other people just like him.

The mantra was, **"Lead by example."**

New businesses sprang up. Old businesses retooled and reinvented themselves.

"Never doubt that a small group of thoughtful, concerned citizens can change the world. Indeed it is the only thing that ever has," said Margaret Mead, author and cultural anthropologist.

As JWF Industries grew, Bill surrounded himself with an advisory board and a group of capable managers.

"I always thought I didn't need to be the smartest guy in the room, but I'd better have the smartest people in the room."

Reflecting on his company's roots, Bill says he wouldn't do anything differently. "I think it's the struggles that we go through and the hurdles we overcome that define our character."

Story about Bill was published in Sept, 6, 2004 issue of *Forbes*.

"What people don't know is the bad things -- the challenges associated with building a business, the struggles you go through in owning your own business."

"If I had to go back and tell myself anything, I would probably tell myself that everything is going to be okay. Just keep doing what you're doing. **Do the right things, and good things happen.** People get behind you, and people help you succeed."

"The greatest secret for eliminating the inferiority complex, which is another term for deep and profound self-doubt, is to fill your mind to overflowing with faith," wrote Norman Vincent Peale in his book, *The Power of Positive Thinking*.

Faith in God, Peale wrote, "will give you a humble yet soundly realistic faith in yourself."

There was little in Bill's childhood to suggest that he would or could become a successful entrepreneur. **Yet, he became a guy who thirsted for success and dreamed that, one day, he would own a magnificent and successful business.**

He did what Donald Trump, the businessman, has long advised: "As long as you're going to be thinking anyway, think big."

Although Bill's father did have moments of thinking big, he never acted on most of them, the really big projects, that is. Big John wasn't afraid to take on a project he'd never done before, but he didn't have the equipment or help he needed to be serious about it.

Nevertheless, Big John wanted to tackle a local ballpark job that would require removing the steel in the top tier of seats and cutting it up into scrap.

"John backed off on that one," says Joe Polacek, the family historian. "To manhandle all of that, that would have been a job." John's father, Martin Polacek (Bill's grandfather), talked him out of it. "You don't have a crane. You can't do that manually. Somebody's going to get killed. You don't have insurance. If there's an accident, what are you going to do?"

Even so, some seeds may have been planted in the back of Bill's mind. The seeds of thinking big. The seeds of being a major employer. The seeds of becoming a leader.

David J. Schwartz, in his book, *The Magic of Thinking Big*, says **"the main job of the leader is thinking. And the best preparation for leadership is thinking."**

Lou Holtz, the bespectacled and quick-witted former football coach and TV analyst, says, "Virtually nothing is impossible in this world if you just put your mind to it and maintain a positive attitude." Known for his ability to inspire players, his 1988 Notre Dame team went 12-0 and was the consensus national champion.

Like Lou Holtz, entrepreneur Ryan Parman believes a person can do anything they put their mind to. He publishes a missive (blog.ryanparman.com) called "Flailing Wildly" where he writes about ideas longer than 140 characters -- the length of a modern-day message on Twitter.

He wrote a special series to his children entitled "Life Lessons," wherein he draws an analogy between being smart and hustling.

Incredibly smart people don't always do well, says Parman. In fact, many are doing badly. Why? he wondered. **"Because they lacked *hustle*.** By being smart, they'd gotten lazy in school and never really learned how to apply themselves."

That was never the case for Big John. The word 'lazy' was not in his genes or vocabulary. True, his generation was different and special in many ways. Going off to war had to impact his concept of responsibility. After all, men's lives depended on his welding skills.

M.J. Gottlieb, author of the book, *How To Ruin A Business Without Really Trying,* places emphasis on working smart, not just hard. "Quality works at a thousand times the pace of quantity," he wrote in a creative business strategy article for his company, Hustle Branding (hustlebranding.com).

Even as a teenager, Big John's nephew, Charlie Polacek, was skilled in sanding, priming and painting vehicles.

In the early 1960s, Charlie was helping his uncle weld on the back fender of a late 1940s Plymouth coupe at the two-car garage when the upholstery caught fire.

The blaze was quickly doused with a water hose. John sent away for an upholstery kit and fixed the mess he had made. John could have been more careful. It was a lesson learned.

The accident was his fault, he assumed responsibility, and he repaired the damage; not just good enough, but better than new.

Charlie Polacek holds 1950s-style vinyl-covered chair similar to one his uncle melted.

On another occasion, John was distracted while holding a torch and accidentally melted the vinyl seat of a chair he was repairing. These mishaps didn't happen often.

No one knows for sure if the two accidental fires were the result of his being in a hurry, or being distracted by his chewing tobacco habit.

But no one could ever accuse Big John of lacking hustle.

And he was going to complete every job professionally, even if he had to do it over before returning it to the customer.

Strive for worker safety, zero accidents
CHAPTER 21
Lucky I'm Breathing Today

Bill Polacek wasn't even born when his mother's father, Frank Whatmore, a 43-year veteran railroader and a Pennsylvania Railroad conductor, lost his left leg while switching a cut of cars in the Morrellville yards near Johnstown in Cambria County.

It was 7 p.m. on Saturday, May 24, 1952. Whatmore had grabbed a steel handrail and was climbing up a moving car when an unexpected jerk of the train hurled him to the ground. His left leg was sprawled across a rail.

The limb was severed well above the knee before Whatmore could squirm to safety.

Bill's grandfather lost a limb but it could have been worse. He could have gone off into eternity while lying on the dirt and stone ballast beside the railroad track as his life-blood squirted from the stump on his leg.

Instinctively, the old-line railroader whipped off his leather belt and improvised a tourniquet which he used to stop the flow of blood. It was a technique Whatmore learned during beginners' and advanced first-aid courses taught by the U.S. Bureau of Mines.

It wasn't Whatmore's first encounter with performing life-saving first aid.

A year earlier, he was working in the Pitcairn yards of the Pennsylvania Railroad, 15 miles east of Pittsburgh, when a brakeman suffered a foot amputation. Relying on his training, Whatmore administered first-aid, and saved his fellow railroader's life.

Tragedy striking in one's own family can have unexpected results.

Both of these railroad accidents happened before Bill was born. Bill only knew his grandfather to have one leg, a pair of wood crutches, and a positive attitude. However, Bill also observed that "Grandpap Whatmore" was never bitter. Instead, he was profuse with his praise for the bureau's first-aid training program.

Dave Willis blogs on a website (sixseeds.patheos.com) that discusses truths to remember when tragedy strikes.

Willis maintains that no simple clichés can erase unimaginable pain of tragedies. But you will get through it, he says, and God will bring something good out of the tragedy.

This was the case with Frank Whatmore.

There were a lot of innocent but dangerous and harmful activities taking place in and around Johnstown; the coal mines and steel mills were danger zones, and anywhere cutting torches and welders were being used, there was the potential for fires and explosions.

Bill's first cousin, Joe Polacek, worked with Bill's dad doing boiler repairs up to 1974 and much of the time his wife was "raising hell" with him, fearful he was going to kill himself.

"You come home from the mill and you go to work with John. That's enough," she demanded one day, "I don't want you doing this anymore."

The two men worked two years steady at the Sanitary Dairy mainly installing and repairing pipes in boilers, milk tanks and freezing rooms.

"Hey, I'm even lucky I'm breathing today. At that time, all those boilers were all asbestos. I think that's where John got some of his asbestos from. He couldn't breathe," says Joe.

Of course, John was also exposed to asbestos wrapped around pipes on ships during his service in the Navy.

"Well, we didn't know nothing about that then. Same way with welding rods," Joe added. "They never put on the box that the smoke was dangerous to your health until years later."

Breathing asbestos dust was a long-term health hazard.

But one particular mishap was instant and nearly took Joe's life.

It happened at an auto dealership that sold Chrysler, Plymouth, Dodge and Desoto cars. Bill's father, John, was working alone at Sanitary Dairy and Joe was working alone on a boiler at the dealership. Joe opened the flues because the night before they had cleaned everything out in the boiler.

"I crawled in. I took the hoses and everything in, and I cut the whole inside out. Then I closed the doors and came outside." Joe climbed up the scaffold and started cutting the first tube "and the whole damn room went up in flames. Fire went everywhere. I just got out. It filled that room instantly, just like that."

Joe jumped off the scaffold and scaled 20 steps, unable to see anything, to escape the flames.

He shut off the oxygen and acetylene tanks and pulled his torch up from the boiler room. "I didn't want the hoses to catch fire and then make a bigger fire with the oxygen and acetylene burning."

By some miracle, Joe wasn't burned.

The fire chief was angry: "You ought to know better than to burn in there where there's flammables."

Joe responded: "There's nothing in this boiler room. It's all concrete, the walls, the floor, we (John and Joe) were here the night before, we drained the boiler out, there was nothing. I don't work where there's papers and stuff. The fire was coming out from under the steps and was going up the steps. I just barely made it out of there."

Firemen extinguished the blaze and sucked the smoke out with a fan. That's when the fire chief found a sump pump underneath the steps and discovered the gasoline.

A quick investigation revealed that an outside tank was leaking gas and it had run underground and accumulated in the sump pump; the owner of the dealership had been blaming his employees for stealing gas.

"But I was lucky that I had the doors shut in that boiler, cause if I would have had them open, I'd been trapped inside with that fire and I wouldn't be here today."

Bill's father would never have forgiven himself had Joe died in that fire.

Yet God brought something good out of the near tragedy, an awareness that safety and zero accidents are the responsibility of every businessman, every company, and every worker.

Joe Polacek, family historian, worked on many tough jobs with Big John.

Keep workplace clean, organized
CHAPTER 22
Uncle Ray, Diamond In The Rough

Some would count excessive generosity, or giving the benefit of the doubt to people who don't deserve it, among Bill's faults. He's known to give employees every opportunity.

To his regret, he has elevated people to positions they were not qualified to handle. He once hired a woman who couldn't do the job, but Bill wanted her to succeed so he provided a tutor. She still couldn't do the job.

Some people would call his action a mistake, as in to err is human. Others see this as a reflection of a businessman with a big heart.

Bill has also reluctantly hired workers that turned out to be diamonds in the rough, a metaphorical phrase that relates to the fact that naturally occurring diamonds are quite ordinary at first glance because their true beauty is only realized through the cutting and polishing process.

This is the story of one man, who might have been viewed as shy and ordinary, who emerged as the proverbial diamond in the rough. But first, an analogy.

One U.S. motel chain apparently got tired of some customers making off with towels and pillows and did something about it. In the bathrooms of their lodging facilities you will now find a plastic card addressed to "Dear Guest."

"Due to the popularity of our guest room amenities," the card says, "our Housekeeping Department now offers these items for sale." The card puts a price tag on towels, bath mats, washcloths and pillows ranging from $2-$15.

It's a nice way of saying, you take it, you pay for it, and it establishes accountability for missing amenities.

"Each guest room attendant is responsible for maintaining the guest room items. Should you decide to take these articles from your room instead of obtaining them from the Executive Housekeeper, we will assume you approve a corresponding charge to your account."

As JWF entered an early growth spurt, missing amenities became a serious problem for the manufacturer.

Tools were being abused or mysteriously disappearing, just like the pillows and towels that went missing in the motel rooms. This isn't to imply that employees were stealing; more often, the tools were simply misplaced and couldn't be found when needed. Regardless of the reason, it was a problem that needed to be remedied.

Bill used this challenge as an opportunity to employ an uncle who needed a job. He had to pray about the solution; he didn't immediately connect the dots between the missing tools and his uncle who was out of work and down on his luck.

Ray Rheel was the husband of Bill's mother's younger sister, Sandy. Ray manhandled huge sides of beef and other slabs of meat at the Armour Meat Packing plant in Johnstown, which became Con-Agra, and lost his position when the plant closed in the late 1990s.

On several occasions Ray asked his nephew for a job, and Bill didn't have one suitable for Ray at the time, but he wanted to help and kept asking himself, "What would Dad want me to do?"

I ran across a blog posting by children's author, Donna Perugini, in which she talked about the phrase "cleanliness is next to godliness." Although she says John Wesley used similar wording in a 1778 sermon, the phrase is believed to have originated with Rabbi Phineas ben Yair.

It got me to thinking about another phrase, *organization* is next to godliness.

Well, neither phrase is in the Bible. But I know from my own hobby woodworking experience, organization in my shop is worth its weight in gold. I am not productive in a disorganized environment. It appears that JWF employees were in the same boat.

Bill eventually found his answer. He devised a plan. He created a job -- a job that did not exist before -- and made his uncle the caretaker of all tools.

And the blessings flowed.

It wasn't long until there was order where there had been chaos.

Under Ray's watch, every tool was accounted for, every day. If a tool wasn't checked back in, Ray went looking for it. Employees weren't offended; they were grateful as production efficiency improved. There no longer was down production time while workers searched for missing or misplaced tools.

He took his job seriously. "You'd thought the national security depended on Ray and that tool room," Bill observed. The overhead expenses for tools went down dramatically.

Some workers teased Ray, saying he really owned the company and Bill was just a figurehead. Although everyone knew this wasn't true, it made Ray feel good.

Then something akin to a miracle happened. Employees at JWF Industries and Ray became like family. Ray came to have purpose. He now worked at a company where he was respected.

A mutual respect developed.

On the floor, he was "Uncle Ray" to all the workers. Newcomers would ask, "Uncle Ray, why does everyone call you Uncle Ray?" His response was always the same: "Maybe because Bill's my nephew and he owns the company."

Everybody loved Ray.

And why did this happen?

Well, Ray was a kind, down-to-earth guy. It was easy for his co-workers to respect him.

But the structure and efficiency in the workplace was striking, once tools were accounted for. A professional atmosphere emerged, and that led to increased morale.

Organization is next to godliness!

Ray was not a person to be outspoken; however, on one occasion he surprised Bill, who was addressing the subject of waste with a group of workers.

"All of a sudden, Ray got up and said, 'I'm going to tell you guys something. Bill doesn't have to do half the stuff he does for you. He gives you profit sharing, he gives you bonuses. You guys don't understand what it's like to work for a company that gives you nothing, doesn't care about you.'"

Ray doubled down. "The least you guys could do is show appreciation by taking care of the stuff he lets you use and be more mindful of waste." That was way out of character for Ray, says Bill.

In the summer of 2001 Ray became terminally ill with lung cancer and had to give up his job.

Before he died, Bill drove him through the factory in a golf cart. Ray stood in the cart, waved to co-workers and said he was coming back to work. He was proud as a peacock.

You're in a win-win situation Ray, Bill told him. Get well and you'll get your job back. "If you don't get better, you'll see God."

Perhaps for the first time in his life, Ray felt genuine appreciation in the workplace. Bill assured Ray his job would be waiting. Ray lived about three months after his diagnosis. He's still fondly remembered.

"When I created a job for Ray, I thought I was helping him; he was really helping me."

Even today, any visitor to JWF's buildings quickly notices the emphasis on a clean, safe and healthy workplace. There's no clutter. There's a place for everything, and everything is in its place.

Cleanliness and organization are a permanent memorial to "Uncle Ray."

If something can go wrong, it will
CHAPTER 23
Safe Work Practices, Zero Accidents

"If mama ain't happy, nobody's happy." I don't recall when I first heard the expression, but it has been used in a variety of contexts in recent years.

Teacher, counselor and website blogger Brenda Yoder (notaloneministries.com) contends that children and families are only as happy as mama. If mama ain't happy at home, chances are there's tension in the air and kids know it.

Anyone in a leadership position should ponder how the expression fits into their workplace. If the leader isn't happy, it seems likely followers aren't happy either.

If mama ain't happy, the family is likely to be in trouble -- chaos, insecurities, frustration, sadness, dissension. The parallels to business seem rather clear. **If employees are not happy, the business is likely to be in trouble, and quality is likely suffering.**

When employees aren't happy, the door is also open to carelessness. And carelessness leads to more than poor quality; it leads to accidents.

Think about this: Leadership is never an accident, quality is never an accident, and neither is safety! **Having a safe workplace takes effort; it doesn't happen by accident.** Having a safe workplace makes for happy and contented employees and spouses.

Lord Robert Baden-Powell, founder of the Boy Scouts, died in 1941 at age 83. In his final letter to scouts, he urged youngsters to "try and leave this world a little better than you found it."

Baden-Powell was also the inspiration for the Boy Scott Motto, **"Be Prepared."** A reporter once asked him, "Be prepared for what?" He replied, "Why, for any old thing!"

Danger is lurking everywhere, especially in a business that focuses on metals and often weighs it by the ton rather than pounds.

Greg Dugan was one of Bill's original employees, a trusted and experienced manager. He was in charge of "cribbing up" a 40-ton beam so blocks could be placed beneath and the steel could be lifted with a crane. He didn't crib it up properly and the load shifted. Dugan lost a part of his right foot.

The injury to Dugan, who had a ton of experience, prompted a movement for more vigorous safety education.

Today, Bill never misses an opportunity to promote workplace safety, even while touting career opportunities at JWF Industries.

"Manufacturing is growing in the U.S. and hopefully some of you will one day work with us and help us build more products and build this town," he frequently tells school groups, like sixth-graders who often tour JWF facilities wearing yellow hard hats, safety glasses and ear plugs.

As a visitor you can't get in the front security gate without picking up your safety equipment. "The purpose of JWF Industries is to have healthy and prosperous employees and retirees," Bill says.

These words go to the heart of his vision. He sees his employees as family, and he wants them to work at JWF until they choose to retire.

"We all know that in order for a business to survive, it must cover expenses and make a profit. No mystery there," he says, "but whether or not an organization is successful depends on a completely different calculation."

"In my view," Bill explains, "success is defined by more than just profit and loss. If we define our success only in those terms, as Wall Street does, then we would be a much different company with dramatically different values. Whether caused by illness or injury, both management and employees suffer when employees can't work."

Hence, **safety is Job One** at JWF Industries.

"The initiative must start at the top and be viewed by all as the top priority," says Bill. This concept is drilled into employees: "No production number is so important as to sacrifice your safety."

Safety success and preventing accidents at JWF is "an epic journey," says Alex Polacek, safety administrator, that requires utilizing the eyes and ears of your employees "by empowering them to enforce and correct safety hazards, as well as reporting unsafe conditions and near misses."

He adds, "If employees are constantly letting you know about something they did or they found without blaming anyone, you will know that safety is second nature and is important [to workers] for all the right reasons."

As with all industries, JWF's workplace is constantly fighting Murphy's Law, for which there are many variations:

- If something can go wrong, it will (the original version).
- Whatever can happen, will happen.
- Everything that *can* go wrong *will* go wrong.
- Anything that can possibly go wrong, does.
- If there is any way to do it wrong, someone will.

The law's namesake was Captain Ed Murphy, a development engineer from Wright Field Aircraft Lab, who, in 1947, was involved in a rocket-sled experiment in which all 16 accelerator instruments were installed in the wrong way.

Murphy observed: "If there are two or more ways to do something, and one of those ways can result in a catastrophe, then someone will do it."

The concept may actually be as old as humanity. Similar statements were recorded in the 1800s. Here are some examples of other modern-day variations:

- You never find a lost article until you replace it.
- Matter will be damaged in direct proportion to its value.

- Smile. Tomorrow will be worse.
- Left to themselves, things tend to go from bad to worse.
- A device will fail at the least opportune possible moment.
- If a device cannot malfunction, it will.

Instead of observing the pessimism in these time-worn adages, Bill and his team seized on the cautionary aspects:
- Don't overlook quality control.
- Don't accept mediocrity.
- Involve everyone in safety, all the way up the ladder of authority.

Bill demands accountability. No one is exempt. He expects that safe work practices and hazard recognition become part of the day-to-day expectation for all those in a leadership role, too. "And it will start with me," he insists.

Prevention is the focus. **"We start every meeting with a safety moment so people are thinking about what could be a potential safety issue,"** explains Bill.

JWF tracks the Total Reportable Incidents rather than lost days. "We measure it every day, and each work area knows the company is keeping score." This helps create a culture and awareness regarding safety, "and everybody is involved, not just the guys on the floor."

"We focus on what could be an accident and prevent the accident." Employees create safety slogans, such as: "A safe move is a good move. What's your move?"

"There are companies whose work is more dangerous than ours but who have gone years since they had an OSHA Recordable accident. I am defining our success with a safety culture that is so concerned about safe work practices that accidents and injuries are both rare and treated as a major event from which everyone studies and learns."

Says Bill, "I strongly believe that Zero Accidents should be our standard."

Where there's a will, there's a way
CHAPTER 24
Never, Never, Never Give Up

Before Bill stepped out on faith and took over his father's welding business, he needed some kind of job, some steady income. Unemployment was at an all-time high in Johnstown.

There were few jobs for people Bill's age, but he found one opening advertised, and he and 299 other anxious job seekers applied for it. He got a first and second interview.

"I was 20 years old at the time, and it came down to me and another guy." Bill knew the area and had the personality to sell things. "That's what the guy liked."

The employer admitted he was struggling between the two candidates. Bill chimed in, "I've got an easy answer, hire me." The employer replied, "Boy, that's what I like about you. Ask for the order."

A salesman asking for the order is a basic principle of Sales Training 101. "I need people with that kind of energy," the employer admitted.

"Seriously, what's the problem?" asked Bill. "Well, you have all the tools, you have a great personality, you're relationship-building oriented, you're smart, you know the area, but the other guy has four kids."

Bill was single. His only contender for the job had a wife and four children to feed. Bill was raised to have concern for others, not be selfish and self-absorbed. Had he taken the position, Bill would have lived to regret it.

Herman Cain, the former U.S. presidential candidate and onetime chief executive officer of Godfather's Pizza, wrote a book, *CEO of Self*, that helps us better understand Bill's dilemma.

Referring to the book on one of his radio shows, Cain told a listener to "be in charge of your own life, you won't be happy until you are."

"I had options," Bill thought. The inspiration of his parents was more compelling than the fear of not having a job. He immediately declined.

Someone said courage is not walking through life without fear, it's walking through life in spite of fear.

"Courage is doing what you're afraid to do," said fighter pilot and Medal of Honor recipient Eddie Rickenbacker, America's most celebrated air ace of World War I.

Walking away from a job where he had the upper hand doesn't mean Bill abandoned his fear. Those demons followed him throughout his career, but Bill kept walking through life.

Fast forward a few years.

When Bill's older brother, John, first heard about the expansion plans for Johnny's Welding, he was skeptical of the trappings of an upstart enterprise. After all, John had seen no future in Johnstown and after high school graduation, he enlisted in the U.S. Marine Corps.

But over the years he secretly kept his eye on an opportunity to return, and he watched his brother's progress.

As time passed Bill realized he had to expand the supporting cast and diversify his revenue streams if his new company was going to realize its potential. He definitely needed to hire someone with a defense background, someone he could trust.

"I decided very quickly if I'm going to get defense business, I needed to hire a COO (chief operating officer). I needed someone who understood this language, has the stripes that can talk the language and teach me how to do it."

Bill's courage was about to shine.

"If you're always at the head of the class, then you're in the wrong class," says leadership speaker John C. Maxwell in his book, *The 15 Invaluable Laws of Growth.* **"The best place to learn is always where others are ahead of you."**

John Polacck had assets that his younger brother needed, and Bill was smart enough to recognize it.

Already onboard were an accountant with defense background, and a supply person with defense background, and now Bill needed a COO that had some marketing capability but also understood manufacturing.

Bill called his brother and revealed his plans to build a team.

"I asked John to meet with our team and give us his thoughts on what we could be doing from the defense side." John knew a lot about Bill's turf. He could speak with some authority when he met with Bill's executives. Bill thought his brother "walked away impressed with the team we had."

John graduated from Conemaugh Valley High School (Johnstown) in 1974 and received a bachelor's degree in business management from the University of Phoenix in 2004. He was vice president and general manager of defense and defense intelligence for BAE Systems in Herndon, Virginia, one of the top three defense companies in the world.

After the meetings, John told his brother he knew someone he thought would be interested in this new position, "in fact the guy's really smart and he's from Johnstown." Bill took the bait. "It's me," John announced.

John submitted his resume and Bill found himself with two qualified applicants. The other guy had more manufacturing knowledge, but John had more marketing, proposal-writing experience, and leadership skills. And John brought a wealth of knowledge in the area of standardized best practices.

John also had 30-plus years in the defense industry and the more he and Bill talked, the more both brothers realized it was a good fit -- an exciting growth opportunity and an opportunity for John to return home.

It wasn't a sudden decision on John's part, as he was already actively involved in the global war on terror. John had a young family and needed to be home more, but his assignments took him all over the globe.

His wife understood the choices he faced. Michelle says John and his siblings were raised with good values, and the Marine Corps only enhanced those core values.

The official website of the U.S. Marine Corps describes three long paragraphs of values; among them are concern for others, being accountable for their actions, fulfilling their obligations, and commitment.

John was seeking a way to apply these values to his wife and children.

Although there were many reasons to return to his roots, one of John's main reference points was his automobile drive to work.

He had chosen to reside in the countryside in Warrenton, Virginia, but, even then, "on a good day my drive was one hour one way, and the average was probably 90 minutes, and on bad days it could take as long as three hours. It takes me eight minutes to get to work now."

"I was tired of the rat race," says John, who was traveling extensively, at home and abroad, and wasn't able to spend time with his children. That ended on his 50th birthday.

After being gone from Johnstown for 33 years, John announced he was bringing his rich defense department experience and contacts back home and joining his younger brother, Bill, as chief operating officer of JWF Industries and JWF Defense Systems.

"The really neat thing in coming back is seeing the renaissance we've had here in Johnstown. I think being removed for so long has given me a real appreciation for all the good things that have and are taking place here."

For certain, John was "taken back" by the sheer size of the manufacturing space that was available for production.

His wife, a lifelong Virginian, is equally appreciative when it comes to quality of life. "We love being around family. Instead of visiting Johnstown, we now call it home."

"Bill has an unbelievable ability to look out for the next business opportunity and to align JWF to go after that opportunity to grow the company. He truly cares about all his employees and is so giving to them, his family and the community. He is the epitome of 'never give up' and 'where there is a will there is a way,'" says Michelle.

"Never give in. Never, never, never, never -- in nothing, great or small, large or petty -- never give in, except to convictions of honor and good sense. Never yield to force. Never yield to the apparently overwhelming might of the enemy."

The World War II statesman Winston Churchill said this on October 29, 1941, when he visited Harrow School in London, where he had been a boarding student and almost flunked out.

It's still good advice.

Don't be afraid to try something new
CHAPTER 25
Job Creation Is A Priority

What is an entrepreneur's most important job?

Work hard, follow your passion, embrace risks, insist on excellence, trust your instincts, don't make excuses, all of these are possibilities. To be sure, not every entrepreneur will have the same answer.

The jacket cover on Donald J. Trump's book, *Midas Touch,* written with Robert T. Kiyosaki, poses that simple question: "What's an entrepreneur's most important job?" Their answer might surprise you: "Creating high-quality and stable jobs."

Once an entrepreneur identifies their most important job, which is job creation, they must figure out how their job is to be implemented. Bill knew he wasn't interested in being a one-man show. He needed a workforce, and that meant one thing: creating jobs.

Next came the real challenge.
- How do you create jobs?
- How do you find the right people to fill these jobs?
- Was Bill focused enough to pull it off?

I had not entered grade school when I learned a valuable life lesson from my grandfather about being focused. It was quite a few years before I applied the lesson, but it was a lesson I never forgot.

Although my grandfather worked for the railroad, his spare time hobbies were raising earthworms to sell for fishing bait, raising chickens, and tending his vegetable garden.

Well before spring each year, a soft-spoken neighbor wearing blue denim overalls would arrive on his squeaky buckboard, unhitch the mule, hitch up the plow, turn under the weeds, and turn the rich dirt back into useable garden space.

As a child I didn't fully understand the purpose of those silly looking weathered leather flaps the farmer fastened over the mule's eyes.

"The mule is a 1,000 pound brute with hot donkey blood," according to blogger (budmanrants.blogspot.com). Bud Hearn.

"It's impossible to handle if its mind gets distracted by the neighbor's greener grass or a greater interest in the barn. It must plow its proper row, straight and narrow, no diversion, no independent thinking. Blinders keep its eyes focused on the dull duty of plowing."

Various dictionary definitions of 'blinders' speak about people who are only able to see things one way and are unwilling or unable to consider other possibilities. Having an extremely narrow point of view is also known as tunnel vision.

Although Bill had what's often called an 'open mind' as he built his business, he was perfectly willing and able to wear blinders when he needed to in order to stay focused.

"Enthusiasm is a necessary piece of the personality puzzle for a startup founder," says Robert Gerov, founder of VokSEO (vokseo.com), a Web design, online marketing, and reputation management company based in New York City.

Your ideas have value, Gerov says. You can be confident about them without being egotistical or cocky. Your business was started "because you believe in it."

I figure he and Bill must have broken bread together. They seem to have the same ideas.

Bill wasn't afraid to try something new. He didn't mind getting his hands dirty. And he took working long hours in stride. **He wasn't afraid to buck the system nor was he afraid to fail, which is perhaps one of his most enduring traits.**

Like so many authors of self-help books about starting and building successful businesses, Donald Trump and Robert Kiyosaki also address fear of failure in their book, *Midas*

Touch, a fear that prevents many people from becoming entrepreneurs because their fear outweighs their desire to win.

Trump had desire but his success was not guaranteed.

He committed to run for President of the United States in 2016 and fearlessly and successfully took on all challengers -- other presidential contenders, the Democratic Party, members of his own Republican Party, and the news media.

"Life has its ups and downs," Trump says, **"which means that if you want to win, you have to accept losing too."**

Even though Bill's company was starting to get some business from Bethlehem Steel, his primary livelihood depended on the work he got from Sani-Dairy. In effect, Bill was working a full-time and a part-time job to make a living.

Losing the account when the dairy company downsized was no different than Bill losing his full-time job.

Bill had too many eggs in one basket. He allowed himself to become satisfied with the business he had, and in a flash, it was gone.

"I had to figure out how to cut corners and get other business." It was a lesson in not being complacent as well as being a motivator.

Truth is, Bill didn't blink an eye. He had to replace his full-time job, or go hungry. Like a mule wearing blinders, he stayed focused.

"The best entrepreneurs on earth never lose that hunger," according to entrepreneur Tony Robbins, of Robbins Research International (tonyrobbins.com). "They are hungry to grow, hungry to give, hungry to contribute." Hunger is essential for entrepreneurs.

"There's nothing that will stop a person who is hungry enough," Robbins says.

Timing, timing, and timing
CHAPTER 26
What Really Runs In His Veins?

In the real estate business, the axiom is location, location, and location. In the welding and fabrication business, the axiom often is timing, timing, and timing.

In the mid-1990s, Bill installed a new $300,000 drill line. One employee could do in 15 minutes what used to require six hours for four employees to finish. The new specialty drill, purchased in Germany, was faster and more accurate and could drill different diameter holes at the same time.

If you're thinking this purchase was made for the purpose of cutting JWF's payroll by eliminating some employees, you'd be wrong.

The preciseness of this piece of equipment was a prerequisite for improving efficiency so Bill could keep JWF's current employees working, acquire more business, and continue growing.

There's a line in the blockbuster movie *Die Hard 2* that says, "As far as I'm concerned, progress peaked with frozen pizza."

Bill could have been satisfied with the amount of business he had. But the purchase of the versatile drill unit was about more than buying sophisticated equipment. It was representative of changing times.

As Bill is so fond of saying, "This isn't your grandfather's steel mill."

A report emerged about a year after the purchase of the German-built specialty drill that stated: Five companies honored at an Economic Summit *together* employ more people than Bethlehem Steel Corporation's Bar, Rod & Wire Division when it shut down in 1992 in Johnstown. These companies didn't eliminate taxes or offer free healthcare.

But they did accomplish something earth-shattering.

Community leaders say these companies demonstrated the ability of the Johnstown area to recover from the loss of coal and steel jobs, to diversify, and to attract entrepreneurs who are starting new businesses.

Bill's company was one of the five.

In the early years, JWF's efforts to acquire more buildings for expansion weren't always easy acquisitions. "I did a lot of praying."

Bill's two and a half year environmental battle to purchase the former Griffith-Custer steel building ended in late 1992. His successful effort is being used as an example of how newly introduced state legislation could help businesses.

Bill's efforts to buy this building were stalled in 1990 by the Department of Environmental Resources, which required certain environmentally hazardous areas be cleaned before a loan could be approved to assist in the purchase of the building.

New legislation was aimed at limiting the liability that potential buyers would have in cleaning up contaminated sites left by previous owners.

Without common-sense legislation, there are thousands of similar sites throughout Pennsylvania -- indeed, across America -- where economic development opportunities and jobs could be lost to communities.

Bill testified at state hearings on the subject in September 1993. State Sen. William Stewart, quoted in *The Tribune-Democrat*, said there are countless William Polaceks out there and "literally thousands of these kinds of sites."

"No one is trying to dodge the environmental responsibility," Sen. Stewart said. "You just have to be reasonable."

A compromise with the Department of Environmental Resources allowed Bill to complete the purchase and enabled him to expand his workforce.

Bill accepted that there will always be regulations, and he'll have to engage with government to deal with them.

That's a daunting task for any business. How did Bill navigate the minefield of challenges he had to constantly negotiate?

I'm not sure what runs through my brother-in-law's veins. Ice water? Black coffee? Red wine? Craft beer? Rock music? Salty sweat? Raw honey? Irish blood? Even members of his family and inner circle aren't certain at times.

His former VP of business development, Matt Hughes (no relation to the author), isn't sure either. "Whatever *it* is, you won't find *it* in your Average Joe," he observes.

Bill has tempted fate many times, didn't always win, but came out of it no worse for the wear.

"Bill taught me the process he uses when making critical decisions," Hughes explains. **"He starts by evaluating what's the worst thing that can happen if you make the wrong decision, then working backwards from there to do his analysis.** This simple tactic helps take worry out of your life. It doesn't mean there's not an abundance of thoughtful discussion about important matters, but having your staff worry about things that are often out of their control does no good."

"This creates a natural vetting process," says Bill, "to see if you're making the right decision."

Looking back at what runs in my brother-in-law's veins, blogger Amber Dugger (amberdugger.com) chooses to ignore the blood and look at the brain, where she characterizes a businessman's headspace as his special and sacred workspace, and the source of ideas and momentum.

"As the sole protector of this precious space, **you want to do everything to keep the creative juices flowing."**

Michael Michalko is a creativity expert and author of the book, *Thinkertoys*. He encourages playing to win and warns that worry and confusion will kill creativity.

Bill learned to avoid these two killers when possible, and deal with them when necessary.

Be humble enough to ask questions
CHAPTER 27
The Man Was A Hero

Television sitcoms over the past half century have presented iconic versions of fathers, none more memorable, perhaps, than Andy Griffith playing the role of Andy Taylor on the Andy Griffith Show, or Robert Reed playing the role of Mike Brady on The Brady Bunch.

Even without using the word, Bill views his father as a hero because of his unselfish acts and other exemplary qualities such as integrity and "quiet leadership."

John Polacek was blessed to return from World War II with his mind, emotions and limbs still intact.

His boyhood friend, Jim, wasn't so fortunate. Jim returned with a severe case of "shell shock." He would stand for hours on the streets of Daisytown where Bill lived, staring into space and smoking one cigarette after another.

In the mid-1950s, Jim borrowed $5 from John. That was a lot of money in the fifties. A U.S. postage stamp cost three cents, compared to today's 55 cents. A gallon of regular gasoline cost 18 cents.

In purchasing power, $5 in 1950 was worth $51.15 in 2017 buying power. Let these figures sink in!

Sally, John's wife, was visibly upset, not with the fact that John cared about his friend, but that she and John were struggling, almost by the hour, to make ends meet. At the time they had four children and another one on the way, and John was working two jobs.

"You know, John, he's not going to pay you back."

John answered quietly, "I know."

Time passed, and, to their surprise, Jim repaid the $5 and reinforced the notion that people are judged more by their actions than what they say.

The World War II British prime minister, Winston Churchill, famously said, **"We make a living by what we get. We make a life by what we give."**

Roy T. Bennett shares positive thoughts about giving in his book, *The Light in the Heart.* "Always have a willing hand to help someone; you might be the only one that does."

There's a biblical admonition in the New Testament, too, about sharing. It's found in Chapter 13 of Hebrews: Be mindful to entertain strangers; for some have entertained angels without knowing it.

Giving from the heart was an act of love in the Polacek household. And so was praying.

John and Sally's children have vivid memories of their parents kneeling by the bedside and teaching them to pray. There's a very old but very true saying for imperfect people who live in an imperfect world: "The family that prays together stays together."

Bill speaks unashamedly about his faith in God and the role of family in his personal life. He lives by the creed, faith is the key that unlocks the storehouse of God's resources.

In the book of Psalms, Christians are commanded to declare God's glory among nations, and God's wonders among people.

"I owe every day to many people," he says, "and the first debt is to God the Father and our Savior Jesus Christ."

And Bill is never hesitant to **give credit to others where credit is due.**

Most people will look at the success of JWF's meteoric rise as a major player in Western Pennsylvania manufacturing, "but what you don't see," Bill says, "is the blood, sweat and tears of a lot of people, and a lot of praying and tough times." He has survived four recessions.

Real estate developer and now president, Donald J. Trump, says his father, Fred Trump, was the most important influence on him growing up, teaching him toughness in a tough business and how to motivate people.

In his book, *The Art of the Deal,* written with Tony Schwartz, Trump says he "learned about competence and efficiency: **get in, get it done, get it done right, and get out.**" Ultimately, it's about "what you accomplish."

There's no denying that everyone has their own definition for the American Dream.

We can look to the United States Declaration of Independence for one universal description: "We hold these truths to be self-evident, that all men are created equal, that they are endowed by their Creator with certain unalienable Rights, that among these are Life, Liberty and the pursuit of Happiness."

Of course, being equal before the law does not mean that all men are equal in ability, says my friend Robert Palmer, who wrote the Epilogue in this book.

An entrepreneur is a unique individual who is not satisfied to be benched on the sideline. The only place they can function well is in the driver's seat where they are responsible for starting, stopping, direction, and speed.

A successful entrepreneur, Bill says, recognizes problems and meets them head-on, and is always pro-active when facing tough situations by learning from them.

Learning is the key word. As Bill Gates, co-founder of Microsoft, said, "It's fine to celebrate success, but it is more important to heed the lessons of failure."

Bill has been chosen as entrepreneur of the year, a businessman who shows innovation, financial performance and personal commitment -- a modern-day example of the American Dream.

Although he's a third-generation Johnstownian, Bill is a true first-generation entrepreneur. Although his father and grandmother Eva generated extra income at home, they weren't interested in expanding, and took no risks.

From the very moment Bill took over his father's welding business, he exposed himself to risks. **"I hated the details and had to recognize what I didn't know, and be humble enough to**

ask questions. You have to be introspective enough to understand your weaknesses."

Bill's sense of fairness came naturally because of his parents, who worked incredibly long hours to offer nine children a wealth of intangible assets, always impressing upon them the values of family, faith and hard work.

"When I think things are getting tough, I always look back at what my mom did and what she accomplished." Sally Polacek embodied the definition of determination. She was also gifted with the ability to see problems as possibilities.

How on earth could she raise nine children, keep up with the laundry when she didn't even have a clothes dryer, prepare meals for 11 people, manage her husband's side business, and take college courses?

Sally's solution was to get up in the wee hours of the morning and head to the basement at 4 AM to study. She changed her perspective and viewed the pre-dawn quiet as the ideal time for her to learn.

The small, dingy basement was home to a makeshift workout room where the boys could lift weights, a workbench for Big John, and a single light bulb with pull-chain where Sally could study. "It was dark everywhere else," remembers Bill.

"My mother worked part-time. She traveled to Mount Aloysius College which was a 30-minute drive, and it was up on a hill where the weather was always worse. It didn't matter what the weather was, my mother went." The route to the college -- Pennsylvania Highway 22 -- had a reputation. Because of the numerous wrecks, it was called Killer Highway.

"She taught us, without saying a word, if you don't like the situation you are in, do something about it."

You're not a victim, stop making excuses, and don't give up.

Big John could have easily given up at the time of his accident. The family's bread winner was put on crutches and told to keep his leg elevated as much as possible. The fall from a ladder prevented any significant compensation; it didn't happen on company time. He missed work for months.

While John was out of commission, Sally was determined to control her own destiny. For the family to survive, it was up to her. She took a job at a dress-making factory.

Referring to the demands on every minute of Sally's time, Bill says, "I don't think she ever gave it a thought. **When you're focused on a goal, you're not focused on how hard it is. When you have that mindset, you'll figure out a way to do it.**"

Sally always taught her children "to keep looking ahead, to have goals and keep working toward them no matter what happens," says Bill.

German performer Kathi Gultini, whose career started in 1908, is considered one of the greatest female jugglers of all time. If you think juggling a few balls is difficult, Gultini could balance a couch on her forehead while juggling four cushions.

Sally wasn't a juggler in that sense, but she became a master of multi-tasking, something that many studies show women are better at than men.

By the time Sally entered college, she and John had nine children at home. Every moment of every day was a balancing and juggling act.

To endure, Sally became forceful and determined. She pulled no punches. One day life would be heartwarming, another day life was tear-jerking. Perhaps because it was in her own past, Sally despised bullying; she became an advocate for those who were teased and humiliated.

Sally taught her boys never to pick on younger children, realizing full well that her own sons were sometimes subject to bullying by older boys in their neighborhood. Sally never promoted violence, but she had no tolerance for bullies -- none. Her boys were encouraged to stick together and watch out for each other.

Translation?

"If a bully starts picking on any one of you, I want all five of you to gang up and beat them up." There was also a stern warning: "But don't you ever start it!"

The day of reckoning came. Sally's worst fears were realized. One of her boys got the full treatment from the neighborhood's biggest bully. Marty, John and Jim responded, beat the older kid up, and sent him home bleeding and crying.

Someone abusing her children, verbally or physically, made her fighting mad, but Sally held no punches when it came to handling the family's laundry, either. Her children couldn't have cared less how their clothes ended up at the washing machine in the basement, but their mother did.

There was method to the madness. Sally insisted that all clothes be turned right-side-out in order to help streamline the washing/drying process on Mondays. She yelled for each child who didn't do it correctly.

Unfortunately, the famous line by Malcolm Kushner, author of *The Humor of Ronald Reagan,* did not work. Kushner said: "There are three ways to get something done: do it yourself, hire someone to do it, or ask your kids *not* to do it."

Sally yelled even louder -- the whole neighborhood would hear her -- if the children weren't home from playing when the street lights came on.

God has a plan for your life
CHAPTER 28
Bill's Decision To Reinvent Himself

It wasn't until the 19th century that steel manufacturing became a dominant industry, fueling America's growth as a world economic power. Pennsylvania had solidified its position in the American iron industry way back in revolutionary times.

From an early age, Bill understood the importance of steel. Growing up, he picked up bits and pieces of historical background because of where he lived in Johnstown. After all, nearby Pittsburgh isn't called the Steel City for no reason.

It's a miracle that Bill survived some of his early business encounters though, given the condition of most of his equipment, situations he now calls "those defining moments" in your business.

The floor boards in his father's Ford pickup were deteriorated and the valves were bad, but he kept it running the old fashioned way with chewing gum, bailing wire and some luck -- lots of luck.

A series of distressing incidents accumulated to steel Bill's resolve to succeed. In reality, though, **many successful businesses were started under worse conditions.**

Adolf Coors was orphaned at age 15 and earned support for his younger siblings by working at a brewery in a small Prussian town.

He arrived in the U.S. in 1868 with no money as a stow-away on a ship. The German immigrant worked his way westward to Colorado, where he discovered the perfect ingredient for brewing beer: water from the Rocky Mountains.

Revenue of Coors Brewing Company, which is in the billions, became another example of an immigrant success story. Persistence, timing, and smart investments can pay off big.

Bill's father's half-ton 1972 Ford pickup was badly rusted. John had installed a different bed and new fenders, but the floor boards were rusted out. Bill and his brothers carelessly tossed firewood in the back.

"Chunks of wood would bounce off the sides, putting all these dents in it." Well, later on, Bill got the truck.

He had used multiple colors of putty on the many dents and the work truck was an attention-getter on the road, especially with a 1,500-pound welder in the back. "Then you put all your tools on it, and I had over a ton."

Although Bill beefed up the springs, the standard-shift vehicle did not have power steering or power brakes. "It was carrying more weight than was intended." A lot more weight!

Bill tells this story: "For those of you who don't know what happens when your valves are bad in your vehicle, when you go down a hill, smoke goes everywhere. I had big holes in the floorboard, a big welder in the back. It was really heavier than it should have been."

The floor boards were gone; you could see the highway.

It was a hard winter and Bill was headed to Johnstown from his Daisytown home, downhill on the steep, slippery two-lane Frankstown Road with limited guard railing and "smoke gushing into the cab so bad I had to wind the window down and stick my head out to drive because I couldn't see."

"It looked like something from Wile E. Coyote and the Road Runner cartoons; you're in a vehicle, it's on fire with all the smoke, and your head's sticking out while you drive."

His face was freezing as he was gearing down to make a left turn at an intersection, but his momentum was too much. "I couldn't stop. I had to overshoot it because of all the weight." It could have been the wreck that ended his career, much less his life.

Another defining moment, maybe even the final straw, came on a cold winter's morning as the temperature dropped to 10 degrees. With wind chill, it was well below zero.

A timber customer summoned Bill to the top of a mountain to weld a broken part under a logging machine.

"The guy I did it for was sitting in a warm truck drinking hot coffee."

Bill to timber customer: "Would you guys give me a hand? I can't do this myself."

Timber customer: "No, it's too cold."

Bill (under his breath): "This is bullshit."

Bill to timber customer: "I'm going to get this thing tacked up so [you can move it and] you can bring it to my shop, or forget it. I thought, I've got to do something else."

On this savagely cold winter day, Bill *almost* gave up. "Can I do this?" he asked himself. "Can I be successful? Should I do something else?" The experience with the timber customer was a major moment in Bill's journey.

"So, **I decided to reinvent myself.** I knew I couldn't depend on the small Johnstown area for my living so I decided to go into manufacturing because I could ship products anywhere and not have to rely on local sales."

Bill didn't need or ask for anyone's permission or approval. He made a decision. He was taking his career in a different direction.

A retired U.S. Navy Seals commander, Mark Divine left a high-paying corporate job while accepting his potential for failure in the military, even death in training or combat. He endured his family's disappointment with his career shift. But deep inside, he wrote in his book, *The Way of the Seal,* "I knew I was on the right path." Divine says he has been rewarded "many times over" for his decision.

Divine's training led him to **think offense, all the time, and develop unwavering confidence.** As for fear, he wrote pointedly about embracing risk, loss and failure.

Even though Bill's father was dying of inoperable cancer, Big John accompanied his son to see the buyer at Bethlehem Steel. Bill made his pitch. A month later, he got "some stuff to quote."

Meanwhile, his mother and father went to Florida. Bill was working up a quote for Bethlehem Steel. "It was a big job." The next day, Big John called Bill.

As Bill recalls the incident, "Dad was worried that I was going to screw it up, and screw up the business. He was all shook up."

John was due to return to Johnstown from Florida on Valentine's Day, but he passed away that night. Bill and Shari had been married less than three months. "It was a tough time in my life," Bill admits.

He didn't know it, but the tough times were about to get worse.

Bill looked at the blueprints he was preparing to bid for Bethlehem Steel. "I don't know why. I looked at the date and the bid was due the same date we were burying my father. I started going back and forth with the drawings." Under the circumstances, should he submit the bid? he wondered. After some brief hesitation, "I bid it."

The $6,280 bid was for a heavy-duty steel staircase.

The U.S. Olympic hockey team's win over the Soviet Union -- the Miracle on Ice -- may be the single most indelible moment in all of U.S. sports history. The steel staircase may be the single most indelible moment in Bill's business career.

More than a quarter of a century later, he publicly acknowledges the irony.

"That staircase is the staircase that's in the building that today I own." It's in a building his father worked in for Bethlehem Steel. Each time Bill walks up or down that staircase, he says, "I feel my father's presence and the genuine integrity he left our entire family."

Bill acquired his father's welding business in 1987; 12 years later he bought the building the staircase is in; 19 years later he was up-armoring Humvees for the U.S. military.

In a way, the successful bid on the steel staircase energized Bill and expanded his fledgling vision. "I started bidding projects. **Sometimes I bid projects and I wasn't even sure we could**

do it, but I didn't care. I knew we had people who could figure it out. And we did!"

Successfully bidding the staircase was the time when Bill discovered the "why" of his existence and found the courage to think and grow big.

In his book, *Start With Why*, Simon Sinek tells how President Ronald Reagan invited a hero to sit in the balcony of the House chambers during the State of the Union address in 1982. "Ronald Reagan knew all too well the power of symbols," said Sinek.

Two weeks earlier, according to media accounts, Lenny Skutnik, who was a U.S. government employee, had dived into icy waters and saved the life of a woman who was aboard Air Florida Flight 90 when it crashed into the Potomac River in Washington. "We saw again the spirit of American heroism at its finest," Reagan told the nation.

Sinek writes that Skutnik "became Reagan's symbol of courage." Likewise, Big John Polacek became his son's symbol of courage as the welding shop in a two-car garage developed into a major manufacturer and employer.

After the steel staircase project, Bill built a 3,600-square-foot shop. Within six months, he outgrew it, sold it for $100,000 and prepared to put down money for a bankrupt 60,000-square-foot factory.

"The first two years, you're just trying to get work. You did anything, anything to make a buck." The creativity and expertise in the company developed slowly but methodically. One day, years later, Bill woke up and found his core group "talking about building vehicles from the ground up."

Not just pieces of a vehicle, but the whole thing. That sort of talk was a long way from building that steel staircase in the early years.

In his book, *Courageous Faith,* pastor, author and founder of In Touch Ministries, Charles Stanley says, "Take it from me, you can overcome anything that happens in your life -- regardless of how devastating or hopeless it may seem -- by having faith in God." It's a message Stanley has preached many times.

According to the foreword in Stanley's book, the pastor's children heard the message a thousand times: "God has a plan for your life and you don't want to miss it."

Bill Polacek stands on the famous steel staircase that is an integral part of JWF's history.

Get over the fear of trying to start a business
CHAPTER 29
All Leaders Are Readers

There are literally hundreds of self-help, business start-up, leadership, money management, entrepreneurial and "how to be a success" books on the shelves of Fortune 500 company Barnes and Noble, the largest retail bookseller in the United States, including the latest revision of Dale Carnegie's *How to Win Friends and Influence People,* the grandfather of all people-skills books for more than 80 years.

Carnegie's first printing of 5,000 copies, published in 1937, became an all-time international best seller, and he became the granddaddy of America's self-help movement.

The subtitle on the cover of the 1981 special anniversary edition claims the work to be, according to the editors, the "only book you need to lead you to success."

Even if the claim may be slightly exaggerated, no one has mastered jazzing up people's confidence more than the failed actor from Missouri, and any serious entrepreneur will be well served by reading and studying Dale Carnegie's books, in addition to the many other authors whose works are mentioned in the pages of *Armor of Success.*

The idea of finding a single book that describes precisely how you should start and build your successful business, manage your employees and develop your leadership skills, seems a bit far-fetched.

I prefer the notion that no one source will address every problem, challenge, opportunity, or possible solution faced or embraced by an aspiring entrepreneur. Hence, there is no such thing as a "one-size-fits-all" publication.

Armor of Success is no exception.

In fact, there are some traditional tenets of successful business management and leadership skills that are not even mentioned in this book. Therefore, it is not a be-all, end-all guide, and was never intended to be such.

"Many leaders claim they don't have a minute to read," writes Erica Brown in her book, *Take Your Soul to Work*. "But reading helps us escape, relax, enter another world, critique, argue and think."

Reading is also exciting!

"Facts are sacred," wrote James Delingpole on Breitbart.com (June 2017). "The truth always makes the best story."

If you're a budding entrepreneur who resists reading, you might want to reconsider that attitude. Reading is important to your success!

"Not all readers are leaders, but all leaders are readers."

Those are the words of Harry Truman, the American president who made the historic decision to drop two atomic bombs on Japan and effectively end World War II in 1945.

Reading makes us better thinkers, improves people skills, communications and relaxation, says Michael S. Hyatt, former chairman and CEO of Thomas Nelson Publishers, in his book, *Platform: Get Noticed in a Noisy World*.

According to Hyatt's assessment, reading is in decline, and the author and former publishing executive cringes at the statistics. Yet, he says he's optimistic. Why? "A readership crisis is really a leadership crisis. And for people who know how to respond, *crisis* is just another way of saying *opportunity*."

The crisis in Bill's life was his need to find a job. Creating his own job was his opportunity to respond to the crisis. How was he going to learn? Reading.

The urgency to inspire reading prompted Wendell Byrd to found a non-profit organization called Readers Are Leaders to help struggling elementary students.

But what about struggling adults in times of upheaval?

Everyone knows that international organizations and governments will set up medical outposts, provide emergency food supplies, and hand out clothing in disaster zones when a humanitarian catastrophe occurs. But are we forgetting about mental fulfillment?

While having books available doesn't equate with the basics of food, water, shelter and health issues, they are important enough that an organization called Libraries Without Borders (librarieswithoutborders.org) was founded to meet this need.

The group's website says "that access to books and information resources improves outcomes for displaced persons. Books and expression help sustain intellectual stimulation and promote self-worth and resilience amid crisis."

My two sisters and I were fortunate to grow up in a family where our parents encouraged reading. In fact, for years my father's employer, International Paper Company, paid for a full-page advertisement in *Reader's Digest.*

The monthly heading was always the same: "Send Me a Man Who Reads." The monthly ad copy included a photo and short narrative about employees who had successfully bettered themselves in the company because they had mastered reading and comprehension skills.

Often times the easiest and fastest way to change one's life is to find people who've already achieved what you want, and copy them. You can do that through reading.

Here's a practical example.

In the early days of my newspaper publishing career, I read that it may be the only business where you could pick a man's brain for a dime. Ten cents was the cost of many community newspapers back then.

For that token payment, I could study other publishers' content, writing and editorial styles, font selection, type size, how to effectively use photojournalism (or not), graphics, presentation, use of headlines, paper size and weight, and design elements such as the best number of stories to present on the front page, and how many should be above the fold.

Yes, all this for two nickels.

Later, as an operations and management consultant for community newspapers and small market daily publications, I found that the worst newspaper had at least one idea to borrow.

Everywhere I traveled all across this great country, I picked up a newspaper and studied it. It was a deal for a dime! And it continued to be a deal as newsstand prices inched up over the years -- 25 cents, 50 cents, 75 cents, even a dollar.

"Confidence, optimism, security, creativity, persuasiveness, being a great golfer or salesperson are simply skills to be learned and mastered, and any skills that anyone else has mastered you can learn too," says Paul McKenna, in his book, *I Can Make You Confident.*

McKenna maintains that people learn through a two-step process:

- Copying or modeling how others do it.
- Repeatedly practicing the new skill, whether it's mental or physical, until it becomes habit.

It's doubtful that anyone will ever be able to duplicate *exactly* how Bill Polacek rapidly moved from a two-car garage to one million square feet of manufacturing space. **But anyone can follow their dream by applying the same principles, and one starts by getting over the fear of trying.**

Fear knocked on the door. Faith answered.
No one was there. -- English Proverb

Get the job done, and get it done right
CHAPTER 30
Protect Your Mind From Critics

Anytime Bill's siblings engage in conversation about the early years of JWF Industries, you're likely to hear some slimy tales. Bill often smelled like rotting cottage cheese as he climbed out from inside a steel processing tank at Sanitary Dairy, his biggest client in the early years.

A century before Sanitary Dairy was producing products commercially, Americans were making cottage cheese in their cottages from any milk left over after making butter. During World War I, U.S. citizens were being encouraged to consume cottage cheese as an alternative to meat products for protein.

For the most part, repairs at Sani-Dairy could only be made from inside the commercial processing tanks, and sometimes homemade tools were required to get the job done.

There's a business axiom that seems to apply here: Whether it's the weird methods or medieval tools used, if it's obsolete and works, it's not obsolete.

Get the job done, and get it done right. That was Bill's mantra. And his father's and grandfathers' before him.

Bill's odor gave new meaning to the word gross. There were times he smelled so bad that his own mother turned up her nose.

"I saw Bill come home at night so tired from putting in so many hours in the day, so dirty," she said, "and he'd just sit on the floor against a wall because he just couldn't go anymore." All the while, the offensive smell attached itself to furniture, clothes and bed linens.

Sally Polacek kept vivid memories of her son's smelly career; so vivid, in fact, that she shared the full aroma at the company's 25th anniversary celebration.

"I remember one time Bill came home and the stench in the house was terrible." Sally finally figured out what was going on. Bill had worked all day under a leaky vat that had contained spoiled milk. He not only "smelled to high heaven," it was days before the foul odor left his body and the air in the little house was fit to breathe again.

"In fact, the one guy with whom he worked called him Stinky."

From Bill's perspective, "it was like being sprayed by a skunk," and all the odor-eliminating tricks such as soaking in tomato juice failed to work. When Bill picked up Shari for a date, "she kind of looked at me and said, 'Bill, I love you, but you really smell bad.'"

The only redeeming grace in Bill's repulsive job at Sanitary Dairy was that he was allowed to take home leftover half-gallon cartons of ice cream that were to be tossed. His father would often wrap a carton in a towel, sit down, and eat the whole thing.

Stinky is also called Uncle Bill by some workers, and he takes it as a term of endearment. Sometimes on emails, he has signed UB#1 (Uncle Bill#1).

Such stinky lessons as the cottage cheese episodes prompted a "down-to-earth" headline in Johnstown's *The Tribune-Democrat* where business writer Shawn Piatek declared that Bill "isn't afraid to get his hands dirty."

In fact, **Bill demanded to take the dirtiest jobs. "That's how he started. He started at the bottom of the ladder performing the dirtiest and most difficult jobs to earn a living,**" reflects Debbie, the second eldest child in the Polacek family.

And Bill got down and dirty long before the first pilot for the television show *Dirty Jobs* premiered on the Discovery Channel in 2003.

Mike Rowe introduced each show by saying: "I explore the country looking for people who aren't afraid to get dirty -- hard-working men and women who earn an honest living doing the kinds of jobs that make civilized life possible for the rest of us."

The jobs Rowe tackled were a mix of difficult, strange, dangerous, repulsive, disgusting and messy; everything from rattlesnake catcher to road-kill collector.

During the 1990s, JWF landed a pivotal contract -- a rush job requiring heavy overtime from its employees. In true Mike Rowe-fashion, Bill, a skilled welder, came in on a weekend and jumped right in beside his workers.

"When we got that contract ... we didn't know if we even had the manpower to pull it off," remembered Greg Dugan, a customer service representative who had been with JWF for 16 years at the time.

Dugan told a newspaper reporter, "Bill came in that weekend and went to the foreman of the job and said, 'I want the dirtiest job you have.' The foreman didn't know what to do,'" Dugan recalled.

"But Bill explained to him, **'I can't expect my guys to do something I wouldn't do.'** Not only did he do it, he did it all day long." And he did it right.

Such actions, coupled with Bill's overall treatment of his workers, built what Dugan called a "fierce loyalty" among the company's employees.

President Harry Truman had a sign on his desk that said, "The Buck Stops Here." The inscription didn't originate with Truman, but he certainly popularized it.

Ryan Holiday and Stephen Hanselman note in their book, *The Daily Stoic,* that strong individuals accept responsibility. Truman knew, good or bad, there wasn't anyone he could blame other than himself.

Holiday and Hanselman offer 366 meditations on wisdom, perseverance, and the art of living. About passing the buck, they say, "we would do well to internalize this [Truman's] same attitude."

When Bill was named Person of the Year by the Inter-Service Club Council of Greater Johnstown, his hometown newspaper captured his dirty background in a story headline, "Welding a family." (The award is presented annually to a person born and raised in Johnstown who has made contributions with regional or national significance.)

Servant leaders are not seeking approval or recognition. It is "who they are and what they are meant to do," says Jon Gordon, in his book, *The Power of Positive Leadership*.

Gordon warns that with leadership comes scrutiny, praise, critics and attacks. He wisely says, "Don't let praise *go* to your head and don't let critics *into* your head."

Sometimes, says Bill, a leader can get too much advice. He recalls an old adage: Man with one watch can tell time. Man with two watches is never quite sure.

Learn art of disagreeing
CHAPTER 31
Union Organizes Against JWF

JWF Industries has a history of outgrowing its facilities almost as fast as it moves into them. The growing company eventually became a ripe target to be unionized.

There was a time when at least six United Steel Workers of America locals were powerful in the region, with membership in the tens of thousands -- all actively engaged in steelmaking. Nowadays the remaining locals have memberships in the thousands, not tens of thousands, from a variety of fields.

On August 16, 2012, workers at JWF Industries cast their secret ballots. **It was the union's largest attempt in 30 years to organize a facility in Western Pennsylvania.**

If approved, according to the National Labor Relations Board in Pittsburgh, the union would have represented all JWF's full-time and regular part-time production and maintenance employees.

If the blue-collar workers chose union affiliation, they would become members of the International Association of Machinists and Aerospace Workers Local 2779.

How is it that Bill was prepared to do battle with union representatives?

Surely his history of brawling with his brothers wouldn't help, or would it? He once chased one sibling with an axe. Would Bill succumb to a temper tantrum that would ruin his chances of denying the unionization?

Matt Hughes, former vice president of Business Development at JWF Industries (no relation to the author), reflected on a poem his father shared with him in his teenage years. It has become a personal barometer that he uses to measure others.

"I didn't appreciate it back then, but as I moved forward with my life and career, I realized what my father was trying to teach me."

In describing Bill's management style, Hughes refers to Rudyard Kipling's famous poem *If*:

> *If you can keep your head when all about you are losing theirs and blaming it on you, if you can trust yourself when all men doubt you, but make allowance for their doubting too; if you can wait and not be tired by waiting, or being lied about, don't deal in lies, or being hated, don't give way to hating, and yet don't look too good, nor talk too wise.*

"I've learned that outside of sales, managing people is the hardest job in business," says Hughes. "Bill possesses a great quality when it comes to managing and relating to a workforce."

Perhaps we'll never fully understand the life lessons Bill learned growing up with four brothers and four sisters and how those lessons helped him succeed. But there's a lot of research behind the claim that siblings can shape their siblings more than their parents.

Boys, especially, learn to handle conflict in different ways, and not always with their fists. Some kids rely on brains, brawn, or just bawling. The Polacek girls did their share of hand-to-hand combat, too.

There wasn't a door in the house that didn't have a hole in it from fighting. Boys and girls both guilty!

Bill once owned a front-wheel drive vehicle that had a slew of belts. "I had to take all these belts off to replace the alternator belt and I put them down so I knew where they belonged. I used my dad's truck to go get a new belt. I came back and my car was gone."

It turns out that Bill's brother, Marty, took the car without permission and belts were flying everywhere.

When confronted, Marty told Bill, "You shouldn't have left the keys in it." Bill went after him. "I was going to hit him, and I pulled my fist back ready to tag him, and I turned around and punched the refrigerator."

That wasn't the only dispute with Marty.

Big John was in the woods cutting trees for firewood while Bill was loading the truck and hauling it to the house. "That was hard manual work, and then I split the wood."

And then he asked, "Where's Marty?"

Big John was about to leave for his 3-11 PM shift at the steel mill. Marty was in college and had told his father he needed to study. "Suddenly, Marty comes around the corner and he's in a tennis outfit."

Confronted by Bill, Marty claimed he needed a break from studying and "besides I'm going to college so I don't have to do manual labor."

Bill, with axe in hand, was chasing him. Needless to say, Big John didn't take kindly to the remark about manual labor.

While Bill made it a habit to save his money, his older brothers spent it as fast as they got it. Sally wanted her boys to be independent after high school so her rule was to charge a small stipend to live at home after graduation.

But Bill found out he was the only one paying. Sally excused the other boys because they didn't have any money. Bill retorted: "They don't have any money because they don't save it."

Later in life, Sally admitted to Bill: "I always thought you were stronger than the others."

Out of the verbal spats, sibling rivalries and physical fights emerged a man who learned how to get along with people. But union organizers appeared to be a different breed.

Was Bill equipped?

For several decades beginning in the late 1960s, Bernard C. Meltzer hosted a syndicated radio show, "What's Your Problem?" He was fond of reminding listeners that good people in this world far outnumber the bad.

Callers were as likely to seek his advice about parenting dilemmas or romantic failures as they were to inquire about investment opportunities or clogged toilets.

Meltzer was a jack-of-all-trades on the radio. A city planner by training, he held degrees in civil engineering and business.

Here's one of his most famous quotes: **"If you have learned how to disagree without being disagreeable, then you have discovered the secret of getting along -- whether it be business, family relations, or life itself."**

In addition to his ability to get along with others, Bill also learned to communicate in ways that transcend mere words -- body language, facial expressions, voice tone, eye movement, eye contact, smiles, frowns, raised eyebrows, nods, rolling eyes -- sometimes referred to as a universal or unspoken language.

Translation?

He learned that **managing people is more of an art than a science.**

Bill wasn't given a secret formula nor did he read a set of rules with which to effectively manage people. It was a process that required relentless commitment and constant practice.

And his school-of-hard-knocks education eventually paid off when dealing with an unlevel playing field as his workers were faced with a critical yes or no decision regarding the fate of a sustained effort to unionize JWF's workers.

When the union organizers started a lie-campaign to sway votes in their direction, Bill didn't show any outward anger. He didn't start blaming union sympathizers for their attacks.

"He maintained a cool head, addressed each attack in a confident fashion, and personally talked to any employee that would listen about how the lies were untrue," says Hughes.

"Everybody knew, if we went union, it would really hurt our ability to put the best people on the job and it would really restrict our ability to be flexible with our customers and it would cause our employees to pay union dues instead of keeping the money for themselves."

Bill kept reasoning with employees. "You decide. Who do you trust with our future, me or the union?"

Union organizers "can say whatever they want," Bill acknowledged, "but you have to look at what I've done. You have to decide if you think the union has your best interest at heart and you want to put your future in their hands, then you should vote for the union."

The union lost. And lost big!

When the votes were counted after the last polling place closed, JWF employees overwhelmingly rejected the move to unionize, 194-38.

It was a supreme vote of confidence in the company's founder and CEO. "This isn't a Bill Polacek win," Hughes says. "It's a Johnstown win."

A union rep was quoted as saying he "hadn't been beat this bad since he was a kid and stole money from his dad."

Afterwards, Bill got a soaking usually reserved for coaches of major sports teams following championship victories.

Despite the victory, Bill took the challenge personally.

Even though women and some men were in tears when the vote tally was announced, Bill thought of the plot in the acclaimed Christmas movie, *It's a Wonderful Life,* where George Bailey, the leading character, was reminded how different life in his little town would have been had he never been born.

The union attempt was a "low moment" in Bill's career. Later he found out that a couple of rebel rousers had forged signatures on cards that fraudulently led to the unionization attempt.

By its very nature, manufacturing has its highs and lows; it's not just unionization challenges. Layoffs are part of the process. Bill never forgot when his own father was laid off "and we had nothing. I saw the cause and effect of that. The fear and anxiety almost felt like a death."

Bill learned that **"you don't a lay a person off, you lay a family off."** His own mother cried when his father got his notice.

Bill was determined to do things differently at JWF. Take pay, for example. There were times when bonuses exceeded an employee's regular pay.

One employee, who always had a "glass half empty" attitude, asked Bill, "Why do you do this?"

Bill's reply: "Because I want you to know that I'm going to share in the good times and also don't forget when things are tough, remember when I gave you bonuses."

JWF Industries is not the only company in America where management has successfully established a working rapport with employees. It actually happens quite frequently.

For example, a similar attempt by the International Association of Machinists & Aerospace Workers (IAM) to unionize Boeing's North Charleston, South Carolina aircraft factory in 2017 was handily defeated when nearly three-fourths of the workforce voted to reject union representation.

Is there a lesson here? Of course.

Unions have their place, but union representation may not be the best approach for every company. Some companies perform best when the 'boss' is allowed to be, and functions as, the leader.

Photo is blurry but Bill is definitely getting a Gatorade bath.

Zero defects. No exceptions. No excuses.
CHAPTER 32
Kill Them With Kindness

Part of JWF's vision is to make its employees successful, says Dan Allshouse, who started as an entry-level welder, and years later became a general manager and one of Bill's brothers-in-law.

When the attempt was made to unionize the plant, Allshouse was impressed with Bill's campaign to share facts with the company's workers, both about JWF and union practices.

From his vantage point, Allshouse says the majority of workers trust Bill and believe he factors in their best interests when making business decisions. Repeatedly, **Bill refers to his employees as family; men and women with feelings, problems, and personal lives.**

Work and family can't be separated, Bill says.

Bill encourages his employees to get to know him, because he cares about the individual and their family. He makes himself available and approachable. It's not an act, but rather part of the JWF culture, and it pays huge dividends.

After all, increased productivity means a better living for everyone. This caring attitude is a natural solution to improving everyone's lot in life.

By any measure, the human approach has been critical to JWF's success.

If you want to make something from nothing, help the world be more productive, and create wealth for the masses beyond anyone's imagination, "I can steer you in the right direction," promises Andy Keesler in his book, *Eat People.*

Keesler subscribes to a simple equation: Increased productivity equals better living. "Productivity is really just doing the right things while doing things right."

Bill found that in business, there's never a wrong time to do the right thing. It's a philosophy embraced by the late civil rights leader Martin Luther King, Jr.: "That old law about 'an eye for an eye' leaves everybody blind. The time is always right to do the right thing."

Even after an overwhelming win against unionization, Bill was troubled that more than three dozen of his employees thought they might benefit from union representation.

"I always thought I put the employee first and do everything I can for them and their families. We don't just have a company. We have a family that looks out for one another and the community."

After the vote, Bill moved to mend any broken fences by sending a message to every worker:

"I want to restate that which I have been saying throughout this process. I want us all to work together. Let's move beyond any differences of opinion that have been created by this experience and make JWF Industries the organization that we all want it to be. I know that you are holding me to a high standard and I welcome the opportunity to meet your expectations."

Bill is adept at giving people genuine praise and positive feedback. Remember the saying, kill them with kindness? Well, he doesn't go that far, but he's nice to people because it's a way of life with him. **Genuine compliments build trust.** "Don't overdo it, but do it appropriately."

Physicist Isaac Newton's third law of motion says, "For every action, there is an equal and opposite reaction." It works in human relations, too.

It's like a second nature to Bill. His thankfulness for every worker has exploded into a fierce loyalty among employees at JWF Industries.

When there's uneasiness in the rank and file, or among mid- and upper-level management, he brings calmness and reassurance. He's confident, enthusiastic and transparent, all of which are traits that inspire people.

Most of us have heard the saying the early bird gets the worm, metaphorically speaking. Another common metaphor is putting the cart before the horse. Killing employees with kindness is one thing. Killing innovation is something else.

Erica Brown authored a challenging and timely article posted online that described how perfection can kill innovation (businessmagazinegainesville.com). "The objective of any successful innovation is to create what did not exist, to improve on what already existed and to solve problems -- even if the solutions are infinitesimally small," she said.

To initiate innovation successes, she added, "do not wait for 'the perfect time' to do so; there is no such time."

That's the attitude at JWF Industries. The time is now.

JWF pays non-union wages but shares a portion of any profits that exceed one percent of total sales. **But the profit-sharing isn't free; it requires an in-kind contribution from each employee.**

The in-kind contribution can be described in many ways: pulling together in harmony, unity, in partnership, and in a joint effort.

To put that in one word, the in-kind contribution is teamwork!

Big banners on factory walls declare: Zero defects. No exceptions. No excuses.

A few years ago, after a particularly grueling job for a big customer, Bill flew 100 employees, plus 50 spouses, to Miami and, from there, put them on a four-day cruise to the Bahamas. Some had never been out of Johnstown; some had never left Pennsylvania; and many had never flown.

Bill was sitting near the rear of the plane and didn't realize the number of employees who had never traveled by air until the stewardess rolled a snack cart down the aisle and he asked for a beer, then a wine, and then a mixed drink.

Stewardess: "Sir, we are completely out of alcohol."
Bill: "Is this normal?"

Stewardess: "Sir, I've been a stewardess for 32 years and this is the first time in my career we've run out of alcohol on a first run. Who are these people?"

Bill: "They are my employees."

Many of the employees and spouses were so nervous, they were drinking non-stop.

While the paid vacation for Bill's employees was appreciated, many of them said it was even more gratifying that Bill was on the floor, working side by side, as they finished the demanding project and delivered on time (which was the reason Bill rewarded their unselfish contributions with a paid vacation).

"The way to get the rhythm of the company's culture is by being out there with them," says Bill.

Matt Hughes says Bill has an **uncanny ability to relate to the "guys on the floor" and not come across haughty.**

"He knew that this union drive would be a marathon and not a sprint, so he was patient with his plan of action and used this experience as an opportunity to learn employees' concerns and become a stronger, better company as a result."

Although the French military genius Napoleon Bonaparte was soundly defeated at the Battle of Waterloo in 1815, he understood the role of a leader; "a leader is a dealer in hope."

Bill offers his employees hope and tries to lead every day by example.

Wall-hanging banner says it all.

Don't put all your eggs in one basket
CHAPTER 33
Seriously, What's In A Name?

"The sky is not the limit ... I am," says T.F. Hodge, blogger, commentator and author of the book, *From Within I Rise.*

Bill wasn't going to be the only welding and manufacturing business in Pennsylvania, not even in Johnstown. However, **he decided early on if someone else can do it, he could do it better.**

"Many entrepreneurs strive to build and sell their company. My goal is to grow and sustain my company," says Garcia Desinor, Realtor and owner of Level Properties in Dallas.

Desinor is quoted in an online article in YFS Magazine (yfsmagazine.com). "The more employees you have, the more lives you're responsible for."

"My goal," says Bill, "is to prepare the company so it will be here a hundred years from now."

There are companies that are so caught up in cost reductions that they lose sight of their primary mission; everything to them is about saving money, not bettering the lifestyle of their employees and building better and more affordable mouse traps.

In fact, Matthew Burrows, a best practices expert, wrote an intriguing online article (BSMReview.com) on operational efficiency, and used the comical example of a consultant that promised to reduce costs for his client by 100 percent -- by sending everyone home.

"You will have no customers or revenue," the consultant told the client, "so you'll need to go home, too."

Of course, the example is silly, but it drives home the point.

At the outset, Bill could have relocated his father's business to a city with a larger population base like Pittsburgh, or a metropolitan area where chambers of commerce, industrial development groups, and local governments were already offering financial incentives to new industry, especially those that were advertising help wanted.

Instead, he elected to stay at home. Bill may not have fully understood the ramifications at the time, but the decision to stay put proved prophetic.

"There are no rules about how much experience you should have when you start a business," according to a posting on the website of Smarta Business Builder (smarta.com), providers of an online tool package.

You learn by doing. Your past experiences immediately come into play. You learn about efficiency. You learn how to deal with people, how to avoid problems.

Although he had no previous business experience, Bill had a working familiarity with the people and places where he had grown up.

In reality, Bill and most other entrepreneurs acquired life experience skills just dealing with stress and problems in their personal lives, and unknowingly learned something about the "resilience and emotional experience needed to cope with running a business."

More importantly, he had absorbed his dad's integrity and work ethic in the very shadows of the bulky steel mill buildings Johnstown had become famous for. This rich history begged a question.

As a new entrepreneur, should you build your dream company where you live, doing what you love?

If you answered yes, you're in good company, says Michael Glauser in his book, *Main Street Entrepreneurs*. According to Glauser, "Most successful entrepreneurs have worked in the industry they start their business in, in a related industry," or have personal experience with services, products and problems.

Glauser cites the case of Steve Sullivan, founder of Stio, a mountain lifestyle clothing company (stio.com). Sullivan says he wished he had come up with the idea for Twitter. Who wouldn't? It's now a $2.5 billion company. But Sullivan's story is that he doesn't know anything about Twitter. He does know about apparel for people who enjoy the outdoors.

Even at age 27, Bill's honesty, integrity and family values were evident. "I've always believed in being honest with clients," he was quoted in his hometown newspaper. **"I feel that I've gained a lot of trust from them. People are more cost-minded today, and a business needs to be honest and dependable."**

In the early days, 75 percent of Bill's business was done in the shop, while the remaining work was done on site because the projects were too large to be moved, such as structural additions to buildings or welding bodies of Air East airplanes.

To reduce his financial risks, Bill quickly learned to diversify. He didn't place all his eggs in one basket, so to speak, nor did he depend solely on one product or one service. His company worked with any weldable material including cast iron which most shops shied away from because of its tendency to break.

"You have to be versatile in this field. You can't depend on one specialty or you won't survive."

Bill's training in blueprint reading and welding provided him the basic tools to begin his venture. An ability to find different and interesting ways of accomplishing goals set him apart as he built his business.

Bill believed in himself.

He carried an air of confidence that created excitement that showed through to customers, employees and suppliers. "I found when you're excited about what you do, you get other people excited, too."

Lisa Messenger has a must-read message:

To succeed in life, you "must have an unwavering, insatiable, tenacious belief in yourself. You have to be able to back yourself, to harbor that kind of unbridled passion for winning that will stop at nothing until you reach your goals."

Lisa Messenger is the founder of an entrepreneurial lifestyle magazine and CEO of The Messenger Group (collectivehub.com). The above declaration is found in the first paragraph of her book, *Daring & Disruptive*.

John Kendera, Bill's first employee, had a background in welding but jobs in the welding field were scarce in the late 1980s. Kendera was skeptical when he first drove up to Bill's small shop for a job interview, but left impressed with his future employer's honesty and knowledge of the business.

"One of the reasons I came here was the fact that I thought Bill knew what he was doing," Kendera said at the time.

When it came to welding, no one questioned Bill's skills. But establishing a new company name and logo, that's another story. It became a work in progress.

The power of a name and its value has long been immortalized in prose, poetry, religious ceremony, and songs.

To make my point, "everybody knew you didn't give no lip." If you were older than a middle-schooler in 1961, you probably remember Jimmy Dean singing these lyrics about a miner in the hit song "Big Bad John" (no relation to Big John Polacek).

Everyone recognizes himself or herself by name. The name of any business, large or small, has numerous branding, marketing, and web implications.

A name creates a first impression.

It can impress investors and bankers (or not). And it can make a company's public relations image consumer-friendly (or not).

An example of the latter might be the Edsel automobile, named after the first child of Ford Motor Company's founder Henry and his wife Clara, which was released in 1957 after an intense "The Edsel is Coming" advertising campaign.

I wasn't old enough to drive at the time, but I well remember all the advertising hype about the Edsel, as well as the negative fallout.

Tony and Michele Hamer described the "legacy of failure" in an online article (thoughtco.com) where they contend that customers didn't buy the Edsel "because the car didn't live up to expectations created in prior months of epic advertising."

Even years later, the name, Edsel, brings to mind all the car's failures. According to the Hamers, "The advertising agency involved in the rollout, provided 18,000 names for Ford executives to pick from. In the end they ignored all of these and went in their own direction."

Enough about the Edsel.

"Excellent customer service and high customer satisfaction must start with understanding customer expectations," wrote Ross Beard, who was on the marketing team at Client Heartbeat, the customer feedback tool. "You need to know who your customers are and what they want," he said on the firm's website (blog.clientheartbeat.com).

Beard added: "If a customer feels like you did not deliver a service that was expected, they won't come back."

A name can be confusing and misleading. For example, there is no such thing as an American buffalo. The furry beast that roamed the Wild West was a bison.

Bill learned about confusing and misleading names the hard way. Although Johnstown's population was steadily declining in 1986, more than 32,000 people still called it home.

And by the time Bill bought his late father's business from his mother, Johnny's Welding was a household name, and the name was strictly associated with Bill's father, Big John Polacek.

Johnny's Welding wasn't a national brand name like Coca-Cola® or GE®; it was strictly local. And it was only natural that customers became confused, maybe even exasperated, when John Kendera, Bill's new employee, answered the phone: "Johnny's Welding. This is John."

It got worse when John Kendera tried to explain that Johnny's Welding was owned by Bill, not John. Well, you get the point. Every phone call was like getting a daily dose of The Three Stooges and one of their comedy acts.

The name of your business may not be everything, but it's darn important.

Suffice it to say that choosing a new name for Johnny's Welding became a critically important decision.

"Johnny's Welding sounds like a little repair shop, which is what it was. I'm trying to sell fabrication and manufacturing."

More than one name change and more high-end work were needed before Bill could fully express the scope of his business.

The evolution of the name happened this way:

- Johnny's Welding, 1957, located in the family's two-car garage.
- Johnny's Welding became Johnstown Welding and Fabrication, Inc. "Not only was I proud of the city, but my dad worked for a company called Johnstown Welding."
- Johnstown Welding and Fabrication, Inc., changed its corporate name to JWF Industries to more accurately reflect the company's background, expanded capabilities, and manufacturing space.

Leadership is a decision made in bad times
CHAPTER 34
Laying Off Workers Is Never Easy

After her passing, Sally's children found one of their mother's completed college assignments that required "naming some values you hope your children have."

She and John tried hard to live their expectations in front of their children. They were not always successful.

"No matter the form it takes, we all have episodes of inadvertently teaching our children 'Do as I say, not as I do,'" writes Rebecca Capuano (thehomeschoolmom.com) in an online blog.

"And if we're *really* honest, we'd admit that sometimes we just wish the adage could be true!"

There were many days and nights when Sally yelled at the top of her lungs. Not her proudest moments. Yet, she was still able to feel love and compassion and put a list of important values on paper:

1. Feel love for each other.
2. Speak only kindly of one another.
3. Share with each other.
4. Accept constructive criticism.
5. Be motivated.
6. Be honest.

"Mom's legacy is very visible in these hopes for her children," says eldest daughter, Barbara. It's no wonder that Sally and John were held in such high esteem by their children. It's especially significant when their children are seen publicly embracing these values.

Sometimes JWF went through crazy surges where "we had to keep up with working 70 hours a week," reflected Bill.

"It was good times." But living on the mountain top is

not always easy, and it's unwise to think the good times will last forever.

In order to avoid losing one particular contract, JWF had to substantially cut the cost.

"We did it by talking to employees and making a plan, not by talking to four walls in a board room."

Sometimes the good times are the calm before the storm. A recession can rear its ugly head. "Margins go down in tough times, and manufacturing is not a high margin business to begin with."

Almost overnight, the company found itself in hard times.

"I had to lay off people who had worked hard. That's very difficult." Bill assembled these workers in one room, with all the managers around them. "I wanted managers to see a person, not a number. I wanted managers to look in their eyes and make the commitment they're going to call these workers back."

Laid off employees were facing the loss of their health coverage. If the layoff proved to be temporary, JWF was facing an expenditure of $150,000 to keep benefits in force for a short three months. "We thought after 90 days we would probably get the work back and the workers could return. That was the goal."

It was a risky move. "If our work didn't come back because of the recession, we'd lose the business, lose JWF Industries," said Bill.

"It's easy to be generous when you have the money; it's harder to say you have that leadership character when your back is against the wall."

"Leadership is not the decisions you make in the good times, but it's the decisions you make in the bad times that test your character." This is the character Bill and his siblings learned from their parents.

Russell H. Ewing said: "A boss creates fear, a leader confidence. **A boss fixes blame, a leader corrects mistakes.** A boss knows all, a leader asks questions. A boss makes work drudgery, a leader makes it interesting. A boss is interested in himself or herself, a leader is interested in the group (quotationsbook.com)."

Bill was willing to risk his business in order to keep health coverage in force for laid off employees because it was the right thing to do. It was one of his proudest moments, a time "I felt I was really tested."

"Our faith is so much an important part of who we are," says Bill. "I think it builds your character and it tells us about who you are and who you're going to be."

Faith was also a key element in legendary football coach Vince Lombardi's view of life, along with family and sports.

Lombardi coached the Green Bay Packers in the 1960s and the NFL's Super Bowl trophy is named in his honor, largely because of his unique leadership skills.

"Leaders aren't born, they are made," the coach said. "And they are made just like anything else, through hard work. And that's the price we'll have to pay to achieve that goal, or any goal."

"I agree with Lombardi's statements a thousand percent," Bill says. "Leadership is a product of one's values and life experiences." And like Coach Lombardi, it's not unusual for Bill to speak about the importance of family.

After he discovered the science behind the power of a lever, Archimedes, the ancient Greek scientist and mathematician, proclaimed: "Give me the place to stand and I shall move the earth."

Bill does something similar. Have a business or family gathering and give him a podium or a place to stand and you're likely to hear one of his inspirational speeches.

"What's more important to me is my family, my wife, my children, my brothers and sisters, my associates, my employees. I love you very dearly. You're a special part of our life. You're a special part of something that we built, not just in the business, but in the community and in friendship."

Through all their ups and downs, Bill's wife, Shari, was by his side.

"She has helped me to keep my values focused. Without her, I would have never been successful. She's my inspiration. She's been all the encouragement I've ever needed. She's been my best cheerleader. She's constantly giving me all the confidence in the world. When I come home and bounce ideas off her, it's amazing how intuitive she is about what the real problem is."

"She's my sweetheart. Here's a woman who literally was a beauty queen and I look back and think, 'I can't believe she said yes.'"

One of the things that Shari did for Bill was to keep him grounded.

"That's a tall task at times," he admits. After one particular award ceremony, the accolades were prolific.

All the way home, Bill was thinking, "I'm all that and a bag of chips, right?" Then they walked into the house and Shari blurted out, "Bill, you need to clean up your mess."

Team work, cross-training are critical
CHAPTER 35
It All Started With A Lie

The air in Grandma Whatmore's kitchen was steaming when she pulled the cake pans out of her oven on April 24, 1946, and proceeded to cool and then spread icing on the two-layer Depression version of a Poor Man's Chocolate Cake. Sixteen candles slipped easily into the freshly cooked batter.

Frank and Lillian Whatmore's daughter, Sally, invited her steady boyfriend, John Polacek, to dinner. After all, the relationship was getting serious.

After the guests sang Happy Birthday, grandma blurted out, "Sweet 16 and never been kissed." John, who had met Sally a year earlier, was stunned. "What do you mean, 16? You told me you were already 16. I came here thinking you are 17 today."

Sally was trembling because she had lied to John about her age. "You're not going to break up with me, are you?" she pleaded, with tears streaming down her face. "Well, you already got me hooked now," John replied.

"It all started with a lie," daughter, Vicki, is fond of saying, referring to the courtship of her parents.

You're only sixteen, but you're my teenage queen.

"Sixteen Candles" was a hit song by The Crests in 1958. Three years earlier, Tennessee Ernie Ford's rendition of "Sixteen Tons" was the #1 pop song on Billboard.

A song about loading 16 tons of coal and "whattaya get" certainly rang true with mine workers around Johnstown as did getting older and "deeper in debt."

Ford began his career as a local radio announcer; he served in the U.S. Army Air Corps in World War II as a bombardier on a B-29 Superfortress. He was blessed with a rich bass-baritone voice, and a unique sort of down-home humor

John's high school graduation picture.

Sally's high school graduation picture.

that appealed to miners and steel workers in Pennsylvania and all over America.

I don't know if Tennessee Ernie Ford ever set foot in a coal mine, much less one near Johnstown, but **"sixteen" is a magic number in the life of JWF Industries,** whether you know it or not.

"Football, I don't know. Politics, I don't know," mused Barry Valinsky, as he straightened his reading glasses. "But JWF has been very, very good to me."

The 60-plus-year-old is an original, one of Bill's first 16 employees, who came on board in January 1991 to run the shears and brake presses when the fledgling company operated from a "little, old, rundown building" with dirt floors.

"The roof leaked!" he chided.

"The rain would come in. It would rain harder in the building than outside the building." Pieces of a current project would be moved to a dry spot in the building, only to be moved again when new leaks showed up.

"When it rained, guess what, now we had eight inches of mud. If you were one of the misfortunate ones to drop your hand tools, nine times out of 10 they were gone," Valinsky remembered.

Fortunately there wasn't much equipment in that original building to worry about. There was a "beat up" Ford truck, an old flatbed whose engine had died, and "Bill's dad's Dodge pickup" and some small hand tools.

Having a sparse collection of tools might have been a good thing one winter night when the crew left the shop and headed home for some shut-eye in the middle of a big job.

The next morning the workers arrived, "and son of a gun, the weight of the snow took the whole center of the roof down," said Valinsky. "Everything we were working on ... most of it was underneath the snow, so we had to dig out what we needed and keep moving on."

You couldn't blame Bill's workers if they chose to throw up their hands and leave.

But that's not what happened. "The wind was coming through this hole [in the roof], we were freezing, but we did get the job done," declared Valinsky.

One of the chapters in Chris Guillebeau's book, *The $100 Startup,* tells the story of a struggling sculpture artist from a small town whose studio roof collapsed with him standing on it while frantically trying to shovel off the heavy snow load. When a bank official arrived to assess the damage, he became excited about the artist's work.

Because of that encounter, the young sculptor secured a commissioned project worth thousands of dollars, which he used as a down payment on two buildings he had wanted to buy.

One of the takeaways from this story is that the bank was forced to take a real look at the man's worthy business instead of viewing him as another broke artist.

The near catastrophe with the caved in roof was one of many turning points in Bill's bigger-than-life journey.

"If people believe in themselves," said Sam Walton, founder of Walmart and Sam's Club, "it's amazing what they can accomplish."

It wasn't long after that Bill's business was showing some profit. How did he spend it? Aspiring entrepreneurs need to take note.

Valinsky and his 15 co-workers all know the answer. "We started making a little money, so Bill took this money and invested it back in. We got our first shear, our brake press, a saw, and some new MIG welders. I mean, this felt great. We're like, bring it on."

Like all the employees, Valinsky was cross-trained, "and very well, too," he says. The cross-training made it possible for Bill's workers to tackle projects together that individually they could not do.

In Valinsky's words, "All the brains came together."

"Sixteen guys. Each had their own little talent. Each came together at the right time. **We weren't afraid to try anything.** The more we tried, the more we saw what we could do together as a team."

Valinsky didn't go out of his way to search out his 15 minutes of fame. A large contingent of names was under consideration to speak on behalf of employees at JWF's 25th anniversary celebration.

By way of a drawing from a hat, this honor fell to the sincere, soft-spoken Valinsky, who had never made a speech in public before. With a graying beard and mustache, he stepped up to the podium wearing a big grin.

There might have been a few lazy people working for JWF Industries over the years, but they didn't stay, and for good reason. As Thomas Edison once remarked, "Opportunity is missed by most people because it is dressed in overalls and looks like work."

"It wouldn't be nothing for us to work from five o'clock in the morning to midnight, days on end," Valinsky said, "just to get particular jobs done." He mentioned a few that were critical to the company's early success.

There was Farnham and Phile in Maryland, and Freight Car America. "We were like their savior because they just couldn't handle [all their work]. The particular work we were doing for them was overflow."

Those 16 guys developed a unique friendship and camaraderie and eventually experienced some "sad, difficult times" as death started taking a toll on Bill's core group: Gino Johns, Jack Irwin, Timmy Thomas, John Kendera, Gary Lamer, Jim Bradley and Pat Kilmartin.

That word 'team' would become a critical component in JWF Industries' development.

"When you work here, you become friends," said Valinsky. "It was good to talk to each other. It helped ease the pain [when a co-worker passed]."

"Now, we've got all you young guys out there. This is an opportunity to change your life," said Valinsky. "What's our secret?" he asked. Then he pointed around the room, and eyeballed everyone from welders to managers to corporate officers. "We all made the difference as one."

Team. Team. Team.

Valinsky mentioned how Bill had stood behind him and helped him during some personal leave, and he insisted that **"we [employees] really do matter."**

Test for skill, hire for attitude, character
CHAPTER 36
Blue Collar Workers, Intelligent People

Before Bill ever hired his first employee, he had a sense that choosing the right workers was critical to his success. Testing the welding skill of an applicant was quick and easy. Asking questions about blueprints was straight forward. But Bill wanted a deeper understanding of the person applying for a job.

Is he a family man? Does he take his family to church? What does he do for entertainment?

"I didn't ask those specific questions but got a sense of a person by asking what's important to them and they would tell me things that helped me understand their character. I also got a sense if they were willing to learn."

"Why do you want to work for our company?" Bill would ask.

Their responses let Bill know "what people outside of our company thought of our organization. It also let me know if they're leaving a former job for more money, or because they want to build a better future."

Ultimately, Bill learned to "test for skill, hire for attitude and character."

As a boy, he used to listen to the conversations between his father and his father's friends, all steel workers. The men often analyzed a work day at Bethlehem Steel and frequently mentioned "the floor guys" with admiration and respect, perhaps even a reverence.

They observed guys on the floor with innovative ideas, but nobody would ever listen. They talked about things they could do if management would let them, better ways of doing things.

This was a management lesson that did not go unnoticed by Bill.

"I always said I have a secret. My secret is that blue collar workers are intelligent people and they have a lot of good ideas, so we very purposefully go out, ask for their feedback, which also helps empower the employees and create ownership."

"When you're told what to do, you stop thinking, when you're asked what to do, you come up with a better solution. **A good idea fails when the people you need to do it, don't own it.** A mediocre idea that they thought of, they're going to make sure it's successful."

"The biggest mistake management makes," says Bill, **"is thinking they are smarter than their subordinates and they have to be right. It's not about being right; it's about creating a team atmosphere where everybody has a stake.** It also creates respect and trust."

Steelmaking has existed for millennia, but these guys took the ancient craft to new levels of perfection. Bill was a quick study. He grasped the work ethic of these guys who made good things happen.

"I know the guy on the floor is very bright, and if you tap that intellect it makes you more successful. So you bring him in and make him part of the solutions, and that gives him ownership." This technique evolved into standard operating procedure at JWF.

Too many employers think they know everything -- that they know what's best for the employees -- but all that does is create a wall of distrust, Bill maintains. A strong workforce culture is one of the reasons that JWF Industries has been able to grow and diversify.

Although the company's mainstay of business is still fabricating components for original equipment manufacturers, it is no longer just a tier one or tier two contractor for the defense department.

Instead, JWF bids directly for contracts, such as up-armoring Humvees.

It hasn't always been that way -- diversification, that is. Bill learned his lesson at a time when his small business was almost totally reliant on one big customer -- Sani-Dairy.

Work was steady. Paychecks were on time. Bill worked 50 hours a week for Sani-Dairy, and it was as simple as clocking in every day and billing them at the end of the week.

"They always paid on time, and I began wondering, 'What's so hard about being in business for yourself?'"

"Then one day, they stopped me before I left and told me they were making cutbacks."

When that company began to sink, smaller firms with which it did business got caught in the undertow. Bill's company was one of them. Better than 90 percent of his work was about to go away overnight.

Bill had met his day of reckoning. It was a day he would never forget. It was a day that altered his destiny.

If you're old enough, you remember where you were the day Elvis died; you remember the Apollo 11 mission when America landed the first two men on the moon; you remember what you were doing when you heard that President Kennedy was assassinated.

It might as well have been the day after the Empire of Japan attacked the U.S. Naval Base at Pearl Harbor on December 7, 1941. In Bill's mind, the devastation was about the same.

The day after the Japanese attack, President Franklin D. Roosevelt made his famous seven-minute speech that included the words, "a date that will live in infamy," and the course of American history was forever changed.

Many years have passed, but Bill still remembers that fateful day at Sani-Dairy: "Your services are no longer needed."

So, how did Bill react to this unexpected news, and what did he tell his wife?

"I didn't tell her," he says matter of fact.

"The way my brain works is, I first think about the worst thing that can happen and how to deal with that, and then I go back and think about how can I change that. Now I've dealt with the reality. I know what I'll do if I have to deal with that. I put a plan in place, with whatever help I need to create that plan."

And Shari agrees. "He does not dwell on the negative at all." People understand that bad things happen, says Bill.

He has faced multiple recessions. "I let my employees know the facts. This is what we're faced with. Here's a plan to get us out of it, and I need your help to get us there. The best way to predict the future is to create it."

"People want to know the truth," he says. And there were a few occasions when Bill did tell Shari about dire situations, especially at times when he was going without a paycheck.

"When things go bad, you can't just have hope, because hope is not a plan. You have to prepare for the worst. You have to make a plan."

Christian pastor and radio preacher Chuck Swindoll once said, "We are all faced with a series of great opportunities brilliantly disguised as impossible situations."

The unexpected announcement that Sani-Dairy was cutting back turned out to be a landmark event for Bill.

"I learned from that experience that you can't have all your eggs in one basket, because if you trip and fall, they're all gone."

In the year 2019, Sani-Dairy is long gone. Bill Polacek and his welding and fabricating operations are going strong.

Bill also learned that everything is not always black and white in business, both literally and figuratively.

One of JWF's buildings used to be painted black. "It was dreary and depressing and didn't really represent what is taking place here," he says.

A fresh coat of paint was in order, high-tech paint, that is. The new sky-blue coating for JWF's facilities is actually a combination sealant and insulating material to keep employees from being exposed to scorching heat in the summer and numbing cold in the winter.

Bill views these improvements as a symbol of the vast investment JWF has made in its facilities and, more importantly, its people.

"I think we've blown a breath of life back into these buildings, and that feels good. Though the mills our fathers and grandfathers worked in aren't here anymore, we took something from our history and made it work in our world today."

Sabrina Son, a blog writer (tinypulse.com), revealed that one recent survey found "only one in four workers feels valued at work."

Anastasia, another blog writer (cleverism.com), said, "There is absolutely no one in the world who doesn't like being rewarded and recognized for the hard work they do."

JWF has invested millions in equipment to keep up with technology and to keep costs down. In Bill's world, **"If you don't keep investing in your facilities, sooner or later technology will catch up with you, and pass you by."**

The company also continues to invest in its workforce, also known as Work Fighters, on the defense side of the business. One recognition program involves buying large ads in the local newspaper and recognizing workers by name along with their years of service.

Ian Hutchinson, former motorcycle mechanic and English professional motorcycle racer, who crashed several times and required many surgeries, made a dramatic comeback.

He's credited with saying, "Your number one customers are your people. Look after your employees first and then customers."

Don't be afraid to take some risks
CHAPTER 37
Leaders Can Make Employees Better

Coal mining started in Pennsylvania in the mid-1700s. Nearly one-third of America's abandoned mines are found in Pennsylvania. Just a few years ago there were still 7,500-plus miners employed in the coal industry. Does coal have an important history in this state?

"Look, if you didn't have coal, America wouldn't have (had) squat," according to Carmen DiCiccio, University of Pittsburgh instructor, historian and author. "It fueled industrial America."

Not everybody is suited to work outdoors, and, in spite of coal's importance, far fewer are suited to work beneath the outdoors.

A mining company needed some steel fabrication, and Bill's company was given an opportunity to submit a quote. Bill arrived on the job site and was met by an official who walked him to a nearby shed that covered an elevator shaft.

Mine official: "Okay, we're gonna go down in the mine and you can measure the job."

Bill: "I'm not going down there."

Mine official: "What do you mean? If you don't go down in the ground, you can't measure, and if you can't measure, you won't get the job."

Bill: "I don't get the job. I'm not going underground."

This event happened in the latter years of the 20th Century -- the late 1900s, to be specific. A similar event occurred in the early years of the 20th Century. And there's a family connection.

It was 1912 when Bill's grandfather, Martin Polacek, turned down his first job in America. "My grandfather and I have something in common," says Bill, "we both refused a job because neither of us wanted to go two miles underground in a mine."

One of the plots in Lori Greiner's book, *Invent It, Sell It, Bank It,* is the idea of sticking to what you know as you develop your business.

Bill knew what had worked in the past, and he wasn't afraid to take some risks in order to grow. He was good at what he did.

"The risks of change always seem to be more real than the risks of standing still." That's a widely circulated quote attributed to Carly Fiorina, former CEO of Hewlett-Packard and former presidential candidate. "Leaders have to be willing to make tough choices at the right time, which means before they are obvious to everyone else."

Bill didn't need to descend into the bowels of the earth to get work. He could find jobs on the planet's surface where he was comfortable.

"Expect the best. Prepare for the worst. Capitalize on what comes," advises Zig Ziglar, renowned motivational speaker. Bill knew where he was drawing the line and it wasn't deep in a mine.

Creating a plan to change and improve his hometown is part of Bill's vision. "It's bigger than you, this company, this valley. **My purpose is to help people succeed."**

Daymond John's book, *The Power of Broke,* suggests a "competitive advantage" goes to the entrepreneur with barren pockets, a strained budget and a yearning for success, which were a reflection of John's own starting point.

He was broke, had a heart full of hope, and was forced to think more creatively because of his circumstances.

John tells the story of Tim Ferris, who was working feverishly to publish his first book, *The 4-Hour Workweek.* The two men apparently had something in common. Ferris was turned down by 27 publishers. John was turned down by 27 banks.

Being rejected is not the same as being a failure.

John points out that Walt Disney was turned down 302 times before getting financing for Walt Disney World. The family theme park, measuring 43 square miles and featuring the Magic Kingdom, Animal Kingdom and Epcot, has become the most visited vacation resort on the planet.

Thomas Edison's teachers said he was too stupid to learn anything. He was fired from his first two jobs for being non-productive. Then he invented the phonograph. Edison was not afraid of rejection or failure.

"I'm very humbled when I see the things Bill does for the community. It's always about what he can do for others," says Tom Polacek, an engineer and the youngest sibling and one of two brothers who work in management capacities for Bill.

"There's no doubt in our minds from the eight brothers and sisters ... we can't say enough about what Bill has done for us, for our mother, for our families, for the community."

"Leadership is not how you can manage people and tell them what to do, it's about how you can build them up and make them better people, and be a role model and make them better at everything they do. That's truly servant leadership," says Tom.

It's a theme not uncommon to successful businessmen all over the globe.

"I feel I'm successful when people who work for me, or are around me, are more than they thought they could be," says Bill. "I'm doing more than I ever thought I would."

Leaders assemble the best team by recruiting the best people, says Eduardo P. Braun in his book, *People First Leadership*. "Great leaders love hiring intelligent people, but, interestingly, they are particularly keen to seek out people who are even more intelligent than they are."

And great leaders work hard to develop people they hire.

Bill was quiet and almost never asked for anything while he was growing up, according to his brother, Marty, but he developed into a goal-oriented, caring man.

Marty believes the main reason Bill succeeded "is the fire he developed within himself," perhaps because people did not believe in him.

While this "fire" is recognizable in certain individuals, it is not something mystical. In fact, the trait of finding one's passion and identifying what's important in life is described by courage coach Peter Hobler in his book, *Courage to Find the Fire Within.*

To state it bluntly, Hobler says, **"Success takes courage,"** and he identifies various principles of courage.

Bill has been characterized in many ways by many people.

Take charge leader. Generous. Considerate. Professional. Good guy. The genuine American dream. Good insight into employee issues and human relations management. Likes to share. A fun guy. Athletic. A man with purpose.

Even the moniker, 'good ole boy,' has been applied to Bill.

Never stuffy. Down to earth. Successful. Rags to riches. Family oriented. Caring. Natural leader. Bright. Involved. Concerned about others. Continually learning and growing. Started with nothing. Truly cares for his employees and Johnstown. Philanthropic. Ambitious. Honest.

It was John Quincy Adams, diplomat, statesmen, and sixth president of the United States, who said: "If your actions inspire others to dream more, learn more, do more and become more, you are a leader."

Selfless acts are hallmarks of great leaders
CHAPTER 38
Sally And John's First Christmas Train

It's impossible to dissect and understand Bill apart from his parents. His father passed far too young, his mother was widowed far too young.

Bill and his siblings went through the last six months of 2014 without their mother.

Sally's death brought on a strange and empty feeling, especially when some 70 immediate and extended Polacek family members gathered in Johnstown to honor their heritage during an annual Christmas Eve dinner that traces its roots back to the Old Country.

"Grandma (Eva Polacek) was born in 1888," commented Barbara Hughes, the eldest child of John and Sally Polacek. "We don't know exactly how long this tradition has been passed down, but we do know it's been at least 126 years. Traditions don't last forever. They only last as long as we keep them alive."

The annual celebration exposed another lesson about how life can throw you curveballs, challenges you can never adequately prepare for, and the long, tiresome journey of grief. Until you experience grief, you don't realize how mentally and physically overwhelming it is.

Someone said it takes a combination of strategies and remedies to comfort a broken heart. The passing of a parent is a reminder to keep life simple and family close.

Sally wasn't prepared for what one particular Christmas would bring. She became painfully aware that her children would not be receiving any presents.

Bill was six years old when he learned the true meaning of Christmas. An untimely accident a few months before the Christmas holidays brought fear and despair to the Polacek household.

Big John fell down a ladder, fractured a heel, and was laid up for months, unable to work, much less walk without crutches.

It was the only time in their marriage Sally ever saw her husband cry.

"The only money coming in was part of his supplemental pay from Bethlehem Steel. We weren't going to have much of a Christmas that year," Bill remembers.

John and Sally Polacek at his retirement party in 1983.

Ten people in the household were in school. Sally was in LPN school; the two oldest girls were in Registered Nursing school; and seven of their siblings were in high school and grade school.

Sally began dipping into Christmas savings to feed the family. By December, there was no money left for presents. The children didn't realize how grim the financial picture had become.

Their mother's most memorable crying episode was about to occur. The family came home from midnight Mass on Christmas Eve and found money, bags of groceries, and presents on the front porch.

To this day the source of the gifts remains unknown. Between her tears and sobbing, Sally told John and the children, "See how God takes care of us."

No one in the family has ever forgotten that Christmas miracle. It prompted Bill to give back to his employees and community in numerous ways. "I decided that I wanted to do something to help people in the same situation."

That's the reason that every year, Bill donates a present to each man, woman and child who comes to Christmas Eve dinner at St. Vincent de Paul Family Kitchen in Johnstown.

Each Christmas you'll find a mountain of presents stacked near the door of the pantry, and you're likely to see Bill and his wife, Shari, and their four children busy distributing gifts.

"If you're in a soup kitchen on Christmas Day, you're not going to get any presents because either you don't have anyone, or you don't have anything. I bought practical Christmas gifts for everybody that was there," appropriate gifts for adults and toys for a range of ages.

On February 1, 2000, this warm and tingling Christmas story became a permanent part of the Congressional Record when the late U.S. Representative John P. Murtha, from Pennsylvania, introduced an article from the December 27, 1999, issue of *The Tribune-Democrat* (Bill's hometown newspaper).

"It's these kinds of selfless acts helping individuals that are such a hallmark of the principles that have made our nation great, and of the personal spirit that must dominate our nation not only during the holidays but throughout the year," wrote Murtha.

Bill's family started the Polacek Family Human Needs Foundation in 1997 to be the last resort when the region's less-fortunate citizens fall through the proverbial cracks of the human services safety network.

The private foundation is a division of St. Vincent De-Paul Society's Operation Touch and follows the scriptural direction found in I Thessalonians, "and we urge you, brothers, admonish the idle, encourage the fainthearted, help the weak, be patient with them all."

Its main function is to provide meals and clothing. A secondary function provides the needy with money for funerals, winter heating bills and other non-food requests.

Before she passed, Bill's mother reflected on that fateful Christmas. "We believe divine intervention helped us and we must cast bread on the water by taking care of other people that don't have anyone to help them."

After John's accident, Christmas was never the same again in the Polacek household.

Sometimes, comfort can be found in the oddest situations. A piece of furniture or a major kitchen appliance is often the first acquisition by a newlywed couple. Not so for John and Sally.

Although they were struggling financially at the time of their first Christmas together, Sally bought her husband an O-gauge Lionel electric train set with enough track to form an oval around their first tree.

The December gift, complete with a remote-control whistle and a miniature village, became a family tradition set up beneath the tree that continues because the youngest sibling, Tom, inherited the heavy die-cast steam engine with tender, a few cars and a caboose and had the set restored.

As an impressionable young boy, Bill may have breathed whiffs of the engine's white smoke and thereby absorbed some of Joshua Lionel Cowen's business acumen. For a toy manufacturer, he was one smart guy. Cowen founded the Lionel Corporation in 1900 in New York City.

By the end of World War I, Lionel was one of three major U.S. toy train manufacturers, and, in a brilliant marketing strategy, Cowen linked Lionel trains to Christmas.

Writing in the May 1997 collector and operator magazine, *Classic Toy Trains,* Arthur Zirul, a frequent CTT contributor, noted that Cowen ran Lionel from the floor, not just the boardroom.

"Heads of some major corporations remain aloof from their workers, trying to keep their distance and to present an imperial aura," says Zirul, who was employed by Diorama Studios, an advertising and model-building firm under contract to the Lionel Corporation.

He said Cowen **"could often be found in the showroom, business offices, or wherever the action was."**

Sounds a lot like Bill's leadership style.

The biblical names Moses, David, and Solomon often evoke thoughts of great leaders. Characteristics of great leaders are mentioned throughout the Bible.

Jack Wellman, a pastor who posts articles online (whatchristianswanttoknow.com) and author of the book, *Blind Chance or Intelligent Design,* says great leaders "must possess the meekness of Moses, be a man or woman after God's own heart, must live a life of obedience to God, must learn to suffer and suffer well, have boldness to do what they know needs to be done, have the courage to do it, and know that when they fall (not if) that they can be forgiven and restored by the grace of God."

Melanie Pinola, a blogger (lifehacker.com), wrote that life is "full of awkward and uncomfortable moments. We can't avoid them altogether, but we can handle them with grace."

Obstacles are teaching situations
CHAPTER 39
Fired Up But Fair

"One of the greatest lessons Bill taught me was Emotional Intelligence," says his former VP of business development, Matt Hughes.

"On the surface that sounds like a fancy way to say 'keep your cool.' In reality it is so much more than that."

"Sure, I've seen him get fired up," says Hughes, "but he's never lashed out in spite. In fact, his level of patience is extremely rare in today's business world. But that's only one part of a person's emotional quotient. Choosing the right words to say and how to say them is another trait he possesses."

"The delivery is often as important as the message," adds Hughes, who then refers to the famous poem *If*, by Rudyard Kipling, written more than a hundred years ago.

> *If you can talk with crowds and keep your virtue, or walk with Kings -- nor lose the common touch, if neither foes nor loving friends can hurt you, if all men count with you, but none too much; if you can fill the unforgiving minute with sixty seconds' worth of distance run, yours is the Earth and everything that's in it, and -- which is more -- you'll be a man, my son!*

How important is a skilled leader in the business world? In his book, *The Art of Leadership*, J. Donald Walters maintains that genuine leadership leads and involves people, it doesn't drive or coerce them.

Walters says **genuine leadership "never loses sight of the most important principle governing any project involving human beings, namely, that people are more important than things."**

"Another part of one's emotional quotient is looking at conflict with a win-win mentality," Hughes says. "Often times Bill will put more energy into figuring out a way to avoid a conflict, instead of entering into one just to prove he's right or stroke his ego."

In Bill's mind, every obstacle and every opportunity provide a teaching situation. Schooling situation. Training situation. Tutoring situation. Coaching situation.

Coaching may be the single most important situation. That's the conclusion of Larry Bossidy, former chairman and CEO of Honeywell International, and Ram Charan, who also authored the book, *What the CEO Wants You to Know.*

"As a leader, you've acquired a lot of knowledge and experience -- even wisdom -- along the way," the men wrote in their book, *Execution, The Discipline of Getting Things Done.* Pass it on, they say, that's part of your job.

Every businessman has heard the fish analogy: Give a man a fish, and you'll feed him for a day; teach a man to fish and you'll feed him for a lifetime. Bill uses the analogy frequently.

I've heard that saying all my life, but always in the context of helping others. This is the first time I've ever seen the fish analogy described as coaching. Bossidy and Charan are spot on. That's exactly what it is.

My pastor once worked into a Sunday morning sermon a comment that has stuck with me. **"Everything rises and falls on leadership."** In a separate sermon a few weeks later, he reminded us that our purpose in life is not to live for self, but to serve others and bring honor and glory to Jesus Christ.

It's the same message that reporters heard at a news conference before the start of the 2019 college football season from Dabo Swinney, head coach of the Clemson Tigers, the defending national champions. "I know what my purpose as a man is. That's to glorify God, be a great husband and father, and use the game of football to equip young people for life."

But serving others doesn't automatically remove us from the challenges of life.

As a Christian, Bill gets a full dose of battles to fight, battles that are certainly easier fought when everyone is on the same page with the same goals and aspirations. It's that old admonition, **a house divided cannot stand.** Bill has created a culture at JWF Industries that, among other things, helps to avoid the pitfalls of a backstabbing workplace.

"A great culture doesn't just happen. It must be built deliberately," says David Novak in his book, *Taking People With You.* "It's the job of every single person in the organization to create a positive culture and make it a big idea."

Christian employers must view work and leadership "as a gift and not a god," say Eric Geiger and Kevin Peck, in their book, *Designed to Lead.* **"We must not value productivity over people."**

"The people of God are different," the writers say. "Our values are different." Geiger and Peck say Christians are "commanded to live honorably among people who are far from God," but can know God "by your good works."

In their book, *Leadership 2.0,* authors Travis Bradberry and Jean Greaves highlight an old axiom: **"People don't care how much you know until they know how much you care."**

"Take the risk," they insist, "and stop keeping people at arm's length."

"It doesn't matter if Bill is talking with heads of state, church leaders or the common man. His leadership stems from his Christian values and he's not afraid to share his faith regardless of the audience," says Hughes. "I've also seen Bill's moral convictions carry the day on more than one occasion."

Bill's actions mirror the scriptural advice shared by Jesus in Luke 18: If we inflate ourselves, expect to be degraded, if we humble ourselves, we'll be exalted.

That's leadership, the kind that can correct and prevent an environment that's toxic and fearful for employees.

If you don't show up, expect to fail
CHAPTER 40
An Imagination In Overdrive

Bill wasn't born when Shepherd Mead published his humorous and instructional 148-page manual, *How to Succeed in Business Without Really Trying,* in 1952, although he heard about it later when he became a budding entrepreneur.

Mead climbed the corporate ladder from mail-room clerk to a vice presidency of an advertising agency, all the while writing the book in his spare time. The book inspired a musical satire of the same name, as well as a 1967 movie.

In a *Psychology Today* blog, Fredric Neuman, M.D., described Mead's book as "amusing because it alluded to certain aspects of business that we all recognize. People sometimes *fail* their way up the corporate ladder," while others rise to the level of their incompetence.

It was a prescription for what an ambitious person without skills or talent or brains might accomplish, and it raises some legitimate questions. For example:

- Is business success a matter of being in the right place at the right time?
- Does business success come from saying the right things to the right people?
- For that matter, what is business success? Have you defined it?

Tom and Gloria Ward are editors (Partners in Ministry) of a magazine called *Dwell.* "Most people think of success as the Siamese twin of wealth; if a person is labeled successful, then they must be wealthy, and vice versa," the July 16, 2018 daily devotional says.

"But it's not true that every wealthy person is successful; nor is every successful person wealthy."

Competence is often considered the most relevant issue in creating a successful business.

But there's no denying the fact that **in certain circumstances, one's network of personal contacts can trump one's knowledge and skills.**

Bill readily acknowledges that he was short on formal education and his raw talent -- competence, if you will -- was originally confined to welding. And in the early days, he had no connections.

But what he possessed the most of was a high degree of God-given common sense and unstoppable imagination.

"Logic will get you from A to B," said Albert Einstein. **"Imagination will take you everywhere."**

After all these years, Bill's active imagination remains in overdrive. "Imagination creates vision and common sense creates the plan," he says. His wife agrees. "He's that way, even with the children. No is never an answer; he'll figure it out."

This 'incompetence process' as outlined by Shepherd Mead is a little akin to another idea: "It's not what you know, but who you know."

References to this statement appear in literature as early as 1914, but its origin is really not clear. However, the meaning in modern-day business is. Clear. Crystal clear.

On the other hand, it doesn't make any difference who you know, if you don't show up. **Entrepreneurs know that keeping appointments, being punctual, being dependable, and being prepared are basic ingredients to success.**

Many years ago I was searching for an unusual-shaped hickory handle to repair a treasured axe given to me by my father. For weeks I had no luck finding the specialty handle I needed. This was in the days before the Internet.

Then I spotted an old-timey, dilapidated-looking general store and stopped to browse around. The aisles, shelves and even the ceiling were jam-packed with merchandise. The selection of replacement wood handles for axes and tools was superior to anything I had found previously.

But the handle I needed wasn't among them.

I was about to give up when the proprietor, a man well into his 80s, asked if he could help me.

I didn't see the purpose because I hadn't seen anything even close to what I was looking for, but I told him what I needed anyway. It took him less than 60 seconds to jerk open a rickety closet door and return with the axe handle I had given up hope of ever finding.

I learned several important lessons that day.

You have not because you ask not. That was my first lesson. I told him how surprised I was that he had this particular handle in stock. I'll never forget what he said. "Son, if you ain't got it, you can't sell it."

That day, I also learned to avoid making assumptions. I couldn't find the axe handle I needed. I assumed it was not in stock.

Over the years, I've thought about many variations of the old gentleman's statement regarding selling. In my newspaper businesses, there was never much tolerance for employees who failed to show up, especially on the busiest days of the week.

"Son, if you don't show up, expect to fail." This is true for employees who are perpetually late, and it's true for make-believe leaders who attempt to lead while embracing that faulty old truism, obey my instructions, but don't imitate my behavior.

It's good that life's trials and tribulations usually come with a silver lining.

I came to have a better understanding of what former president Calvin Coolidge, a man known for few words but decisive action, meant when he said, **"Nothing in this world can take the place of persistence."**

Do quality work at prices that can't be beat
CHAPTER 41
Risking Everything To Grow A Business

"Uprising in the Rust Belt."

That was the headline of an in-depth article datelined Cambria County, Pennsylvania, in the June 2016 issue of *Politico Magazine* (politico.com), published on the web and in print.

"Donald Trump's road to the White House begins here," the article declared, "just east of Pittsburgh, past the roadside taverns, burned-out gas stations, and parking lots choked with weeds ... and then down into the valley that was once home to steelworkers, coal miners and party-line Democrats."

Aware of the frustration with Washington among his employees, Bill was not surprised at the outcome of the presidential election. He observed that manufacturing costs were escalating, especially health insurance, and wages were stagnant.

Workers were tired of talk. In random polling within his own company, Bill found a new sense of hope in Donald Trump.

Although Bill credited U.S. Rep. John Murtha, D-Johnstown, for helping JWF Industries in its pursuit of growth in government work, **the congressman was always quick to point out that his influence only worked when it was supported by companies offering quality work at competitive prices.**

"People like to say that these companies only come here because Jack's going to take care of them," Murtha once said. "No," he added, "they come here because we have quality companies doing quality work at prices that can't be beat. I may be able to open some doors, but this is a perfect example of how our local companies are competing at a very high level, offering quality and cost that is on par or better than can be found elsewhere in the country."

Bidding on defense projects demands an arsenal of certifications and paperwork. JWF previously had no luck. "We'd bid, we didn't get the job, and no one told us why," Bill remembers.

Then, JWF became involved in a reverse auction to acquire a military contract. The procedure required an initial bid, and all bidders could see how they stacked up with each other. Bidders had 30 minutes to lower their bid, should they choose to do so. Final bids were placed secretly with two minutes remaining in the process.

"We didn't think we got it," says Bill.

But a month later he got a call from the low bidder, a mom and pop shop that realized they didn't have the sophistication to handle the intricate, high-tech project.

"That was our first contract in the defense industry."

Then came a private meeting in Murtha's office. "I'm going to tell you something Bill. You do a quality job, I'll open doors for you, but you're on your own. You better do a quality job, you better deliver on time, you better never embarrass me."

According to Bill, "This was Murtha's way of saying he wasn't going to be here forever. Make sure you're competitive so this is sustainable."

Bill added, "When you stood in a back room with Jack Murtha, he didn't pull any punches, you knew exactly where you stood, he communicated exactly what he wanted, he didn't mince words. Of course, that's the Marine Corps colonel in him."

Murtha, who was born into an Irish-American family, grew up in Westmoreland County, a largely suburban area east of Pittsburgh. As a youth, Murtha became an Eagle Scout, delivered newspapers, and pumped gas before graduating from an all-male boarding school. He easily identified with young entrepreneurs.

The congressman never hesitated to defend his practice of helping local companies, either, and detractors of the practice never hesitated to malign it. Most of Murtha's constituents understood it. As for Bill, he never got an earmark.

"The prince of pork?" questioned the headline prominently displayed above the fold on the front page of the Sunday, March 29, 2009 edition of the *Pittsburgh Post-Gazette.*

"This city once had a steel-based economy and critics now say it has a John Murtha-based economy but, in what used to be the 11-inch rolling mill of Bethlehem Steel, nobody's apologizing."

"When you ask about the late congressman and his earmarks, tell that to the 2,000 families in this valley that are being supported largely by the defense business that would have gone somewhere, but came here instead," Bill says.

The reporting, by Dennis Roddy, stated that Johnstown made Murtha the king of earmarks.

According to an accumulation of magazine and newspaper articles, and personal letters kept in boxes by Bill's wife, as well as friends who knew him, Murtha had multiple passions, including care for wounded soldiers, and health issues like breast cancer and diabetes, and a distaste for long-winded political speeches.

Murtha was described by some journalists and friends as a political master, dedicated public servant, and fearless soldier. To others he was a back-slapping joker, a devoted gardener, loving and tender husband and father.

"During the recession of the 1980s, unable to get a job," wrote Roddy, Bill Polacek turned his father's part-time welding firm into a full-time job.

"This guy is something," Congressman Murtha once said of Bill. "He did this on his own."

"I had no other choice," answered Bill. "It was either that or leave town [to find a job]."

Build your business on a solid foundation
CHAPTER 42
Can One Man Make A Difference?

History is full of close calls. One *vote* made Thomas Jefferson president of the United States instead of Aaron Burr. One *vote* made Rutherford B. Hayes the 19th president. One *vote* brought Texas into the United States.

Can one *man* make a difference?

One thing's for sure. Businesses that were assisted by Congressman John Murtha used the help wisely, unlike the $247 billion in wasteful government spending exposed by Senator James Lankford (R-Oklahoma) in 2016.

Over $500,000 in taxpayer money was wasted texting people encouraging them not to smoke. Nearly a half million was wasted on studying the sights, sounds, tastes and smells of the medieval period.

These two stupid projects alone wasted over $1 million! And $1 billion was spent on hospitals and infrastructure in Palestine at a time America's veterans were in crisis.

Murtha represented Pennsylvania's 12th congressional district in the U.S. House of Representatives. In doing so, he earned two unique political distinctions:

- A former Marine Corps officer, Murtha became the first Vietnam War veteran to be elected to the U.S. House of Representatives.
- Two days before his death, Murtha became the longest-serving representative ever from the state of Pennsylvania.

When Murtha died, there was some concern that defense contracts might dry up in the region. But it turns out that local defense-related companies like JWF Industries **were thriving on their own merits.**

How was this possible?

Bill Polacek understood the answer: "John Murtha **taught us to stand on our own two feet** in the defense-contracting arena."

Three business school professors -- Michael Mazzeo, Paul Oyer and Scott Schaeffer -- discovered invaluable insights at out-of-the-way small businesses when they set off on a series of cross-country road trips. For most businesses, competition is a fact of life, the three men concluded in their book, *Road Side MBA.* It's true in politics, too.

Two years before he died, Murtha faced a Republican challenger. Polls showed the race was much closer than most would have expected. Some area business leaders contemplated what life without Murtha would be like. There were a few doomsday predictions. No doubt, some considered Murtha's influence and leadership irreplaceable.

All of the hullabaloo pointed to a central question: Did one man really make a difference?

When Murtha died at age 77 of complications following gallbladder surgery, newspaper headlines reflected his impact. "He was a giant," said one banner. **"He was like a father to the community. He tried to raise us correctly, with a responsibility to the community and responsibility to our fellow man,"** said Bill.

"When Jack died, people asked, 'What are we going to do?'" related his widow, Joyce.

JWF's employees heard her comments at the company's 25th anniversary celebration. "We're going to build on what Jack Murtha started. He laid a great foundation, and it's up to us to continue what he started, and this community has done exactly that. Bill is a perfect example."

The culture at JWF Industries gives us a glimpse at how one man, even one company, can make a difference.

Bill quickly learned to be flexible -- change rules, change directions, change resources, modify goals -- in order to remain competitive.

"It takes 20 years to build a reputation and five minutes to ruin it," said Warren Buffett, one of the world's most successful investors. "If you think about that, you'll do things differently."

Several years after Murtha's passing, Bill spoke to a packed pavilion where workers, family members and friends of JWF Industries had gathered.

"That question [about one man making a difference] by the late Jack Murtha challenges our very soul and declares that you have a God-given purpose."

In 2011 members of the Veterans Park Project began a tangible tribute to the late Congressman Murtha and all area veterans.

The help of "Wild Bill" Polacek of JWF Industries fame was enlisted for a "Celebrity Roastee" fundraising dinner. Bill 'foolishly' agreed to the no-holds barred event. His mug shot on a WANTED poster was plastered everywhere.

It's no secret that Bill will do just about anything to promote and advance his hometown.

And Bill's wife, children, siblings and employees are not a bit above buying newspaper space to poke fun at the CEO on special occasions.

"Who would have thought that sweet Bill Polacek would turn out like this?"

Advertising hype included a photo of Bill as a child dressed as an altar boy, "innocent" hands folded, and wearing a traditional white vestment.

WANTED poster with Bill's mug was widely circulated.

Have a plan, make people part of solution
CHAPTER 43
Anyone Know How To Kill Dracula?

Not everything in Bill's journey proved to be a bed of roses. There were ups and downs, peaks and valleys, ebb and flow. And the occasional tight turns, steep slopes and inversions.

Yes, the classic rollercoaster ride, especially one that inverts you and delivers a bonus adrenalin rush.

James Clear, author, entrepreneur and photographer, writes a blog (jamesclear.com) where he shares self-improvement tips, including the crucial thinking skill known as inversion, "in which you consider the opposite of what you want."

For example, what would things in your company look like if everything went wrong tomorrow? he asks.

Getting employees and managers engaged to consider such questions hasn't always been easy.

"When things go bad, you can't just have hope. You have to make people part of the solution and carry out a plan, otherwise everyone is in the same boat," Bill says.

"If you don't do anything different, it's like shuffling chairs on the Titanic; the chairs may be in different positions but the boat is still going to sink."

According to Bill, **"You can't help people fix a problem if they're not fully engaged."**

No one understands the ups and downs that Bill faced better than his wife, Shari.

"When the economy would go bad, he'd struggle." Bill hated having to lay workers off, and he lived for the day they could be called back to work.

"More than once, he stopped taking a paycheck so he could be sure bills would get paid." In fact, Shari says, there was a time Bill never cashed his paychecks. He accumulated them in his dresser drawer.

"When he loses good employees, he really struggles," emphasizes Shari.

In the early days, Bill was gratified to have the services of his youngest sister, Sally Ann, at the reception desk. Details about phone systems, copy machines, coffee machines, and office protocols can be taught, but you can't teach genuine friendliness.

Sally Ann was known for her ever-present smile and what one visiting congressman described as her "bubbly" personality. **She was gifted at making customers feel welcome.**

Because she was family, the background of how the business started just flowed from her tongue. She often referred to the picture of her father hanging on the wall in the reception area.

Sally Ann was a good ambassador for Bill's company. One of Bill's hires was not so good.

Imagine hiring a man who was getting a doctorate in operational management who expressed public empathy for employees and their families, but privately was arrogant and smug to workers, actions that were repugnant to Bill. He was a bad leader, but no one was telling Bill.

"I found out later, it wasn't that he wanted to be president of my company, he was filling his resume."

If Bill had more information from his employees about what was really going on, the new hire would have been fired much sooner.

Bill shouldered the blame. "I learned from that to never take my leadership's word for things; I go down on the floor and I see if what they're saying matches the rhythm of the main work environment."

We can get a feel for Bill's frustration by examining two of the fictional characters in a famous horror show.

Professor Abraham Van Helsing, the main champion from the 1897 Gothic novel *Dracula*, was a vampire hunter.

After his first failed attempt to kill Dracula, the professor had an exchange with a female character named Ann Valcrious.

Valerious is condescending as she speaks to the vampire hunter: "A silver stake? A crucifix? What, did you think we haven't tried everything before? We've shot him, stabbed him, clubbed him, sprayed him with holy water, staked him through the heart, and *still* he lives! Do you understand? No one knows how to kill Dracula."

The professor's reply, after his failed attempt, was short and to the point: "Well, I could have used that information a little earlier."

What was meant by his response? I had a hearty laugh when I read that story. And here's why.

Bill's brother Jim was getting married in 2017. In the days preceding the ceremony, a handful of family members descended on Jim's home to buy groceries, cook a meal and make desserts for about 80 people.

Among the dozen different homemade sweets being prepared, the ladies baked nine dozen chocolate chip cookies, but it was the 13 dozen mini-cheesecakes that caught my eye.

Wafer cookies were dropped into the bottom of the mini-size cheesecake baking cups and the helpers were directed to drop the batter into the paper cups, a task they undertook with meticulous care. As a blob of batter filled the last cup, one of the sisters walked over and announced, "They're too full. They'll boil over!"

The volunteer worker bees were stunned. Their facial expressions were priceless. "Why didn't you tell us how full to make them to begin with?"

All of us have experienced frustration and wasted time because our instructions were confusing, incomplete or even non-existent. We've all made decisions, or formed opinions, that we regretted, often because we didn't have the right information at the right time.

How many missteps and calamities might have been avoided in early years if Bill had more information and had it sooner?

Strategies may involve fighting the system
CHAPTER 44
Embrace True Meaning Of Success

The *Small Business Journal*, a supplement to the *Pittsburgh Business Times*, asked the 1996 Entrepreneur of the Year winners to share the strategies that put their businesses on the map.

"When you're starting your business, you have an eye and vision on being successful, and making money, and getting sales, and that sort of thing," said Bill. "When you get to that point, that you're doing well, you look back and realize what really is important. That's when you're truly successful."

Because of his faith, Bill measures success in different ways, and it starts with realizing what's really important in life.

George Boiardi, a lacrosse player at Cornell University, had a reputation for doing everything to the best of his ability. He was a "terrific person, a great team leader, an excellent student," said Cornell's director of athletics and physical education.

He was competitive, humble, a difference-maker, says Jon Gordon in his book, *The Hard Hat*. During a game, Boiardi took a ball to his chest, stepped toward the sideline, staggered, and fell to the turf. Efforts to resuscitate the young man failed.

The next day, Boiardi's grieving mother spoke to her son's stunned teammates in the locker room, most of them in tears, some sobbing. As Gordon told the story, it was the young man's mother who was comforting her son's teammates, while encouraging them to spend time with friends and love family.

Bill believes success is trusting God, doing His will and accomplishing what He put him here to do. Biblical success is not measured by how much stuff you own, or how much money you have in your bank account.

Bill believes God wants us to be successful, enjoy, AND share the fruits of our labor. Humility is the key.

- What will it profit a man if he gains the whole world and forfeits his soul?
- Those who give to the poor will lack nothing.

None of us has the market cornered on problems, says Bill, problems that can come in almost any form, including regulations.

"We were growing our business, and 75 percent of it came from the local steel mill. We moved to another facility and did a Phase One study. They found some water soluble oil and metal shavings."

Oops! Is this going to be a problem?

"At first, it wasn't thought to be a big deal. They're indigenous to any fabrication facility. Well, we went to move in, and the government regulators said, 'Hey, hazardous waste,' and stopped the whole process. It was going to cost $2 million to clean up.

Not two dollars, not two thousand dollars, but two million dollars! "I had sold my other buildings, and I was sitting there faced with moving into this building."

This was worse than being up the creek without a paddle. Bill was flat out of options.

"I figured I had no choice, so I moved into the building in 1990 and took my chances and figured because the economy is so bad in Johnstown, they weren't going to throw jobs down the drain."

As the saying goes, all's well that ends well.

"We ended up getting other customers and turned a black cloud into sunshine, because we worked hard with a local senator to get a grant to clean it up. And on top of that, government regulators changed the brownfield regulations."

Bill was left with a new appreciation for the challenges of regulations.

Businesses will always have regulations to deal with. Bill's message is to work within the system, and, when necessary, try to change it.

Lessons learned. Be skeptical of excessive regulations because they can stifle growth. Be pro-active when the situation calls for it.

When fighting the system, it's a matter of not giving up, says Bill. "I wouldn't quit."

For new entrepreneurial enterprises, it's important to be aware of which states impose ever-more burdensome regulations. Regulations are like grains of sand at the beach. There are too many to count. Operating a business in some regulatory environments makes it almost impossible to turn a profit.

Businessmen, beware!

Wayne Winegarden, writing in *Forbes* in 2015, referred to the 50 individual states as "laboratories of democracy" and notes that some states have imposed regulations that *slow* business growth and development while other states have regulations associated with *fast* business growth and development.

Do your homework!

"By my third year, I doubled my sales. I thought this was great -- I doubled my sales. But I made half as much profit. What that meant is I worked twice as hard for the same money," says Bill. Not too bright, or sharp, or wise.

Part of Bill's expanded vision is to grow smart, identify new products that his company is equipped to design and produce, and create possibilities. Unlike working twice as hard to earn half as much, that's bright!

When motivational speaker Randy Gage wrote his manifesto for entrepreneurs, *Mad Genius,* he defined the two specific words in his book title: "Genius is knowing what your customers want." The Mad part "is knowing what they will want the moment they discover it exists."

Gage, the author of numerous self-help books, tells a story about Henry Ford, who famously quipped that had he asked his future customers what they wanted, they would have just said, "Faster horses."

With that jibe he illuminated the mystery of entrepreneurial innovation: the ability to envision something that has never been seen before, because it doesn't exist. Yet.

Bill's company is already known for building things that never existed before.

High tech! This is a 55 Dual Arm Robotic Weld Cell (two-sided double-arm robot).

Besides growing smart, having a vision, and creating possibilities, Bill also heeded Albert Einstein's wisdom: **"Imagination is everything**. It is the preview of life's coming attractions."

Who would ever think of a welding and fabrication company being home to high-tech engineers and robotic machines?

Companies that build the cockpits of a single-engine Piper Cub, commercial airliner, or flight deck of the space shuttle Atlantis rely on sophisticated technology.

So does JWF Industries.

Bill's company produces custom work for clients as well as engineers its own designs as one means of influencing its growth. Engineers can work with a simple sketch, 2D prints, or 3D models, and often design and fabricate parts from the "ground up" based solely on a customer's description.

Imagine, this business was started in a two-car garage!

"Apart from the tech sector, American innovation has underperformed since the early 1970s," says Tyler Cowen, in his book, *The Complacent Class.* "That's right; for all the talk about Silicon Valley, we are less a start-up nation than before."

Furthermore, Cowen adds, a smaller percentage of start-ups are succeeding.

Bill places a lot of faith in the people he employs. "One of the key benefits we have is that we create an atmosphere where everyone can control his own destiny." JWF is always striving to get employees to buy into the company's vision. And it's working.

Michael Gerber, who has been referred to as the world's top small business guru, explores people strategy in his book, *The E Myth,* where he responds to the most frequently asked question by small business owners: How do I get my people to do what I want?

Gerber's answer is blunt: "You can't." But you can if you "create an environment in which 'doing it' is more important to your people than not doing it. Where doing it well becomes a way of life for them."

In spite of a company's best laid plans, says Bill, "workplace culture kills strategy any day of the week. **That's why it's so important to create an atmosphere where everyone has the ability to do their work well and create their own destiny."**

Being foolishly funny can be good business

CHAPTER 45

Humble Polacek Humor Factory

A Registered Nurse in San Diego promotes therapeutic humor as a magic charm to relieve tensions, put a smile on a worried patient's face or inspire a grumpy nurse to lighten up. Now an entrepreneur, Karyn Buxman was an early researcher in the applications of humor.

If the power of laughter works in hospitals, can you imagine its potential impact in industry?

Yes, it's true, **a little levity goes a long way.** It can break down communication barriers, relieve stress and boredom, and open doors for businessmen. Utilizing humor has potential in almost any situation.

Comedy always came natural to the Polacek family. Big John was a jokester extraordinaire. Bill was always a funny man, and still is; his brothers are jokesters, too.

Bill's Uncle Mike -- one of his dad's two brothers -- was an early fan of slapstick comedians Stan Laurel and Oliver Hardy. Laurel was a thin Englishman who had appeared in over 50 films when he and Hardy, a heavyset American, teamed up in 1927.

Laurel had a penchant for personally replying to every fan letter. He did not, however, develop a close personal friendship with all of his fans.

But Mike Polacek was different.

He mailed a fan letter from his home in Huntington, West Virginia, and Stan Laurel answered. It was the beginning of a long friendship.

Mike flew cross-country twice to visit Stan at his resort hotel apartment overlooking the Pacific Ocean in Santa Monica, California.

By the time Mike passed, he had accumulated a wealth of memorabilia, including personal letters and autographed pictures of himself with Stan and other celebrities.

The celebrities included comedian Soupy Sales, whose pie-in-the-face gimmick became his trademark, and actor Orson Bean, who appeared on TV game shows for three decades and was a long-time panelist on "To Tell the Truth."

Too many guys and gals are trying to run their enterprises straight-faced and void of any humor or humility.

It's a tough assignment to work all day around people who rarely crack a smile.

One of the best stories about humility comes

Big John's brother Mike (left) was a friend of comedian Stan Laurel.

from the author's friend, Bill Irwin, who died in 2014; he left behind a legacy unmatched by anyone.

Bill Irwin is the only blind person to thru-hike the full length of the Appalachian Trail, the longest, continuously marked hiking trail in the world, with a Seeing Eye® dog.

Totally blind, and only able to distinguish night from day, Bill Irwin followed his guide-dog Orient for 2,168 miles, step-by-step, from Springer Mountain, Georgia, to Mt.

Kitahdin in northern Maine, starting in early spring and arriving in the dead of winter.

In his book, *Blind Courage*, he described hiking the trail as akin to being a guest in someone else's home. "My Host controlled the thermostat and arranged the furniture the way He wanted it. His invitation was, 'Make yourself at home.'"

"It didn't take long," Bill Irwin said, "to realize that this wonderful wilderness was a tool in God's hands, sometimes gentle and sometimes harsh, to put me in my place."

Prior to his Trail journey, he had "always equated humility with weakness or subservience," and thought "humble" was about the worst thing you could call someone.

On the Trail, Bill Irwin was learning another side of humility.

"First, I wasn't in charge out here. The weather, the terrain, and the animals were out of my control. This was God's world and he was in charge. My choices were limited: To hike or not to hike; to accept or reject; to cooperate or complain."

Bill Irwin also learned to laugh at himself. A lot! Bill Polacek is willingly and foolishly funny at times. Like Bill Irwin, Bill Polacek has come to understand the true meaning of humility and God's sense of humor.

He's known to dress as a pilgrim at Thanksgiving -- white shirt, black pants, black jacket, black wig, black top hat -- and hand out hundreds of frozen turkeys to employees and laid-off workers.

Bill's brother, John, who manages the defense company, has been seen in similar garb. John Skelley, former human resources VP, has also been spotted in a turkey outfit. Bill is able to laugh at himself while doing silly things.

Rita Davenport is an internationally recognized expert in principles of success, time management, goal setting, creative thinking, self-esteem and confidence. In her book, *Funny Side Up*, she talks about being raised poor and wearing clothes made from sacks.

She overcame a speech impediment and learned to laugh at herself, especially her "under-endowed figure," as she describes it.

Her family's struggles taught her profound business principles.

"Poverty is a gateway to the most powerful success secret I know: being grateful," she says. "One of our most important jobs is to help others reach their greatest potential," she adds.

When Bill hit the half century mark in 2011, a one-third page ad in the local newspaper invited the public to his birthday bash held at a local conference center.

In a letter printed on the editorial page of *The Tribune-Democrat,* he answered the following question: "Why would I subject myself to the abuse I'll get in doing the Bill Polacek 50th Birthday Bash?"

"First, our community needs to take care of itself. As many people know, I started my business in Johnstown as a one-man show and grew it tremendously. The reason I was able to do this was because of the dedication and devotion of JWF's workforce and through the help of the community."

Besides, the birthday bash was intended to be roll-on-the-floor hilarious.

Laughter is part of the universal human vocabulary, says laughter researcher Robert Provine. Ironically, laughter has been linked to better health, too.

Proceeds of the birthday boy's party were designated for local initiatives that "bring jobs to Johnstown and beautify the area, respectively," noted Bill.

Workplace laughter increases job satisfaction
CHAPTER 46
Giggles Just What Doctor Ordered

My mother, who grew up in the South and married a naval aviator whose roots were stretched across Pennsylvania, New Jersey and New York, despised ironing and so does Bill's oldest sibling (my wife). Hating ironing apparently is something most men and women have in common.

To disguise the drudgery, my mother, a home economics major, often unfolded her ironing board in a corner of the living room directly in front of the Olympic console radio, the first piece of furniture my parents bought after they married -- a beautiful mahogany cabinet that enclosed a big, deep-throated speaker.

She dialed in the Arthur Godfrey program on an AM radio channel, turned up the volume, and shifted back and forth from laughing, chuckling and simply grinning for an hour or two until the ironing was done.

It was the 1950s. Godfrey was well known for his sympathetic, neighborly and sometimes emotional conversation with his listeners.

Later she ironed while watching Art Linkletter's television show (black and white TV).

Linkletter was known for eliciting hilarious remarks from guests, especially children. His broadcast presence was therapeutic for a lot of people, whether dealing with the stresses of ironing at home or manufacturing products in the workplace.

Linkletter once asked a young boy what ever happened to Adam and Eve. The youngster responded: "God sent them to Hell and then transferred them to Los Angeles."

I can still hear my mother laughing as boys and girls answered Linkletter's amusing questions.

But there's a lesson here about being a successful entrepreneur, businessman, and boss: **Never take yourself too seriously.**

Whether a person is a brain surgeon, bank loan officer, school teacher or unclogs toilets, everyone puts their pants on one leg at a time. Humor helps maintain one's perspective.

Even the prestigious Mayo Clinic confesses that more giggles and guffaws are just what the doctor ordered.

The editors of *Reader's Digest*, which has been around since 1922, published the book, *Laughter the Best Medicine*, about 20 years ago, which is filled with a laugh-out-loud collection of the magazine's funniest jokes, quotes, stories and cartoons.

Humor occurs in many forms. Lines from job evaluations are especially funny.

- When he opens his mouth, it seems it is only to change whichever foot was previously there.
- If you give her a penny for her thoughts, you'll get change.

Then there are jock jokes.

Jack Ham, who played high school football in Bill's hometown, is considered one of the greatest outside linebackers in the history of the National Football League. He retired from the Pittsburgh Steelers in 1982.

Bill had vowed to get a Pittsburgh tattoo if the Steelers won a Super Bowl. So he did, on the left back shoulder, where no one but family was likely to see it.

Ham was a 225-pound, 6 foot 2 inch native of Johnstown and a 1988 Pro Football Hall of Famer who made it to four Super Bowls with Pittsburgh.

He was a classmate of Bill's oldest sister at Bishop McCort High School in Johnstown, was blessed with tremendous quickness, known as a ferocious hitter, and had a flair for the big play.

Bill and his oldest brother John were relaxing at a resort. John was facing the pool and Bill was sitting with his back to the water when he heard a kid say, "Steelers suck."

"Where did that come from?" he wondered to himself.

As Bill turned around and looked at the boy in the water, he remembered the tattoo on his shoulder.

John chimed in: "You obviously don't know who this is. This is Jack Ham." The ruse was on.

Bill looked the part in height and weight -- 6 foot 4 and 230 pounds -- and happened to be sporting a Super Bowl-look-alike ring. Ham was considerably older than Bill, but once you're over 40, everybody's old to kids.

When Bill was named Entrepreneur of the Year in 1996, he was given what looks like an NFL Super Bowl ring, complete with a spray of stars and a diamond in the middle. It's even called a Super Bowl ring by the entrepreneurial organization.

Bill flashed the ring in front of the boys. Immediately, one of the kids wanted an autograph. "No, you said that Steelers suck and I'm not going to give you an autograph."

"Oh, come on Mr. Ham," the boys begged.

Bill pointed to one of the other kids -- there were four of them -- and said, "Your buddy said the Steelers suck." As soon as the words came out of Bill's mouth, "the other kid thumped his buddy in the chest, and the air went out of his lungs."

"I told you not to say that." The other boys left, all yelling at the smart-mouthed kid.

"Ten minutes later, 20 kids come with pen and paper in hand wanting my autograph. How am I going to get out of this one?"

"Look kids, I'd really love to give you my autograph. Here's the deal. My agent does not want me signing a lot of autographs because if you sign a lot of autographs they lose their value, and if they lose their value, my autograph and signature are not worth as much, and people pay for it."

"You have to understand the economics," he said to the boys, as that remark sailed over their heads.

Aside from relieving boredom, maybe the ruse also released some creative and productive thought!

"The workplace needs laughter," wrote Alison Beard in the Harvard Business Review (May 2014). "According to research from institutions as serious as Wharton, MIT, and London Business School, every chuckle or guffaw brings with it a host of business benefits. Laughter relieves stress and boredom, boosts engagement and well-being, and spurs not only creativity and collaboration but also analytic precision and productivity."

It took me years to realize why my father, who worked in a supervisory capacity for his employer, so thoroughly enjoyed listening to entertainment and comedian legends Jack Benny and Red Skelton. My dad often watched well-worn VHS tapes of both comedians, who believed their life's work was to make people laugh.

I can't speak for other families, but it worked for my father. **Thinking back on it, my dad probably embraced the power of laughter long before I could pronounce the word.**

"Laughter increases productivity, teamwork, employee retention, and job satisfaction," writes U.S. Army Special Operations veteran and blogger, Shane Schreck. "It's also amazing for your health. It actually lowers your blood pressure. Just by doing that [hearty laughing] alone will reduce your risk of stroke and heart attack." (stormlakepilottribune.com)

Once when they were in Florida, Bill and his brother Marty worked out at the gym and barely made it to church on time, arriving in their sweaty and smelly gym clothes -- shorts, tee shirts, socks and tennis shoes.

They were raised Catholics and weren't going to miss Ash Wednesday. They waited in line until the priest looked at them and said, "I'm not giving you ashes because I don't like the way you are dressed."

Even back then, if he thought he was right, Bill didn't hesitate to say so. "I come from a family of nine children and my parents taught us and my religion teaches us, God doesn't specify whether you wear shorts or not."

Bill never forgot the lesson of that incident. "I always felt you should respect authority. That doesn't mean you can't question it. And just because you're in a position of authority, it doesn't always make you right."

Bill also realized that when he complained, he better be willing to do something about his complaints.

When opportunities arose to speak to leaders, he needed to be honest. "That encouraged me to give them my thoughts, and what I feel is going on in our country and, ironically, that's what they want to hear."

Leaders from all walks of life seek his opinions because they know his answers are coming "for the right reasons without a hidden agenda," and this opened the door to meeting four U.S. presidents.

Author and syndicated columnist Harvey Mackay, who writes career and inspirational advice, encourages laughter in times of stress.

"When you are tempted to fight fire with fire, remember that the fire department usually uses water," he says. "Throw a little water on those situations and douse the anxieties before they spread like wildfire into other areas of your life."

While many women have experienced the frustration of asking their husbands to complete a project on a deadline, only to have it fall by the wayside, perhaps only the mothers of brides-to-be can appreciate the irony of this story.

For months, Bill's mother had begged her husband to paint the kitchen in preparation for their second-eldest daughter's wedding. Nothing happened.

The wedding date had finally arrived. A steady stream of visitors from out of town was expected. Debbie's mother demanded a spotless house and was trying to put the finishing touches on the cleaning when her mother had a meltdown.

"John," Sally screamed, "why are you painting the kitchen today?"

In her later years, Sally enjoyed the attention that accompanied her son's success. She appreciated clean humor and was very much aware that her children, especially the boys, could morph into clowns or stand-up comedians at the drop of a hat, without cause and without so much as a dare.

She leaned over the podium and eyed the audience at JWF's two-day 25th anniversary celebration.

Without hesitation, the late matriarch of the Polacek family embarked on her favorite biker joke.

A long-haul driver eased his 18-wheeler into the parking lot outside a diner. After setting his brakes, he stepped down from the elevated cab.

Four bikers, all wearing black leather jackets and bandanas tied taut around their heads, parked their cycles nearby and followed the driver inside.

"They were the rough kind of people," Sally mused. Before eating, "The truck driver made the sign of the cross, put his hands together and said his prayer."

"Look at that wimp," chided a biker, "he's not a real man, praying and blessing himself in public." The biker proceeded to pick up the truck driver's plate and dumped his food on the table.

"I don't want any problems. Let's just forget about this," said the truck driver. He paid his bill and left.

The waitress watched from the window as the trucker climbed into his big rig.

"He's a lousy man, he's a wimp," snorted the biker.

"Well, I don't know what kind of man he is," observed the waitress, "but he's a lousy driver. He just ran over four motorcycles."

Don't under-value your time and expertise
CHAPTER 47
Take This Job And You Know What

United States skating champion Scott Hamilton, whose feats on ice are legendary, was the 1984 Olympic gold medalist.

"What was really funny," he says, "is that as I got older all those guys who called me sissy in junior high school wanted me to be their best friend because they wanted to meet all the girls that I knew in figure skating (brainyquote.com)."

The rigors of figure skating definitely are not for sissies. Fabricating heavy steel plate wasn't for sissies either, and neither was it a job for Bill's four sisters who were all older than the five boys, but sometimes their father desperately needed assistance.

Barbara, the eldest, once helped her dad lift onto a truck a welding machine that was a handful for two stout men.

Later in the evening she developed a pain in her side and started vomiting bile. Toxins were already flowing through her body when she arrived at the hospital's ER. She was rushed into surgery to repair a strangulated hernia.

Big John loved his children and the thought that the machine's weight might injure one of his girls never crossed his mind. He was focused on the work he had to do.

A loyal union man, Bill's dad made $10,000 a year welding iron for Bethlehem Steel in the late 1960s, not enough to support nine kids. Even with Big John's $5,000 in supplemental income from his side business, his family of eleven stretched his take home pay razor thin.

We'll never know if Big John had secret aspirations that he never shared with anyone.

Was he fed up with being a company man at the steel mill?

Was he entertaining thoughts of quitting?

To have such thoughts wasn't unusual.

As a teenager in high school in the early 1960s, I held a part-time job as a disc jockey and announcer at the local radio station. That's when I heard a co-worker and frustrated employee tell the station manager to take his job and shove it.

It was the first time I witnessed a face-to-face confrontation between a manager and an employee.

Songwriter David Allan Coe penned similar words to a song popularized in 1977 by country music star and Grand Old Opry member Johnny Paycheck. No one could fault Big John if he found himself humming the catchy tune quietly under his breath: "Take this job and shove it!"

Was Big John seriously contemplating working there no more?

Maybe, maybe not, but Big John did not have a vision.

"Good business leaders create a vision, articulate the vision, passionately own the vision, and relentlessly drive it to completion," says Jack Welch, former chairman and CEO of General Electric.

God used visions in the Old Testament to reveal His plan, to further His plan, and to put His people in places of influence. After all, it was in a dream that God gave King Solomon the famous offer: "Ask what you wish Me to give you." Solomon chose wisdom.

It was about 1986 when Bill decided to make welding a full-time venture. His mother already had a vision, of sorts, that someone would spearhead a change in Big John's operations. "In her mind, it was me," says Bill.

Before this happens, let us travel back in time more than two centuries to March 23, 1775.

"I know not what course others may take; but as for me, give me liberty or give me death," declared Patrick Henry, the great orator and promoter of the American Revolution and the fight for independence.

In that same address, Henry, one of the 56 signers of the Declaration of Independence, made another memorable statement that relates to entrepreneurs: "I have but one lamp by which my feet are guided; and that is the lamp of experience. I know of no way of judging the future but by the past."

On April 19, 1775, a few weeks after Henry's discourse, "the shot heard round the world" was fired on the Lexington, Massachusetts Common, and the American Revolution began.

Philosopher, poet and novelist George Santayana is often credited with a similar statement concerning **the past and future:** "Those who cannot remember the past are condemned to repeat it."

Over the years, there have been many paraphrases and variants including this one: "Those who fail to learn from the mistakes of their predecessors are destined to repeat them."

Learning from our mistakes is a critical component of being a successful entrepreneur and businessman.

Bill loved and respected his father, but the one mistake he was determined not to repeat was under-valuing his time and expertise.

How do you charge what you're worth? Understanding the value of one's time is the subject of an online article by Morten Rand-Hendriksen (mor10.com), in which he asserts, be hired for your expertise, not your price.

"The ultimate pricing strategy to charge what your time is worth," is the subject of an online article by Noah Kagan (okdork.com). He advises to charge based on the value of the results you create. "Recognize that people are buying your time," he says, and "people value what they pay for."

Surprisingly, it isn't that unusual for business people to feel guilty about charging for their time.

Bill tells the story about working for his father at Sani-Dairy and Big John being unnerved to ask for an increase in his welding fees. His father was charging $7.50 per man hour.

Bill: "I got my calculation and said, 'Dad, you're losing money. You can't pay me $7.50 an hour.'"

John: "They won't give me any more money."

Bill: "Dad, you've got to ask them for more money."

Bill recalls how nervous his father was to ask the head of maintenance for a small pay increase.

Bill: "My dad literally shook. The maintenance guy made my dad feel like he wasn't worthy of 50 cents an hour more, and that really infuriated me. I thought, I would not take my father's dignity away again. I'll do this myself next time."

Bill: "Within a year I was charging 21 bucks an hour."

Bill's assertiveness offended his father, a man who favored the status quo. Even as children, Bill and his siblings were told to let sleeping dogs lie and let well enough alone rather than making an issue of something.

Bill's father had worked hard and burned the proverbial candle at both ends, but as the months and years wore on, he failed to account for his increased costs of doing business, much less making a profit, and he failed to set a goal to do something about it.

The old axiom, **failing to plan is planning to fail,** was at work. Stated another way, dragging your feet can hurt your business.

Bill's push for a more equitable wage wasn't popular with Big John. He had his own way of doing things, and rocking the boat wasn't one of his favorite activities.

Keli Hite McGee, a strategic planning consultant, submitted an article to the *Daily News-Miner* in Fairbanks, Alaska, that deals with making unpopular decisions and having success through conflict.

The opinion piece that was being reprinted appeared in *The Washington Post* in September 2010 written by Patricia McGuire, president of Trinity Washington University. The article was published in the aftermath of proposed strategic changes at the school which were opposed by protestors.

"Conflict is an inevitable part of change, and learning to work with conflict is an essential skill for success," wrote McGuire. She added, "Fear of conflict can inhibit change. Failing to make necessary changes can be more harmful than the conflict that comes with bold decisions."

Says Bill, facing conflict head-on is often "the difference between success and failure."

One time Bill was asked to quote repairs on a damaged fence at Sani-Dairy. Bill quoted a price, but the head of maintenance suggested adding more material.

"He basically told me where the numbers were going to be, and it was higher than I bid." Bill was told, "If your bid is a little higher, maybe we can get you to do some more things."

At the time Bill didn't understand the payoff scheme, but the manager cornered Big John and asked for a kickback. "That was against my dad's moral fiber and character. He wanted my dad to give him money. My dad was friends with this guy; he'd known him for years."

John gave the man a hundred dollars and said he'd never do this again. Bill's father was basically told, "If he didn't pay, the company would stop doing business with him. Dad did it for me."

Bill was furious: "Dad, don't ever do that again. I'm with you. **Our values and our character are more important than dollars.**"

When Bill approached Bethlehem Steel for new bidding opportunities, he was again faced with a kickback scheme, and was told he wouldn't get much business if he wasn't a player.

Bill refused. **"I want companies to do business with me because I'm competitive, I do a great job and I'm giving good service."**

"The guy smiled at me, and said, 'You're exactly what we're looking for.' I was in the right place at the right time and they were trying to stop the kickbacks. They were looking for new suppliers that had the integrity and the right character and we got business very quickly and very honestly."

Bill was aware that other workers were stealing things from Bethlehem, but he's certain his father never took one item, tools or anything else. People who worked with him knew Big John was honest.

"If anybody could have used the tools, he could have," reflects Bill, "but there was never one thing in my dad's garage from Bethlehem Steel."

Craig Rouzer, who worked for one of Bill's competitors, suggested a young applicant seek employment with Bill, an action for which Rouzer was later fired.

Rouzer's boss was given to yelling, screaming and belittling workers. Rouzer hired on with JWF Industries.

Rouzer was used to working with equipment that cost hundreds of thousands of dollars. Bill was surprised a guy with that talent would even consider coming to work for him. "Craig had knowledge of equipment we didn't have. All I had was a chop saw and some welders."

But Bill's shop was run differently; employees were respected and well treated. Bill's operation had a heart and soul, and Rouzer sensed it.

Jim Rohn, who publishes a free weekly newsletter (success.com), posed a question in an online article: What is a substitute for heart and soul?

"It's not money, because heart and soul is more valuable than a million dollars." He added, "Heart and soul is like the unseen magic that moves people -- moves people to make decisions, moves people to act, moves people to respond."

Seven years later, Rouzer became one of Bill's key general managers, heading up the bending and burning department. A couple of Rouzer's friends came to work for Bill, too.

Find customers' needs, provide solutions
CHAPTER 48
If First Impressions Matter

It was Thomas Edison who said, "To invent you need a good imagination and a pile of junk."

When Bill Polacek changed his focus from repair welding to manufacturing, virtually everything he had was junk -- junk tools, junk vehicles, a junky building with too little space.

Before Tom Selleck hit it big with the television series Magnum P.I. in 1980, the actor supplemented his income by appearing in commercials as a spokesman for products like Pepsi® and Close-Up® toothpaste.

The sportsman magazine *Field & Stream* recently hired a spokesman to pitch its product; country music star Jason Aldean is the magazine's first celebrity marketing partner and brand ambassador.

But in today's Information Age, a company's website is often the first connection someone has with a business organization, not a celebrity spokesman.

Therefore, the website is a type of brand ambassador and is largely responsible for shaping first impressions. With the click of a mouse, anyone can use a search engine and find out about JWF's facilities and capabilities.

Not so in 1987 when Bill acquired his father's business.

The Internet was in its infancy. Bill couldn't afford a celebrity spokesman much less television commercials, and his local daily newspaper, which boasted a top-flight newsroom staff, didn't have the global reach of the Internet when he started his journey.

If first impressions matter so much, **how was Bill going to sell a two-car garage as a manufacturing facility?**

He might get away with it in Johnstown, his hometown, but not Pittsburgh (PA), Plattsburgh (NY), Newburgh (NY) or Alburgh (VT). And not Harrisburg (PA), St. Petersburg (FL), Gatlinburg (TN), or Parkersburg (WV). Bill had to have a better first impression than an old garage.

Back then, there was no instant way to learn about a new company's capabilities, much less the principles upon which the company was founded. But today, for example, JWF's core values are prominently posted on its website (jwfi.com) for the world to see:

- We will act with honesty and integrity in everything we do.
- We will satisfy our customers with uncompromising quality, value and service.
- We will value and develop our employees' diverse talents, initiative and leadership.
- We will work safely in a manner that protects and promotes the health and well-being of the individual and the environment.
- We will be good citizens of the community in which we work and live.

Although Bill's belief in these pledges was unwavering when he started his company, he still had to overcome the down side of first impressions.

As the saying goes, **"you never get a second chance to make a first impression."**

A series of experiments by Princeton psychologists Janine Willis and Alexander Todorov reveal that it takes less than a second to form an impression of a stranger from their face, and that longer exposures don't significantly alter those impressions.

That's why they call them first impressions. Even if it takes five seconds or 15 seconds to form a first impression, it's still basically instant.

First impressions come in many forms. "Please," "Thank you," and "You're welcome," are always appropriate. Good manners never go out of style; neither do firm handshakes.

In some ways, branding your business is like putting your home on the market for sale.

You give the house and property its best face because home buyers form their first impressions as they pull up in your driveway and then reinforce these first impressions as they approach the front door and enter.

What they see and smell in those few seconds will shape their whole experience. Hopefully, a well-kept yard and inviting front entryway are harbingers of pleasant things to come.

In the business world, face-to-face first impressions of people and products really do matter, but so do first impressions of a company's work space, and Bill didn't have much to see.

Many a youngster made a beeline for the Sunday morning newspaper in the 1950s and 1960s so they could be the first to grab the funny papers and listen in on conversations between Dick Tracy and his partner on the police detective's 2-Way Wrist Radio. The gadget was upgraded to a futuristic 2-Way Wrist TV in 1964.

Regrettably, the comic strip character had more gadgetry than Bill had tools.

But Bill knew he had the goods, so to speak, when it came to welding just about anything -- any material, any size.

However, he did not have a 2.8 million square foot circular-shaped headquarters building that resembled a spacecraft. Apple had not come on the scene yet and built history's most expensive corporate campus in California.

Bill would have been happy for a square foot of green grass, a few blooming flowers in clay pots, a thinly graveled parking lot, and a freshly painted front door with stable hinges. Even that was asking too much.

How did he overcome this deficit? He set about to create a substitute impression.

He had to find a distraction, one that would refocus attention on his character and skills. What was his solution?

He went overboard to learn everything there was to know about his customers. And they never noticed there was no gravel in the parking lot, no pots with flowers, and the front door was peeling paint and falling off the hinges.

Bill was 28 years old when he read a newspaper article containing a statement from an unknown source. **"We'll find what the customer needs and grow and change to meet those needs."**

His reaction was instant: "That really personifies who we are, so I made it our passion statement, because that's what we're passionate about."

"I try very deliberately to go as high in the food chain as I can with our customers," he says, "so I understand what their strategies are, I understand what they're looking for, and I understand how to organize my company in order to facilitate that. So we're ready to be in line with where they're going."

"We formulate a strategy where they know my name, they know my company name. We're part of their strategy."

"Sell yourself," Bill begins, as he encourages his sales and marketing people.

He uses the analogy of entering a shopping mall and being approached to buy some tasty cheese and crackers, but your mission is to find perfume for your wife or girlfriend. Had they been selling perfume instead of cheese and crackers, you might have made a purchase.

Bill's analogy is critically important to any entrepreneur: "The key was listening to my customers, finding out what they needed, and understanding their strategies. Our secret to success has been finding what the customer needs, then growing and changing until we can meet those needs."

JWF's passion statement looks nice on paper, but how does it translate into new business? Well, here's one example.

Bill was aware of three different companies, all searching for a place to outsource their powder coating, a new technology that's superior to conventional liquid paint for many industrial applications.

JWF Industries was able to take the identical need of three different companies and put together one of the largest non-OEM (original equipment manufacturer) powder coat automated systems east of the Mississippi.

"That's how you find what the customer needs. Before that, we weren't painting at all, we had zero painting capability. And most of my competition had zero painting capability."

Do not ignore or underestimate the next paragraph. It's important. It doesn't matter what type of business you have, or its size.

ATTITUDE

It wasn't the $3 million investment that solved a problem for three different manufacturers and created a new revenue source for JWF Industries; it was the *attitude* of finding out what the customer needed.

Recycle abandoned property
CHAPTER 49
Not A Gold Mine, But A Gold Field

When Bethlehem Steel began shutting down its facilities in the 1990s, the company left behind hulking skeletons of buildings with abandoned equipment.

But what some saw as useless, others recognized as an opportunity to turn lemons into lemonade and seized on the potential.

It was the proverbial clash of uselessness versus opportunity.

The concept of something having contradictory qualities to different people has been around for centuries. One man's trash is another man's treasure. One man's mistake is another's gain. One man's loss is another man's profit. One man's meat is another man's poison.

Meandering all about under all those former industrial buildings were deteriorating water and utility lines amid possible contamination from hazardous waste or pollution, a classic "brownfield." Bill's inner voice was listening, and the wheels were turning in his head.

Pennsylvania is the fourth-largest coal producer in the United States, after Wyoming, West Virginia and Kentucky. When the state is producing coal, businesses think "black gold."

As planners studied the former industrial site, the "brownfield" looked more like a "gold field," said Linda Tompson, president of JARI, a non-profit economic development organization which provides financing support, infrastructure grants, procurement assistance, and workforce training.

She was speaking at JWF's 25th anniversary.

The steel skeletons that appeared to be haunting Johnstown's landscape turned out to be a critical component of the Miracle on the Conemaugh River.

Bill was already putting the space to good use, although he had no security, offices were sparse, and the manufacturing floor was dirt-covered. "This is something that economic developers like me truly love," said Tompson.

On the surface, the abandoned structures were messy places, but disorder has the potential to transform one's life.

In his book, *Messy,* Tim Harford says improvising exposes us to new and different risks that even careful preparation can't entirely remove. But practice, a willingness to cope with messy situations, and the ability to truly listen go a long way in helping entrepreneurs remain focused.

For some reason, listening can prove to be very difficult for some businessmen.

"We are failing to listen to ourselves and each other," says Michael Edmondson, creator of Michael's List, a free micro-learning website on personal growth and professional development (mindbodygreen.com).

"We have more devices than ever to put into our ears but the challenge of communicating and listening continues to grow."

Edmondson contends that "advancements in technology seldom translate into improved communication," yet **listening is one of our most powerful resources.** "How often we choose to practice it is up to us."

Of course, country music singers and songwriters have long understood the importance of *listening.* There's a reason that millions of Americans listen to country music.

There's a poster in the Country Music Hall of Fame in Nashville that says "country music *communicates* shared truths and common experiences."

Most songs would simply be meaningless musical notes without the songwriter's message and methods of expression. Take the singer known as "The Man in Black," for example. "Hello, I'm Johnny Cash," the country legend would say when he stepped onto the stage.

But Cash didn't effectively communicate to his live audiences until he began to belt out the lyrics to his signature song, "Folsom Prison Blues."

At this point, his body language, gestures, and facial expressions had his fans emotionally involved. You could feel the electricity. Yes, it was in song, but Johnny Cash was communicating.

Communicating can have many pathways. "Seek first to understand before being understood," says Bill. "Things aren't always what they seem to be."

Expressed another way, "All the known facts are not necessarily all the facts." My grandfather Percy Hughes, a professor at Lehigh University for 35 years, said this to my father because that's where I first heard it.

Once when an employee was about to be booted because of constant tardiness and an apparent bad attitude, Bill intervened. By talking to the man, Bill discovered that the employee's wife was dying of cancer and the employee was her only caregiver, but he never revealed this personal crisis to his supervisor.

This incident led Bill to adopt a policy where he would always make an opportunity to speak privately with an employee before they're dismissed.

The man mentioned in this story remained with JWF and became a valued employee while drawing strength from his co-workers.

Aside from an ability to listen, Bill had desire, determination, and a vision for the abandoned steel buildings. He wanted officials to see what he saw.

In his mind's eye, Bill could see the abandoned property working for Johnstown.

This was not meant to suggest some psychic ability to see events in the future.

Instead, what Bill has is an ability to *imagine* a project in its finished state before it ever happens; he's able to imagine the future after the deteriorating infrastructure is resurrected.

This metal pail kept Big John's lunch safe from rodents.

There was one thing fearful about those cavernous buildings along the river in Johnstown that was home to Bethlehem Steel; they were headquarters to the world's largest rats -- thousands of them.

The rats were there when the steel mill was operational, too. Only an unsuspecting newcomer would have carried his lunch to work in a paper bag.

The only deterrent for workers was a metal lunch pail, most often made of aluminum.

Along with desire, determination and vision, Bill had high hopes!

"When you have hope, you believe that something good is going to happen in the future, even though it seems unlikely," writes Zig Ziglar, in his book, *Born to Win*.

"Without hope, there is depression, stagnation, and negative thought processes that can paralyze you emotionally."

"Hope is the Thing with Feathers" by Emily Dickinson is ranked as one of the greatest poems in the English language. The poem metaphorically describes hope as a bird that rests in the soul, sings continuously and never demands anything even in the direst circumstances.

Bill's high hopes and steadfast vision helped produce huge dividends. Recycling the region's industrial heritage is breathing new vitality into an otherwise stagnant economic climate.

"Today we have productivity beyond compare. I don't think there's a community in Pennsylvania that has as great a use of industrial facilities," says Linda Tompson, the economic development leader.

Just how big is Bill's manufacturing space?

"If I put all my buildings together end to end, it would be a one-mile-long building." That's the equivalent of 20 New York City blocks.

Tompson has described Bill as a great recruiter and a community cheerleader. **"He routinely has the best interest of the community in mind, and when there's adversity, this is when he really rallies."**

"He always took to challenges," says his wife, Shari. When their first child was born, they bought their first house. The risk was unnerving for Shari.

"I was so scared," she remembers. But Bill was very secure in making the purchase. "He was very confident in everything he did."

Stop talking and try listening!
CHAPTER 50
"I Decided To Sink Or Swim"

Listening to his customers became Bill's lifetime strategy and ultimately was the cornerstone upon which JWF built its success. In fact, this principle is so important, that it's the most prominent statement on JWF's manufacturing-oriented website.

The importance of listening can hardly be overstated.

Genuinely listening is easy to say, but it can be hard to do.

"Most people do not listen with the intent to understand; they listen with the intent to reply," says educator and author Stephen Covey. In his book, *The 7 Habits of Highly Effective People*, he also stresses the traits of fairness, honesty and integrity which equate to honor and moral uprightness.

Here's one of the best anecdotal and effective stories you'll ever read about listening.

In the March 2017 bulletin of the American Association of Nurse Anesthetists, the group's president contends that communicating, which includes active listening, is not an inborn skill.

"During my first six years of school," says Cheryl Nimmo, "every single one of my report cards had the phrase 'she talks too much' written on it. My mother tried without success to get me to stop talking and to listen."

"It took a long time for me to first understand the concept of listening," Nimmo admits, "and then to work at actually listening to what others were saying. And then to go to the next step, which is to listen before you make a decision or take a stance."

Listen. Listen. Listen. Hold on to Nimmo's comments; we'll come back to her conclusions in a moment.

As a grade school student, Bill was just the opposite of Cheryl Nimmo. His siblings describe him as more quiet than talkative. Unknown to anyone at the time, Bill was learning his father's well known attribute of being a good listener.

Bill's ability to listen kept his older sister out of some serious financial hot water in the 1990s.

Sensing burnout in her anesthesia job, Barbara felt a need to do something different. Her now-deceased husband had been injured on the job and was getting Worker's Comp.

They accepted a settlement and invested well over half of the $70,000 into a joint craft store venture with a friend who promised they'd both have a windfall. Soon the investment money was gone and there was no money coming in.

Barbara approached Bill. Desperate, she explained her situation and asked to borrow $5,000.

"My brother listened intently and then he turned me down." It was the best outcome that could have happened, although she didn't realize it at the time.

Even though it was a difficult decision for Bill, he had enough business acumen to know that his sister's craft business was going to fail, and all he would be doing was perpetuating that failure.

She was a highly trained nurse with special skills, but she had absolutely no business experience. None. As it turned out, she didn't need to change careers, she simply needed to change her working environment.

She transitioned from a hospital setting with required call time, holiday work and weekend work that led to total exhaustion, to an outpatient surgery center with none of the extra nighttime and weekend demands. "This put me on a good course. Bill did the right thing."

Says Cheryl Nimmo, "When we listen to respond, we sometimes don't hear the entire comment or issue. Thus, our response is fruitless. No real communication has occurred. Likewise, when we are resolutely mired in our own position, we cannot 'hear' or 'see' another viewpoint, consequence, or possible solution."

Bill listened and saw the big picture. A few years later, Barbara thanked Bill for rejecting her plea for help because changing her work environment was all she needed to do.

As for Bill, "He looked at me and said, 'Turning you down was one of the hardest decisions I've ever had to make, but I knew it was the right decision.'"

Sometimes our failure to listen has nothing to do with being disinterested, but rather it's because our minds are somewhere else. We're caught up in our own world at the moment.

Ever been guilty of daydreaming?

Ever found yourself lost in thought, almost oblivious to what's happening around you?

There was a time when mind-wandering was derided as useless, especially when used to escape reality. Surprise, surprise! We now know that short periods of daydreaming can be beneficial.

Researchers have discovered that daydreaming is a strong indicator of an active and well-equipped brain and an essential cognitive tool. Daydreaming was working well for Bill.

Can you imagine daydreaming on a dreary winter's day when the temperature is six degrees below zero and the wind is blowing at 20 miles per hour, and you have to work outside?

His first winter on the job, while working from the two-car garage, Bill traveled around the community and thawed frozen water pipes. What could possibly be more boring?

While he wondered out loud how that would pay the bills and put food on the table, he was also daydreaming. He dreamed about what the business could be, and, in his mind, he became part of the solution.

"Entrepreneurs always like to think of themselves as trailblazers, boldly going where no one else dares," wrote Boland Jones, founder and former CEO of PGi, a telecommunications provider, in an article for *Entrepreneur* magazine (entrepreneur.com).

He offers insight about his friend, Fran Tarkenton, NFL Hall of Fame quarterback, TV personality, computer-software executive, and investor, and a man he admired for tenacity and business savvy.

So what's Tarkenton's secret?

Jones believes the famous quarterback's greatness largely comes from his curiosity and "insatiable thirst for knowledge."

Someone once said, "Some people dream of great accomplishments, while others stay awake and do them." **Bill had an insatiable curiosity,** much like Walt Disney and the company that bears his name.

Disney and JWF Industries kept growing, opening up new doors, creating new opportunities, and doing new things, in part because curiosity was always leading them down new paths.

"My father was my best friend, my best man," Bill says. "He was helping me as a business partner." But the time came, after Big John died, when Bill had to reach deep into his soul to find his intestinal fortitude and to discover what he was truly made of.

In the back of his mind, there were fear, doubt, uncertainty, insecurity.

How would he handle failure?

Could he handle being out of his comfort zone?

Was he willing to lean on the advice of a famous actress and TV sitcom star, Mary Tyler Moore, who encouraged fans to follow their own dreams?

"Take chances, make mistakes," she said. **"That's how you grow."**

For days on end, Bill fought his demons. He knew people thought of him as a nice guy, a funny guy. He had a sense of adventure and was willing to make a commitment.

But was he resourceful enough to pull it off?
Could he be relentless and still be himself?
Could he be different and still be resilient?
Finally, he made a decision: "I decided to sink or swim."

What was Bill thinking?

Chaucer, considered the father of English literature and the greatest poet of the Middle Ages, used a similar phrase, float or sink, in the 1300s.

"Sink or swim" was a phrase associated in the 1600s with the barbaric practice of throwing suspected witches into deep water. If they didn't sink, they were not a witch.

In modern pop culture, young English singer-songwriter Lewis Watson captured the essence of the sink or swim concept in the lyrics of his song, "Sink Or Swim," with the admonition, "don't let *doubt*" hang around.

Bill was no stranger to this axiom about swimming or sinking. It was one of his father's favorite sayings. "I can literally hear my dad's voice saying, 'It's time to sink or swim.'"

Bill had no *doubt* that he could swim with the best of them. His passion was ignited, and he was pleased and positive about his decision to sink or swim.

Bill also realized that he must extend his vision outside of his hometown in order to be successful.

Best-selling author Harvey Mackay captivated businessmen all over the world in the late 1980s with the title of his first book, published nearly three decades ago, *Swim With The Sharks Without Being Eaten Alive.*

On the 20th anniversary of his online column (November 2013), Mackay said the number one piece of advice in his book still remains no contest: The Mackay 66™ Customer Profile, available for free on his website (harveymackay.com).

Mackay says this profile "helps readers humanize their selling strategy and take business relationships to a personal level."

In other words, "know what turns that person on."

Quick response a hallmark of service
CHAPTER 51
The Boy Born On Christmas Day

Each Christmas season Big John assembled a stable scene using rough lumber and straw that he positioned in front of the family home, complete with nativity figures. The elder Polacek would wait until after midnight on Christmas Eve to place the infant Jesus in the manger.

Christmas morning was both solemn and joyous in the Polacek household.

John Polacek, Jr. is the oldest brother, the one who was born on Christmas Day.

"It's kind of symbolic when you think about it," he admits. John wasn't due until the first or second day of January. "I popped out on Christmas," a testament to his parents' faith and God's goodness. His mother, Sally, certainly thought of him as a special gift from God.

Little did anyone know that John would become a special gift to his younger brother, Bill.

In pursuit of defense business, Bill once found himself in a corporate boardroom with major defense contractors. Guys in suits were throwing around acronyms he wasn't familiar with, most of them related to military projects.

"It looked something like a scrabble game. I had no clue what they were saying."

Then and there, Bill knew he needed to take the next steps to be a defense contractor. He needed an already successful person, someone with a network of contacts who was open to new ideas and woke up every day excited about what they do.

But he did not know then that one of his brothers would prove to be the answer to his prayers. "I needed someone I could trust. Who better than my brother?"

John, the Christmas miracle baby, left Johnstown at age 17. He returned at age 50 to become COO (chief operating officer) of JWF Industries and JWF Defense Systems which represent the two faces of JWF: commercial and military.

Someone once said: "I'm great at multitasking. I can listen, ignore, and forget all at once." Operating two companies under one umbrella and remaining balanced is a multitasking challenge.

Leaders must avoid robbing Peter to pay Paul, which means exactly what the ancient expression implies: Don't take something from one to pay another, leaving the former at a disadvantage.

"We decided from the start that we would place an equal level of importance on both sides -- commercial and military. We need to continue to have the diversity that we have always enjoyed in our business," says Bill.

Even in the face of maintaining diversity, the military side of JWF dictates speed. Not all endeavors in life require speed, but some do, and for different reasons.

We turn to magicians for card and coin tricks. I have a brother-in-law who has practiced magic tricks for years; he can make a coin disappear from one hand and appear in another faster than the blink of an eye. Of course, it's called "sleight of hand."

When we think about land speed, we think of race cars. NASCAR drivers approach 200 miles per hour at some tracks. Bill Elliott set the NASCAR sanctioned-event speed record at an incredible 212.08 MPH during a race at Talladega, Alabama in 1987.

NASCAR'S six-member pit crews are tasked with changing four tires and adding fuel in as little as 11 seconds, thanks to technological advances, special tools, incredible hand-eye coordination, teamwork, and grueling training.

The very best tire changers can make a complete tire swap in four seconds. That's quick!

For most fans watching a NASCAR race, it's impossible to tell what pit crew members have done. They work at a blurring speed, which is necessary to win.

Because of highly trained welders and superior technology, JWF is able to fabricate products fast and with great precision. It's a tempo that comes with being a military contractor. And their speed and exactness save lives.

"Quick response to the threats facing our war fighters is mission critical for today's defense contractors." This statement is part of a brochure promoting JWF Defense Systems, and it gets to the core of the challenge for speed.

"The enemy will not wait while you hire employees, buy more materials, and ramp up production."

Even with all the talk about balancing military and commercial work and the speed of completing a project at JWF, here's something else that's hard to believe.

Scientists at the University of California have a defense contract to develop beetles capable of spying. Controlled by computer signals, the DOD hopes to use these technological terrors to assist with search and rescue missions and for surveillance.

No, JWF Industries has nothing to do with the cyber beetles project, but some of its contracts do sound like science fiction. JWF builds so-called 'normal' stuff like submarine cabinets, mining equipment, lifts, above-ground impoundments, portable air compressors, and diesel exhaust fluid tanks.

But, the Johnstown company is also involved in Common Remotely Operated Weapons Systems, Missile Service Units, Dirigible Docking Platforms, Remote Weapon Stations, and TPQ 53 Radar Systems.

Use siblings as sounding boards
CHAPTER 52
Laying Off A Family, Not A Person

The Iditarod may be the most grueling and dangerous race in the world. Mushers and their teams of 16 Alaskan Huskies cover 1,000 miles of Alaskan backcountry from Settler's Bay to Nome in blizzard and whiteout conditions and sub-zero temperatures.

To haul a 450-pound sled for 8-13 days, the dogs may train harder than any athletes in the world for this epic undertaking.

The alpha dog on a sled team is the lead dog, the one with the mystical X-factor.

But this dog can't pull the sled anywhere without help from the other dogs. He might think he can, but he'd just kill himself trying. He needs his supporting cast.

"If a musher turns frustrated or disheartened," writes Jay Bennett in an Internet article (outsideonline.com), "it can affect the dynamic of the whole team."

Bennett quotes one of the Iditarod racers, Elliot Anderson: "You have to stay positive or your dogs will pick up on it and they won't perform. You go through ups and downs mentally, but you need to stay happy for the dogs' sake."

It's the same way when running a business; employees are watching you.

How the leader acts can affect the dynamic of the whole team. How do you stay happy? Try discussing your business ideas with your wife and trusted advisors, and often with your siblings.

In his book, *God is my CEO,* Larry Julian tells the story of Bill Pollard, chairman emeritus of ServiceMaster, who "believes that helping employees find meaning and purpose at work is the key to his organization's success."

Julian quotes Pollard: "God and business do mix."

You'll be surprised to know what else mixes with business! Sure, you're close to your wife. But are you close to your brothers and sisters?

You should be.

Siblings can be effective sounding boards, helping to shape kids more than parents, in many instances.

That's the gist of an article penned by Alyson Schafer online (huffingtonpost.ca). There appears to be consensus among Bill's eight siblings acknowledging his attributes as an effective leader, and they've all been used as sounding boards.

What does this "sounding board" interaction look like in the real world? The answer is quite simple: Bill surrounds himself with people who have his same attributes!

Bill is confident, mentally tough, as competitive as an Alaskan Huskie, and willing to persevere.

If you're a musher guiding a sled in the Last Great Race on Earth, you better have these qualities if you're going to survive gale-force winds and minus 50-degree cold. And you need them to survive in today's business world.

Bill's eight siblings also see him as both patient and decisive. When he's being patient, Bill will think through problems and opportunities in a systematic way. Although he tries to work through problems, he isn't afraid of being decisive either.

His wife says he's a "quick decision guy."

"We make decisions every single day," some more complex than others, and "some will be so routine that you make them without giving them much thought. But difficult or challenging decisions demand more consideration," says the editorial team at Mind Tools (mindtools.com).

So, which is it?

Slowly consider options and consequences, or go with your gut?

Blogger John Sheesley (techrepublic.com) says decision-making can be an arduous task. But, there's a lot of good science supporting snap decisions.

The bottom line is that snap decisions typically favor leaders who already have a lot of decision-making experiences under their belt as contrasted to newcomers who might be better off deliberately thinking through their options.

Retired United States Marine Corps Lt. Gen. Richard F. Natonski is a member of Bill's advisory board at JWF. Natonski's grandparents came from Poland and Lithuania, and they worked in the carpet mills in upstate New York.

"My mother grew up very, very poor," says Natonski. "Her mother died when she was 15, and she helped her father raise her two younger siblings. She wanted to drop out of high school to help her father. Her father wouldn't let her."

Faith, family and community are critically important to Bill, and he conducts his business affairs accordingly.

Natonski says Bill has that "immigrant-kind of mentality" where you work hard, you take care of your family, and you take care of your workers.

Many years ago, an elderly man dressed in tattered clothes appeared on the job site of a union-run company where Bill was employed.

He was wearing a belt that was too big, and tattered shoes were held on his feet with pieces of cord that appeared to be tied together to make one lace. His moth-eaten sweater "was clean but looked like something he pulled out of a dumpster," thought Bill.

To Bill, the visitor looked like a vagrant, but he was being greeted by name by other employees.

"Who is that guy?" Bill asked after the man departed. He was shocked at the answer: "He retired from here."

Bill learned that the former employee's pension consisted of $10 a month for each of the 30 years he worked and his total retirement was $300 a month, not a sustainable income, not even in 1985.

Although Bill did not own his own business yet, he knew in his heart that this practice was wrong.

Life is filled with lessons and blessings. This was one of those inspirational, life-changing moments for Bill.

Lesson: "I never want to do that to one of my employees."

Blessing: God eventually provided Bill with the means to provide his employees with a generous retirement package.

My grandfather worked nearly 50 years for the same company (L&N Railroad). A great-uncle worked his entire career with the same company (Westinghouse).

The retirement for both men consisted of a photograph and caption in the company newsletter, inscribed gold watch and a pension.

That is no longer the rule; it's the exception.

"One of the most notable shifts in the workplace in recent years has been the rapid disappearance of the prototypical loyal employee who would work 30 or 40 years for the same corporation and then retire with a gold watch and a pension," according to a Wharton business school posting at the University of Pennsylvania (knowledge.wharton.upenn.edu).

The modern-day contrast is striking.

"Many workers today hold positions at multiple companies during their careers, and many feel no particular loyalty to remain at any organization for any great length of time," the Wharton article added.

But this is definitely a two-sided coin. **"By the same token, many companies feel no special loyalty to their workers,"** says the article.

This is just the opposite of the culture at JWF Industries, where there's a tremendous amount of loyalty, and it has everything to do with management.

Bill's employees have a special place in his heart, and it's easy to recognize the contrast between JWF Industries and many American companies, where the days of workers staying put for the long haul are long gone.

The culture at JWF Industries can be summarized in 13 words: "You don't come here for a job, you come here for a career."

And layoffs hurt.

"We're not laying off a person, we're laying off a family." Bill has said this many times.

According to his younger brother, Tom, JWF's executive vice president, Bill said it when he decided to reach out to laid off families. He put turkeys on every table for Thanksgiving, gave the families $2,000 for Christmas, and invited them to the company Christmas party.

In Bill's world, he desires that every employee work their entire career with JWF. And he's willing to mentor them for the purpose of helping them better themselves.

While his mentoring skills are shared with people in his community as well, they are most critical within the confines of his company because that's how Bill personally helps to develop his leadership team.

Businesses every day face a new slate of problems. As jazz bandleader Duke Ellington once said, "Problems are a chance for us to do our best."

So, how should we handle problems?

"Just our best, that's it. Not the impossible," concurs Ryan Holiday in his book, *The Obstacle Is The Way*.

Employee morale comes down to leadership
CHAPTER 53
"I'll Never Forgive Myself"

What do these four words have in common: blunder, miscalculation, blooper and flub? They're different ways of describing a mistake.

Skip Prichard's book has one of the more intriguing titles in the marketplace, *The Book of Mistakes.*

According to Doug Conant (conantleadership.com), founder of ConantLeadership and former president and CEO of Campbell Soup Company, Prichard's book is a "helpful reminder about the power of the choices we make in life and leadership."

In their book, *Extreme Ownership*, U.S. Navy Seals Jocko Willink and Leif Babin tell the story of a half dozen boat crews competing with each other in training exercises during Hell Week, one race after the other.

Initially, one crew placed dead last in virtually every race. "Rather than working together as a team, the men were operating as individuals," the authors wrote.

The Senior Chief proposed swapping out the boat crew leaders from the best and the worst crews. Could it possibly make a difference? Amazingly, the last place crew finished first with a new leader.

Why did this happen? There are no bad teams, only bad leaders.

Leadership is critical to success in every walk of life. However, Bill embraces a particular type of leadership: servant-leadership.

Servant what?

Robert K. Greenleaf founded the Greenleaf Center in 1964, according to the nonprofit's website (greenleaf.org). "Not long after, Greenleaf published The Servant as Leader, a landmark essay that coined the phrase 'servant-leader' and launched the modern servant leadership movement."

How is servant leadership different from traditional leadership? The nonprofit provides the answer: **A servant-leader focuses primarily on the growth and well-being of people and the communities to which they belong.**

A servant-leader shares power, puts the needs of others first and helps people develop and perform exceptionally. **This approach leads to teamwork.**

Babe Ruth won fame as a slugging outfielder with the New York Yankees.

A 22-season veteran of major league baseball, the fabled home run hitter had a strong opinion about the importance of teamwork: "The way a team plays as a whole determines its success. You may have the greatest bunch of individual stars in the world, but if they don't play together, the club won't be worth a dime."

Although Bill excelled in the individual sports of wrestling and running, he was also attracted to team sports, so much so that he dreamed of selling his company by age 40 and making enough money that he could open a gym, more as a civic contribution than a money-making enterprise.

His dream almost had the makings of a true story!

At age 39, Bill was offered a mind-boggling amount of money to sell his company, "but something wasn't right" about the deal. Hours before the sale was to be finalized, Bill called his brother-in-law, Dan Allshouse, and asked for help. It was two o'clock in the morning.

Bill relied on Dan, a man who prayed, read his Bible daily, quoted scripture from memory, and lived his faith, to give him honest feedback. The two men rode around in the still of the night for two hours before Bill reached a decision that changed everything in his life.

"If I sell this company and it goes under, then the very people who helped me build this company will lose their jobs, and I'll never forgive myself." The next day, he did not sign the papers.

Bill chose to make a difference.

"I decided from that moment on I would never sell this company, I will always look after the best interests of the employees, we're going to build something together, we're going to make a difference in this valley, and we're going to help our community. And that's who we are."

"There are many qualities that make a great leader," says Rudy Giuliani, former U.S. attorney and former mayor of New York City, "but having strong beliefs, being able to stick with them through popular and unpopular times, is the most important characteristic of a great leader."

"Each of us is the world's leading authority on his or her own experience," according to Marvin Weisbord and Sandra Janoff in their book, *Lead More, Control Less.* "People you lead can accomplish much more in less time with greater enthusiasm when you put them in charge of themselves."

"Leadership begins with you -- and you will not succeed as a leader unless you have some sense of who you are," say Rob Goffee and Gareth Jones in their book, *Why should anyone be led by you?*

The authors cast doubt on a leader's ability "to inspire, arouse, excite, or motivate people unless you can show them who you are, what you stand for, and what you can and cannot do."

Lieutenant General Richard Natonski (retired) says he learned more about leadership from his first company commander in the Marine Corps than he did from anyone else, "and the reason being is because he was the worst leader I ever had. It was 'do as I say, not as I do.' He didn't set the example. He used to threaten people; he browbeat people."

That's a mouthful considering Natonski has a decorated 37-year military history and has witnessed the best and worst in leaders.

"You don't follow an individual like that," says the general, "but Bill's not like that and so I really attribute the success that JWF enjoys directly on Bill's shoulders."

The morale in a company's workforce comes down to leadership, says Natonski. "Bill is as good a welder or better welder than anyone in the company. Employees respect him for that."

Bill has a vision and leads by example.

Bill and JWF built a reputation. "It goes back to quality control," says Natonski. He and his management team protect and maintain the company's reputation, and they protect their workers, too.

"You gotta take care of your people. Safety is critical. You don't want people getting hurt on the job. JWF does everything they can to protect their employees."

Bill was a quick study when it came to taking care of his employees, Natonski emphasizes.

When Bill was an employee working for someone else, he encouraged a co-worker, who was struggling to make ends meet, to make a case for a higher wage. The man finally mustered the courage to ask for more pay.

The company owner seemed to listen, looked the man in the eye, and said, "I'll take care of you." Two weeks passed before the co-worker saw his pay raise, a nickel. Bill knew he would never treat people like that.

"In the military, mission comes first, people come always," the general says. It's the same at JWF Industries.

"I think that Bill has created a culture. That's why I'm very proud to be a part of the JWF team, because it is a team and I don't see that in a lot of businesses."

A culture of success and accomplishment does not accept or embrace greed, which can be a danger zone for a leader who isn't well grounded.

Does anyone believe that manufacturers that push cheap junk food, fast food, and dead processed food want you to lose weight and be healthy? There's no incentive to stop or even slow these rivers of profit.

But there's a big incentive for a leader to keep his workforce healthy and happy.

In keeping with the general's theme, "people always come," JWF Industries recognizes that hundreds of its workers are deer hunters. Pennsylvania has one of the largest tracts of public hunting lands in the country, and some estimates say that one million hunters are in the woods of The Keystone State on opening day.

For JWF employees, the first day of buck season every year is a paid holiday!

There's another angle to JWF's success: complex processes were made simple, and that goes back to leadership, too.

Some of the most successful companies in the world have been built up on a very simple mission, says Ken Segall in his book, *Think Simple,* how smart leaders defeat complexity. Segall advocates finding ways to make your company more nimble, more responsive, more effective, more competitive, and more important.

They defeat complexity, he says, "with that unique combination of brains and common sense." He admits, simplicity rarely is as simple as it looks. "Simplicity takes work."

During our travels somewhere on the Eastern seaboard, my wife and I noticed a roadside billboard: **Some people dream of success, others make it happen.**

My first thought was Bill.

Don't be hobbled by doom-and-gloom
CHAPTER 54
Steel Mill Closes, Panic Grips Town

Time after time, people who know Bill well, and some who only know him casually, mention his "grit."

The first time I ever remember hearing the word was in the late 1950s when several of my boyhood friends sold GRIT, the tabloid weekly newspaper that targeted small towns in America with news and rural know-how and gave kids an opportunity to pick up some pocket change.

I admired those guys. I mowed a few lawns for pocket money, but I would finish each job in an hour or two. My friends would devote several days to hawking their newsy little paper and they could go hours between sales. That's perseverance.

The most famous person in the world ever associated with grit was a larger-than-life actor and American hero. John Wayne exhibited perseverance in the 1969 movie, "True Grit," as he took on the role of U.S. Marshall Rooster Cogburn.

John Wayne's role was pretend; Bill's is reality.

By any measure, Bill has true grit, which means he never quits. His life has meaning and is purpose-driven. He is passionate about what he does. Against any odds, he perseveres.

"Passion and perseverance, it turns out, matter more than talent or intelligence when it comes to being successful," according to Linda Thaler and Robin Koval in their book, *Grit to Great*. "Perhaps what we love most about grit is that you don't have to be born with it."

"It can be learned," these authors say.

When Bill is down, he gets up. He has an abiding hope and confidence that he can make things better in his community, especially for his family and equally important for his employees and their families.

Angela Duckworth, psychology professor at the University of Pennsylvania, has spent years trying to understand the motivation of high achievers. It wasn't related to a degree of IQ, she concluded. They had grit.

Duckworth says highly successful people "wouldn't dream of giving up." She relates the findings in her book, *GRIT, The Power of Passion and Perseverance.*

"Self-confidence is the surest way of obtaining what you want," said General George S. Patton, known as Old Blood and Guts. "If you know in your own heart you are going to be something, you will be it. Do not permit your mind to think otherwise. It is fatal."

In the preface to her book, *Multipliers: How the Best Leaders Make Everyone Smarter,* Liz Wiseman makes the observation that there's "more intelligence inside our organizations than we are using."

In her words, leaders who "saw, used, and grew the intelligence of others" were Multipliers. Other leaders, who "shut down the smarts of those around them," were Diminishers.

Bill falls in the category of multiplying the talents and intelligence of others. His selection as an Entrepreneur of the Year led to his inclusion on a Public Broadcasting System's episode of "Follow That Dream," which was distributed to schools throughout the nation.

Never one to miss an opportunity to brag about his hometown, Bill used his air-time to tell America how Johnstown had "risen above the ashes," referring to its history of devastating floods and the disappearance of the local steel industry. In the video production, Bill advised other entrepreneurs that Johnstown is a great place to start a business or to relocate one.

In his real-life success story, intended to motivate manufacturers, Bill touted Johnstown's survival and recovery from the closing of Bethlehem Steel Corporation's Bar, Rod & Wire Division in 1992.

As word of the steel company's closing leaked out, panic gripped residents of the western Pennsylvania town. It was "like the day the music died."

This analogy appeared in a *Classic Toy Trains* magazine article written by Lou Palumbo. It's a perfect fit for what happened in Johnstown.

Sixty years have gone by since the airplane crash in Iowa that killed rock 'n' roll singers Buddy Holly, Richie Valens, and the "Big Bopper" on a cold night in February 1959. Years later, singer-songwriter Don McLean penned "American Pie" to recall that sad time, which he called "the day the music died."

We all know that music lived after that day, but the song referred to a day when the music world got a real hard kick in the gut that took time to get over, wrote Palumbo.

The steel mill closing was a hard kick in the gut for Johnstown. The shutdown could have been devastating to JWF Industries, which at one time got nearly three-quarters of its business from Bethlehem Steel.

Fortunately, Bill, who was an active and energetic 31-year-old, wasn't hobbled by a doom-and-gloom mentality.

No one told him his company couldn't recover from such a disastrous loss.

So Bill made a plan, went out and replaced the lost Bethlehem business, and ended up with even more business, enough new business that he was named Entrepreneur of the Year three years later.

You're not a loser unless you quit trying
CHAPTER 55
Vision, Determination Get It Done

Effective analogies that can succinctly characterize good leaders may seem few and far between, but they're there if you search for them. This one happens to reference college football, and in many ways it mirrors what Bill has done with his company.

In Tuscaloosa, Alabama, head football coach Nick Saban's 2015 National Champion Crimson Tide started the 2016 season at No. 1 in the preseason Amway Coaches Poll despite a murky picture of a four-way quarterback battle. (Only one of the QBs had ever taken a college snap.)

George Schroeder, sports columnist for *USA Today*, wrote: The Alabama football program "is among the best ever at collecting, organizing and motivating talented players toward **a single goal, which is not so much to win as to improve.** Winning is simply what happens, a result of continuous progress. In Tuscaloosa they call it the Process."

During ESPN's pregame show for the National Championship matchup in January 2017, Saban was asked about the trust factor with his players. "I think you earn trust," he responded. "You've heard me say, players don't hear what you say until they know that you care."

Bill Polacek has developed that same concept with workers and associates at JWF Industries in Johnstown, 70 miles east of Pittsburgh, where steel was made and coal was mined for decades.

Johnstown was named the first "Kraft Hockeyville USA" in 2015 recognizing the community as the most passionate hockey town in the United States.

And passions don't stop with hockey.

"If you liked the *Rocky* movies, you'll love Johnstown."

The claim is made in the Greater Johnstown/Cambria County Convention & Visitors Bureau in their 68-page 2016 Visitors Guide.

"This community was knocked down three times by devastating floods -- in 1889, 1936 and 1977. Each time, our residents honored their dead, rolled up their sleeves, and rebuilt their homes and businesses."

JWF Industries has emerged as a giant among U.S. manufacturers, building on the storied history of an American steel town, and many aspects of the company's successes have been characterized by various sports and patriotic stories.

Bill's brother-in-law, Rick Truscello was an early hippie at age 14 when the Beatles arrived in the United States.

One day he took a short-cut to the second floor at Bishop McCort High School in Johnstown, going up the "down stairway," a no-no especially for underclassmen, and ran into two junior football players, Steve Smear and Jack Ham.

The jocks jokingly blocked his way and eagerly made jabs about Rick's long hair and warned he should get it cut before they saw him again.

Usually, these hair-raising underclassmen incidents are preferred to be forgotten. In this case, the incident became an amusing memory, especially since Rick and his wife, Bill's sister, Vicki, are zealous sports fans.

Smear became an All-American at Penn State and played on a championship team in the Canadian Football League. Ham went on to win four Super Bowl rings with the Pittsburgh Steelers.

Often when watching Steeler games with friends after a good play by Ham, Rick would boast, "Jack was the guy who teased me at McCort." Many years later Rick elicited a hearty laugh when he shared this story in a chance encounter with Ham's famous teammate, Franco Harris.

Although Bill played some team sports and wrestled in high school, he did not play football or ice hockey, yet all three sports became an important part of his adult life, especially in the development of relationships; sports can open many doors.

To say that JWF workers and executives are vocal Pittsburgh Steelers fans would be an understatement.

Pro football hall-of-famer and four-time Super Bowl champion, Franco Harris, talks about Bill's father, John Polacek. "Here's a guy that went out on his own, started a business on his own on the back of his pickup truck."

Harris, who was taken by the Steelers in the first round of the NFL's 1972 draft after playing his college ball at Penn State University, said, "you look for opportunity and sometimes it's just little things" and "hard work and dedication."

As for Bill's father, "little did he know," said Harris, that "one day what he started would be something like this."

Coordinating to get Harris to JWF's 25th anniversary required all the skills of an offensive tactician.

"One of the big feats of the day was getting Franco here," admitted Bill. After all, JWF's anniversary coincided with the 40th anniversary of perhaps the most famous pass completion in Steeler history.

"What we got was the ultimate Steeler, the owner of The Immaculate Reception," a reference to the 1972 playoff matchup with the Oakland Raiders. Often referred to as one of the greatest plays of all time, Harris's catch in the dwindling seconds of the game allowed the Steelers to win.

"Franco couldn't wait to meet my mother," Bill recalls. "He gave her the biggest hug. The two of them hit it off like kindred spirits."

Like Bill, Franco Harris comes from a large family with nine children. Harris calls himself "an Army brat" because his father was in the military for 24 years and fought in World War II and Korea. "He liked to be strict."

Franco Harris thought back to his job with the Steelers and to the founding owner Art Rooney, who started the pro football franchise in 1933 with his winnings at Saratoga Race Course, "and what he meant to Pittsburgh."

Rooney's great-grandparents were Irish Catholics who immigrated to Canada during the Irish potato famine in the 1840s.

The Steelers struggled with playing in a city and era where baseball was king and were treated as something of a joke compared to the Pirates.

It didn't help either that the organization made some questionable personnel calls such as cutting then-unknown quarterback Johnny Unitas in training camp and trading a first round draft pick.

For those who aren't football fanatics, Unitas, who was born in Pittsburgh, went on to a Hall of Fame career with the Baltimore Colts. For 52 years Unitas held the record for most consecutive games with a touchdown pass.

Remember that first round draft trade mentioned a few paragraphs ago?

Well, the Chicago Bears used that trade with Pittsburgh to draft Dick Butkus, who became a member of the Pro Football Hall of Fame in 1979. Butkus was considered one of the most feared and intimidating linebackers of his time.

Adam Von Gootkin, founder of Onyx Spirits, shares his "business principles from the mind of a moonshiner" in his book, *Living Proof.*

College Football and Pro Football Hall of Fame player, coach and television analyst, Mike Ditka, himself an entrepreneur with a line of cigars, wines and restaurants, wrote the foreword in Gootkin's book. Ditka had an illustrious, hands-on career with the Chicago Bears.

Over the years, Coach Ditka has been quoted with rich football-savvy comments that apply equally to aspiring businessmen and seasoned entrepreneurs like Bill Polacek:

- If you are determined enough and willing to pay the price, you can get it done.
- Success isn't permanent and failure isn't fatal.

- You're never a loser until you quit trying.

It was more than coincidence that the 79th anniversary of the Pittsburgh Steelers coincided with the 25th anniversary of JWF Industries in 2012.

Bill's company might be considered the Number One Cheerleader for all aspects of life in Johnstown and Cambria County.

The Steelers, with their iconic yellow uniforms, "were one team," according to Harris, **"and we had one goal in mind, always be the best."**

He added, "We worked hard, we focused on it and every year ... we had the goal that we want to go to the Super Bowl."

That goal must be placed in context. For the first 40 years of the Steelers' existence, they were the *worst team* in NFL football.

The team's fortunes did turn around, says Harris, and their eventual success affected "many, many people, and it's the same thing you have here. You have a guy in the family who took a company, and with hard work and vision and the dedication to Johnstown, that really makes a difference."

Bill's father honed his skills as an underwater welder in the U.S. Navy. Any job in wartime can be dangerous, but in peacetime, some jobs are riskier than others. According to the U.S. Department of Labor, being an underwater welder in 2012 was the number one most dangerous job in America.

But John Polacek's welding career wasn't always dangerous and it certainly wasn't glamorous, and neither was Bill's.

Often, the careers of this father and son were more dirty than anything. But there was one common denominator. Whether it was the demands of the military or private industry, both men had special skills and used them to their advantage.

JWF Industries had a big say in making sure the Pittsburgh Pirates baseball players and fans are safe when playing at home in their new PNC Park. JWF's team filled a major contract to fabricate 60,000 tons of finished steel for fast-track construction at the new stadium.

Raw steel came into Pittsburgh by barge and then was trucked to Johnstown where JWF workers cut, drilled and welded connecting angles and shapes. The finished steel was then trucked back to Pittsburgh for sandblasting, painting and erection.

The baseball stadium work was done in JWF's facility on Iron Street in Johnstown, one of three JWF buildings located in what was once the Lower Works of Bethlehem Steel, known as the bar and rod mill.

The work was being done in a facility Bethlehem used to crush manganese, a resurrected building JWF has been using for 20 years.

Greg Dugan, manager of JWF's Structural Division that did the stadium work, said at the time, the company is highly competitive in landing such orders because of its location. "Working in Johnstown gives us an advantage," he said. "We can fabricate steel and ship it to an area such as Washington, D.C., cheaper than they can fabricate it there."

Although they weren't as big as the roof trusses at PNC Stadium -- five tons each -- JWF did truss work for an indoor shooting range in Washington for the Federal Bureau of Investigation.

"If we are going to have real success we are going to have to grow our own," speculated John Skiavo, former president of Johnstown Area Regional Industries in an April 2000 interview.

Officials of that agency, Johnstown Redevelopment Authority, and Cambria County Industrial Development Authority say most of the growth the area will experience will come from within. The three entities say JWF is a perfect example of how this is happening.

Always make time for family
CHAPTER 56
I'm Not Going To Keep You Very Long

Actor and comedian George Burns, who lived to see his 100th birthday, never experienced a shortage of words, or cigars.

He smoked more than a dozen a day and credited them with his longevity. He joked if he quit smoking when his doctor told him to, he wouldn't live long enough to attend his funeral. He was big on family, too; he had 11 siblings.

Burns was always giving sage advice, such as, "Happiness is having a large, loving, caring, close-knit family in another city."

For many families, Burns was right. Put some distance between siblings, aunts, uncles, nieces, nephews and cousins!

Successful business executives in America are often men who have built their own companies, said Harry Levinson in the March 1971 Harvard Business Review online (hbr.org).

"Ironically, their very success frequently brings to them and members of their families personal problems of an intensity rarely encountered by professional managers. And these problems make family businesses possibly the most difficult to operate."

Yet, six of the nine Polacek children live in or near Johnstown, and in spite of the sage advice of George Burns, they've managed to make it work. Three of the siblings show up at JWF Industries, one as owner and two as partners in high management positions.

Although Bill and his siblings appear to be exceptions to the rule, there's no denying that sometimes working with family can be both a blessing and a curse.

Carter Polacek, Bill's youngest son, describes himself as "a man of very few words, unlike my dad." His older sister,

Madison, has her own characterization of Carter: "He's kind of like trying to wring water out of a burnt piece of wood."

Carter's ways are a reminder of classical Hollywood cinema star, Elizabeth Taylor, who must have warned her eight husbands, "I'm not going to keep you very long."

The phrase, man of few words, literally means what it says, which is rare for most phrases. The phrase has been around for at least 400 years, and its meaning has remained unchanged throughout the centuries.

Playwright William Shakespeare used the phrase in the play *King Henry V*, from 1599: "He hath heard that men of few words are the best men."

Maybe it was his dad's constant banter that caused Carter to be less talkative. He did grow up, by his own account, hearing his dad's stories "countless times."

"But to be completely honest," Carter admits, "when I was much younger, these stories came out to me to be a bit of a brag."

As he matured, however, Carter developed a different take.

"I finally came to the conclusion that these stories he told me were not at all brags. They are life lessons that taught my family and me that if you try the best you can, you will succeed."

"My dad is a role model. He's brilliant, hard working, and tries to help people who need help."

Carter sees his father as the "busiest man" he knows. "Yet, when he has no time, he always has time for family."

There's an anonymous quote that seems to describe Bill's family values: **"Love your family. Spend time, be kind and serve one another. Make no room for regrets. Tomorrow is not promised and today is short."**

Carter says his dad "always tells me the story of how my mom was really sick when she was pregnant with me and she refused to take any medicine because she was afraid it would hurt me in some way. Also, when my mom broke her wrist, I had the flu. She took care of me while I was sick even with a broken wrist. I didn't want her to but she insisted on serving me food, giving me medicine, and making sure I got better."

When Bill and Shari's eldest child, William, was married in September 2016, Bill observed that his son was "always doing the right things for people." It sounds like William learned something valuable from his father.

Pulitzer Prize winning journalist and author, Hodding Carter, once wrote: "There are only two lasting bequests we can hope to give our children. One is roots; the other, wings."

"With all of the struggles my dad has faced in his career, he always kept a strong faith, and never let work interfere with family," says Madison.

"My dad truly believes, as do I, that God has blessed him with all of his accomplishments. He gives thanks to God and prays for more opportunities to help others every day. This is a skill that requires a lot of dignity."

"My dad has always been able to overcome his obstacles with the grace of God, and the strength of family," Madison adds. "After all, he has always impressed upon my brothers and me that God and family are the two more important things."

"Growing up, I only knew Bill Polacek as one thing: my dad. He helped my brothers and me with our homework, cleaned up my scratches when I fell off my bike, and warded off all the monsters under my bed."

Madison was allowed in the family business as part-time summer help when she was 13 and began hearing heartwarming stories about her father. "Men told me that he was their hero; women told me he was the person they admired the most."

All of Bill's children have worked for him.

"We put them in different areas that they wanted to work in, and it wasn't for anything more than to start getting them to have that sense of work ethic and understand they don't get a free ride."

Family photo 2014

Madison (kneeling), (second row, l-r) Bill, William, (back row) Carter, Shari and Blake.

Bill and his siblings never asked their parents for money, because they knew they didn't have it. Bill didn't want his children asking either.

"We are able to afford things," says Bill, "but I don't want my kids to think just because we can afford it, they have a rite of passage."

The lesson was brought home one day when Blake was 15 and Madison was 12. She stepped off the school bus crying and told her parents that "kids on the bus were teasing us."

"Daddy, they called us rich kids. Daddy, are we rich?" she asked.

Bill responded: "Your mother and I are, but you guys don't have anything."

In a joking way, Bill wanted to send a message: **"I'm not handing you everything; you're going to have to earn it. If you're not willing to earn it, you're not going to get it."**

"There were summers they didn't work for me, they worked for somebody else, and I'm just as happy and would rather they did work for someone else. But they're going to work, figure out how to earn money, create a budget, and take responsibility."

Making something out of nothing
CHAPTER 57
Who's Next American Entrepreneur?

Rock musician and American filmmaker, Frank Zappa once said: "Art is making something out of nothing and selling it."

Bill's daughter Madison says her father "has shown me and my brothers how to make something out of nothing." Well, a two-car garage built with concrete blocks is a little more than nothing, but it's pretty darn close to zilch.

"He taught us we can be anything we want to be. From watching my dad in his business, I've learned no matter how big a goal is, I can succeed at it."

Madison, a Penn State graduate, recalls the positive feedback she heard over the years: "Each person spoke of my dad the way children speak to their parents, or siblings speak to their older brothers. These employees looked at my dad as their dad, their brother, their uncle."

Bill isn't just a boss; he's a role model.

Sadly, talking to people in general, and especially employees, requires a skill-set some employers simply don't have.

"Don't just act interested. Be interested." That's the advice of Mark Goulston in his book, *Just Listen.* "Go into the conversation knowing that there is something very interesting about the person, and be determined to discover it."

Madison eventually discovered one of her father's not so subtle secrets: **Treat your employees with respect, and maintain a good relationship with them, just as you would with an older brother, or a father.**

Madison's mother, Shari, has always been the universal support system for the whole family.

"She is the type of person that will attend all four of your musical performances in eighth grade, even if you only have a background role and no lines in the whole production. Yes, that eighth grader was me," says Madison.

Shari, whose soft speaking tone exudes her faith, "is a wonderful confidante to our family," Madison says. "She offers her best advice, even when you may not want it. If my dad ever had a problem at work, she was always there to lend an ear, and a word of advice."

When Madison's parents develop a solution together, it's destined to succeed. "They have a way of filling in each other's gaps."

"When my dad is low, my mom steps right in and lifts him up. Even when times are tough, my mom has been so strong and was able to fill in any gaps. It makes my dad even stronger."

The primary difference between a rich person and a poor person is how they manage fear, so says Robert T. Kiyosaki, in his book, *Overcoming Fear. Rich Dad Poor Dad.* "It's how you handle failure that makes the difference in one's life."

Failure defeats losers. Failure inspires winners.

Madison sees her parents lifting each other when one is down. **"They've taught me to never give up on my dreams. With all of the ups and downs they've experienced, they continue to stay in love."**

William, the oldest sibling, remembers his father's "ability to leave work at work and give his kids his full attention when he was at home."

"He worked tirelessly all week, but still insisted on coaching all four of his kids in any sport they played. He was trying to grow a business with hundreds of employees, and at night I would see him reading books about coaching football, basketball, baseball, or whatever sport we were into that year."

"While he, and most of the family, has a competitive spirit, his reading these books was more about him wanting to be the best coach he could be to us," William added. "This applies to both sports and life."

Looking back on his childhood, William realizes his father "couldn't have had a second to himself. He couldn't do what he wanted to do; he couldn't relax when he wanted to; in his eyes we were more important."

"And that is true sacrifice and love."

Sports connections remain important barometers in the Polacek household. William has attended every Steelers home game in the last five years but one with his father, and had fun being with him, win or lose.

"I've broken a finger high-fiving him too hard, froze to the bone to watch meaningless games late in the season, watched three Super Bowls in person, have been in the middle of a few fights with Ravens fans. But at the end of the day, he was always right by my side and doing it along with me."

Blake, the second sibling, considers himself to be the "black sheep" of the family in that he has chosen to forego the family business.

Being a black sheep has not always carried a negative connotation. There was a time in England when a single black sheep in a flock was considered good luck by shepherds and a mark of integrity.

Black sheep have also been the source of corny jokes:

Bumpkin 1 -- Why do black sheep eat less than white sheep?

Bumpkin 2 -- There aren't as many of them.

Corny, right?

In the sense of entrepreneurship, that corny joke carries a lot of truth. For every dedicated entrepreneur, there may be thousands or tens of thousands of would-be entrepreneurs afraid to even try.

Bill and Shari always encouraged their children's dreams, and they have done so by providing a solid foundation upon which their children can build their own lives.

Blake watched his father chart his own course in life.

"Out of all of the lessons that I've learned from him, this is the one that stuck with me the most," Blake explains.

"I've always admired that he was able to make his life what he wanted it to be. His ability to plan out what he wants to do and not be swayed has been the driving force for me to take that lesson and apply it to my own life."

So called "black sheep" stereotypically see things in life differently, have their own opinions and viewpoints, and seek out their own pathway.

Who's to say that one of them won't be the next American entrepreneur?

"Bill has lived his values through the company, his family and community by truly **thinking of others first** and how he can help those around him and make them better." These are words of his younger brother, Tom, an executive VP in JWF Industries.

Some would say Bill is Mr. Fix It, although what you hear after asking for help may not always be what you want to hear. If he sees someone struggling in their golf game, for example, he'll give advice. "He is a fixer in all that he does," Tom says.

"If you come to him with a problem, you better expect him to give you advice because he believes that it is his duty to help others. I believe that is what's helped make him successful as those around him felt they were helped as he had their best interest at heart so they were compelled to be there for him by helping to make JWF successful."

Enthusiasm gets people focused
CHAPTER 58
Exercise Leadership With Civic Pride

"Opportunities will come and go, but if you do nothing about them, so will you," says Richie Norton, author of the book, *The Power of Starting Something Stupid: How to Crush Fear, Make Dreams Happen, and Live Without Regret.*

"I don't live my life in order to garner material things. I live it to help this community and to help my employees and build something."

With those words, Bill was inducted into the Johnstown West End Lions Club Hall of Fame in January 2015.

It was a thought often echoed by Bill Gates, co-founder of Microsoft, who said, "As we look ahead into the next century, leaders will be those who empower others."

Bill and every member of JWF's management team sit on one or more community boards, giving their time, talent and money to make Johnstown a better place, in keeping with the notion that great companies have great leadership. And JWF is seen as a great company.

And seeing how other companies are run helps broaden leadership skills.

No company is perfect, says Jim Champy, in his book, *OUTSMART!: How To Do What Your Competitors Can't*, "even if it performs well year after year."

But Champy has identified a short list of things he says all companies aspiring to greatness have in common, and his tally includes an ambitious leadership team that focuses on what they know and do best.

Satisfying customers is also on the list, along with plenty of inspiration.

An example of community leadership is Bill's brother John, a U.S. Marine Corps veteran and chief operating officer for JWF Defense Systems and JWF Industries. He was recognized as Veteran of the Year by Veteran Community Initiatives for being heavily involved in the group's fundraising work and for his skills, knowledge, experience, credibility and networking abilities.

The record shows that JWF's donations and committed funds over their first quarter century of business exceed $3,000,000.

Dan Ariely, professor of psychology and behavioral economics, talks about the hidden logic that shapes our motivation in his book, *Payoff.*

"If a kind word can impel people to do better, what other hidden treasures of energy, dedication, and commitment might we find if we only looked for them?" asks Ariely.

Civic pride is another way of exercising leadership.

When it came time for firefighters in the city of Johnstown to have a new training facility, JWF Industries put in the lowest bid and built the flexible structure, which can be adapted to specific types of training at different training sessions.

Bill said his company took ideas from the fire department and developed the plan for a site that offers many different features.

A 12-foot sculpture of a steelworker with a hard hat and shovel was restored free of charge by JWF Industries. The facelift was the dying wish of one of its creators, Charles Zilch.

The sculpture was also moved from its perch on the remains of the "H" blast furnace in Johnstown's Franklin Mills, to the Heritage Discovery Center where it will serve as a reminder of the hard-working men and women who forged a city and a nation.

The sculpture was created by Zilch and fellow steelworkers Robert Scarsella, Dennis Waltz and Larry Ramach, to represent those who survived back-breaking labor in the mills, and multiple floods, recessions, layoffs and plant closings.

The sculpture, known as the "Man of Steel," has become an icon symbolizing the rise and fall of the steel industry in Johnstown.

In my lifetime, I've met very few business people who have not read Dale Carnegie's 1936 publication, *How To Win Friends and Influence People*. The book puts forth timeless human relations principles.

Persuasion is defined in the Dale Carnegie Training book, *The Five Essential People Skills,* as "convincing others to internalize your argument, then embrace it as a part of their own belief system."

Unless your company is a one-man band, it's a skill you best master.

In April 2015, Bill had his eyes on a very focused and specific vision as being the key to Johnstown's future, pushing a plan aimed at getting local businesses and business leaders on the same page. He was bent on selling it, and meshing the best of every available plan into one.

Bill says the project began with eight people "we thought had influence, money, and intellect to help create vision." He adds, "It may be the first time everyone has been on the same page in community development."

Carnegie Mellon University's Remaking Cities Institute was commissioned to conduct an intensive study of Johnstown, and the result is a volunteer-based organization known as Vision2025 that has engaged more than 1,000 people.

The group heeded Benjamin Franklin's sage advice: **If you want something done, ask a busy person.**

Bill accepted chairmanship. He's supported by a lot of other busy people.

"His approach to creating and engaging Vision2025 has been and continues to be very thoughtful and strategic; but to me when he is talking about our projects and goals in groups or one on one, it's his enthusiasm that gets people focused," observes Mike Kane, executive director of the Community Foundation of the Alleghenies.

"At the opening event for Vision2025, Bill spoke eloquently about his commitment to our community and how we should work together for its improvement.

Said Kane, "He kept making the point that **we are not victims, that we can advance our community if we create a vision and work toward it.**"

Kane added, "This thinking really helped make Vision2025 what it has become, and you can look around the various activities of the Vision2025 'CaptureTeams' -- as Bill suggested they be called, but which really are working groups around identified projects -- and see that the sense of optimism and enthusiasm is there."

Kane continued: "The people in the teams are not thinking of themselves as victims. Through his advocacy and commitment to Vision2025, Bill has a lot to do with that. I think that is a really big deal."

"It's a bottom up plan that turned into a movement," says Bill, "which is how we'll be able to perpetuate this plan for many years to come."

On the Foundation's website, we find an old Japanese saying: "Vision without action is a daydream. Action without vision is a nightmare."

While JWF is the recipient of Lockheed-Martin's prestigious Star Supplier Award, which recognized its achievements in meeting some of the most stringent performance criteria in the defense industry, JWF pays the same special attention to its own suppliers as it does to community service opportunities.

Vendors that provide JWF's wares are treated with the same enthusiasm as customers or Vision2025 efforts.

This attitude is corroborated by John G. Miller, in his book, *Outstanding*. He says organizations should "build long-term relationships of loyalty and trust with suppliers" because it's good business.

A good relationship, he says, "returns more value over time than one that's focused only on price and terms."

You can't teach character and pride
CHAPTER 59
The Work Fighters Are Battle Ready

As Bill expanded from his two-car garage roots, the company's initial growth was due largely to its ability to compete in the commercial sector and to exceed customer expectations. The next frontier was government contracting.

Could JWF's workers handle the international stage? Bill knew the veterans were ready, but what about newer members of his company's workforce?

It was General George S. Patton who said, **"A good battle plan that you act on today can be better than a perfect one tomorrow."**

Bill believed his workforce was battle ready. He was relying on a plan he set in motion years earlier.

He expected his new hires to know how to read blueprints, be good welders, have ambition and take pride in their work. Bill's parents took great pride in their work, a trait that rubbed off on all nine children. It's known that pride in one's work helps drive performance. But finding a workforce of this caliber was a tall order.

The concept behind Bill's solution to this problem has followed him his entire business career.

"I find people with the ambition and pride, and then I train them to weld myself. You can't teach character and pride."

He made that statement 29 years ago.

Over the years the training program has morphed and is now called the Apprenticeship Program, and Bill no longer personally does all the training, but he provides input. "I still critique welds, even today."

Want to be a success? Well, know your gut and know what you want. In his book, *It's Your Move*, Josh Altman highlights a handful of suggestions for becoming a successful entrepreneur.

Fall in love with what you do, and let everybody know what you do. Among his other thoughts, have a tough skin, embrace rejection, confront your weaknesses and use your head.

Altman says not every failure is a mistake, but he advances the idea to "let mistakes open your eyes." Remember the big picture, he says, and risk smart, not hard.

Ever wake up from a deep sleep thinking of a solution to a problem you've been contemplating?

Sometimes our subconscious is working overtime on our behalf.

Tap into your subconscious. Malcolm Gladwell, in his book, *Blink: The Power of Thinking Without Thinking,* suggests that "trusting one's gut feelings may be more accurate than you think."

Less than 10 years after starting his journey, Bill was adding a third manufacturing facility in Johnstown, two of which were abandoned industrial sites that JWF had purchased and returned to use.

Bill was at the core of this new economic thinking where development groups were concentrating their job creation efforts on helping local companies grow, rather than just working to attract new manufacturing facilities or other new businesses.

When JWF celebrated its silver anniversary in 2012, PA Business Central, a business publication that covers 16 counties in central Pennsylvania, had recently named the manufacturer a Top 100 organization.

Bill was optimistic about the future of local manufacturing. "More good times are in front of us."

JWF's machine shop was now military-certified to handle defense work, meaning it was meeting quality control standards necessary to do work for the government.

At the time JWF's posture in the marketplace was contrary to some manufacturers. JWF was not experiencing skill shortages. "This is not a problem," said Bill.

Why? "We train our workers coming into the company, and it has worked out very well for us."

However, finding trained welders and metal fabricators to fill jobs at JWF had not always been easy.

That's why Bill took matters into his own hands, forming a partnership with Penn Highlands Community College to provide the classroom training, while the hands-on training was provided at Bill's plant.

If the trainee comes to work for Bill, JWF makes the loan payments for the community college part of the education. "If they go to trade school and they have a student loan, if they come to work for us, we'll make those student loan payments."

For many, being a welder is just the beginning at JWF and its associated businesses. An employee may start as a welder then move into operations manager, an estimator, go into engineering, sales or become a foreman.

Bill is pleased with the workers he is getting and is convinced people in the Johnstown area work as hard as they ever did.

"The work ethic is still there," he says.

Even with his unconventional hiring methods, Bill was seeing a shortage of welders in late 2015 that forced him to turn some business away. Other work has been subcontracted, and JWF is exploring possible technological solutions to the manpower shortage.

In 2017 JWF was able to get employees it couldn't find two years earlier.

As an expression of their desire to be the best at their jobs and meet international standards for quality management and manufacturing, hundreds of JWF's employees and families crowded into a Johnstown mill in 2003 to celebrate a certification that would make it easier to do business overseas.

The ISO certification, which often takes up to four years, was earned in just three months. Note that the certification was not simply awarded; it was earned.

The designation shows that a company has developed processes that everyone in the organization is going to follow to get the desired outcome.

"It basically says you are going to do what you say you're going to do," Bill explains.

"I grew up being taught you're only as good as your word."

"When you have a business, you're in a leadership position, whether you like it or not. And you have to understand people will follow you as long as they feel you have their best interests at heart," says Bill.

This sentiment is expressed another way as anonymously quoted in *The Infantry Journal*: "No man is a leader until his appointment is ratified in the minds and hearts of his men."

Bill's people philosophy is quite simple, and can be summarized in two points:

- "Leadership is not about how successful you are, leadership is about how successful you make other people around you."
- "A guy told me a long time ago that you also have to make tough decisions. If you're not willing to make the tough decisions, then you shouldn't be in a leadership position."

For a leader like Bill with a big heart, one of the most challenging decisions can involve hiring and firing.

Someone has said, **hire slowly and fire quickly.**

Bill's mission strategy for growth is quite simple, too, and can be summarized in four points:

- Right people.
- Right processes.
- Right markets.
- Right customers.

Most companies don't think this way, Bill says. They think a sale is a profit, and it's not.

"Our customers recognize that we have to be competitive." Bill has a different philosophy: If someone, even a competitor, is going to lose money on a particular job, he's not going to take the job.

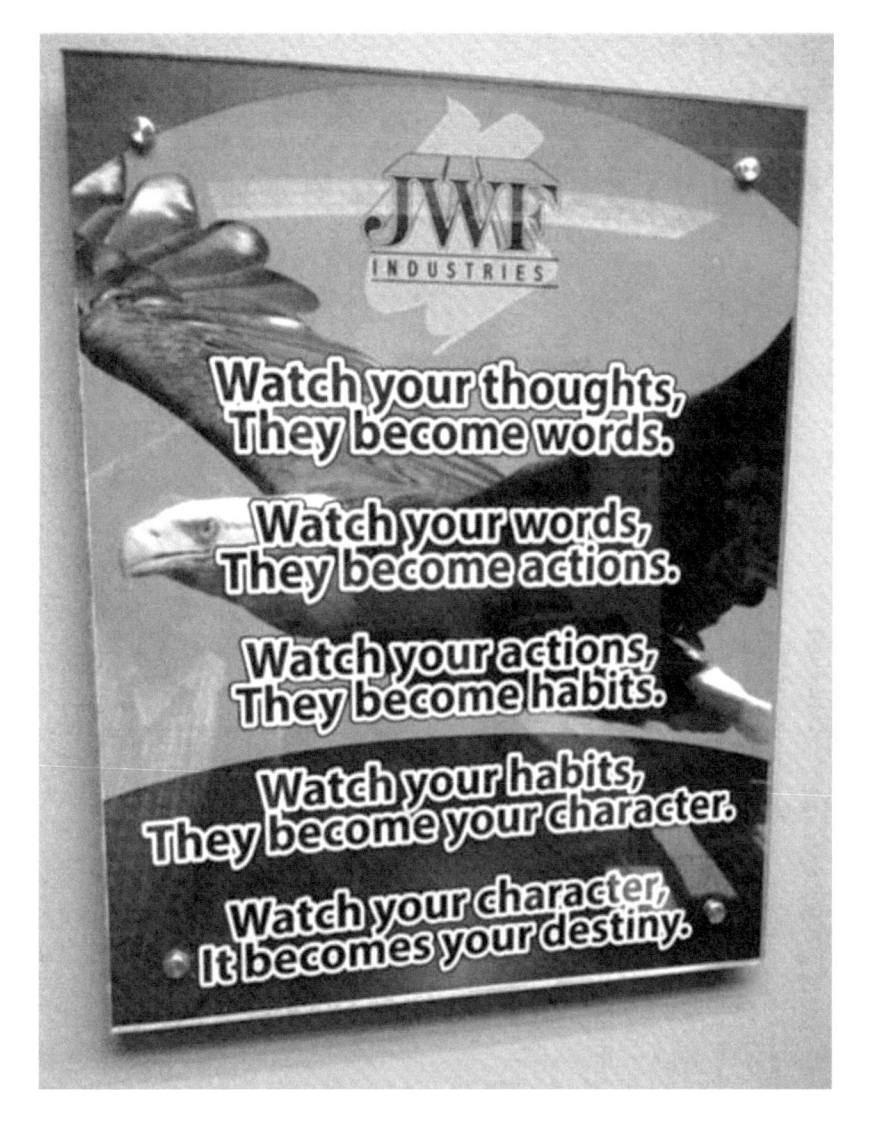

This sign, hanging in Bill's office, is completely self-explanatory.

Focus on solutions, not problems
CHAPTER 60
Some Things Cannot Be Changed

The lyrics of counterculture singer/songwriter Bob Dylan chronicled social unrest beginning in the 1960s, especially civil rights and anti-war movements. His 1975 song, "Money Blues," bemoans his inability to afford basic necessities like rent and groceries.

In essence, he had money, he gave it to his woman, and it's gone.

There's an often misquoted biblical admonition about money posed by the Apostle Paul: "The love of money is the root of all kinds of evil." Notice that money is not the problem, but the *love* of money is.

Have you ever been tempted to define success as making or having a lot of money?

Why is 58-year-old Bill Polacek happy and successful?

"That's an easy one," answers Dan Allshouse, a brother-in-law who has worked for Bill nearly 24 years in a host of capacities -- fitter/welder, crew leader, production manager, division manager, customer rep, and project manager -- and watched him hone his on-the-job training skills.

In Dan's eyes, **Bill has claimed all of the biblical principles about sharing one's God-given, God-recognized wealth, and has been blessed accordingly, personally and professionally.**

At different times, Bill discussed the state of his business with his siblings. There was no pretense. He never acted like everything was perfect when it wasn't.

At one point, Bill thought his business was going under. Even though the cloud of failure was sometimes dark and hanging low overhead, there was one constant: Bill still had a dream.

"The future belongs to those who believe in the beauty of their dreams," said Eleanor Roosevelt, former First Lady of the United States.

Bill recognized that **some things cannot be changed**, and he methodically applied his energy to the things he could alter.

The best example of this philosophy is the Serenity Prayer, the common name for a prayer authored by the American theologian Reinhold Niebuhr.

According to Wikipedia, the free online encyclopedia, the prayer has been adopted by Alcoholics Anonymous and other 12-step programs.

The prayer's best-known form is: "God, grant me the serenity to accept the things I cannot change, The courage to change the things I can, And the wisdom to know the difference."

Bill zeroed in on solutions, not problems.

He did exactly what Anita Roddick did. The British businesswoman, who founded The Body Shop cosmetics company, said: "Nobody talks of entrepreneurship as survival, but that's exactly what it is, and what nurtures creative thinking."

On the occasion of JWF's 25th anniversary, Bill presented each of his eight siblings with a box containing a thank you gift of $5,000. On each box he had handwritten the personality trait of that sibling which helped shape his life.

- Barbara, you look for the goodness in others because of the goodness in you.
- Debbie, you are the one who is always there when the need is the greatest.
- Vicki, you have a lot of love, heart and courage.
- Sally Ann, you don't think of yourself as doing that much, but you do, as evidenced by raising two successful children.

- John, you always make people feel good about who they are and what they have accomplished.
- Marty, you already possess the good traits you admire in others.
- Jim, you are at a place in your life where you need less advice and have the ability to offer sound advice to others.
- Tom, you have the integrity that embodies the Polacek heritage.

"Bill shares his wealth, not only with family and employees, but with others that many don't realize," says Dan, who cites the promise of Jesus in Luke Chapter 6: Give, and it shall be given unto you.

Dan believes that a large majority of JWF employees trust Bill and readily accept his leadership. Over the years, Bill has proven true to his word. He always said, **"I'll take the company as far as the markets and employees let me."**

On the occasion of JWF's 30th anniversary, Bill announced that he was sending his and Shari's siblings, along with their spouses, on a European vacation.

The family boarded the Scenic Amber in Budapest, Hungary and cruised the legendary Danube for eight days.

While passing through Slovakia and Austria on the way to their final destination, Nuremberg, Germany, everyone expected to see the ruins of medieval castles, an 18th century Benedictine Abbey, and Salzburg and the background of the Alps, where the movie, *The Sound of Music*, was filmed.

But absolutely no one expected to make a human relations discovery on this river trip, the discovery of a hidden gem -- a week-long course in the hospitality phase of running a business, and the definition, by example, of exceptional service.

Observing the staff taking care of their customers on this river boat -- attending to small things, small details -- was the equivalent of auditing a graduate school course in human relations.

My wife has to be very diligent about avoiding certain foods. Branislav Arambasic, restaurant manager, caught my eye the first day on the boat as he monitored her menu at each meal. His younger brother, Aleksandar, was just as diligent. Both men have prior work history in one or more of the major work venues in the hospitality business (hotels, restaurants, ocean cruise ships).

As for my wife, all the servers were aware of her needs. So was the chef. On the entire cruise, she had zero food issues. Why? Because every employee on this river boat worked as a team, a cog in a well-oiled machine.

There are a lot of hospitality and human relations secrets, admitted Aleksandar, but one of the most important "is to be very kind."

One former guest on the Scenic Amber was a man with some health issues who was traveling alone. He met Branislav and Aleksandar, two men who were old enough to be his sons, old enough to be his grandsons. On the last day of the cruise, he became emotional and began to shed tears.

"I will never forget as long as I live," said Branislav. "He was crying for three minutes. Why? Because he met two guys serving his food? No! Because he met somebody that cared about him."

How is it possible to assemble such a caring, creative team? It starts with management.

"Give me one guy with the best attitude and less experience, and give me the guy with the most experience and a bad attitude," says Branislav. "I'll always choose the guy who has no idea what he's doing, but with the best attitude."

Refer to the back cover of this book: "Give people more than they expect. No dissatisfied customers, not a single one." This lofty goal is an attitude and a mindset at JWF Industries.

To beat the clock, delegate effectively
CHAPTER 61
Time With Family Is Priority

In a sense, Shari's function in the family is aeronautical, as she's both a gyroscope and a stabilizer, maintaining orientation and bringing balance to every challenge and decision.

One of Bill's sisters lives in North Carolina, less than an hour from Tallulah Falls (North Georgia) where 65-year-old high-wire artist Karl Wallenda twice stood on his head during his quarter-mile balancing act across the 1,000 foot deep gorge in 1970.

That's a balancing feat that demands passion and determination!

Bill's wife, Shari, is not a high-wire artist, but she is passionate, determined, and known for her ability to balance faith, family and Bill's business interests.

Because of Shari's influence, Bill's decision-making abilities were refined over time, and he was able to maintain a sense of balance between work and family. For both of them, family was priority.

Shari accepted her part in this balancing act.

"This is my job. I considered it to be my job, to take care of the kids. That's how I was raised. I considered myself fortunate enough to be with my kids, be here when they got off the school bus, be here for Bill when he got home. I felt very honored that I was able to do what I do."

Bill's best advice came from his father whose biggest regret in life was not spending more time with his children.

"He gave me the best message a father could give his son: 'Nobody ever dies wishing they'd made more money.'" Bill's takeaway was to "begin with the end in mind and do the right things."

"I told my kids hundreds of times," says Shari, "I don't know how your dad does it; he gives a hundred percent at work and then comes home and he still has a lot of energy."

"He's in the thick of it," Shari says of Bill's work, while she thinks of herself as an outsider looking in.

Well before Shari gave birth to their first child, Bill had agreed with his bride that he'd back off the endless 16-hour days at work to be with and help nurture their offspring. Family had to be a priority, no matter what.

That's exactly what happened, and their four children weren't the only beneficiaries of this sacrifice.

"It forced me to trust the abilities of my employees," Bill admits, "and to hire the right people and to delegate."

"I got the business to the point I started hiring employees before my first child was born. I knew what I had to do," says Bill. "Kids grow up fast, life moves on, you understand where your priorities are, and your priorities are the people you love."

Along the way, Bill realized he needed to decide what he was good at and what he wasn't good at, what he liked to do, and what he didn't like to do.

"If I didn't like to do it, I probably wasn't good at it, and there are people better at it than me. So I hired the people that complemented what I did well and helped me become a link in the chain to support the things I didn't do well but were necessary."

This required delegating responsibility. **Bill empowered his employees, held them accountable, and got them moving in the same direction.** He read books and attended seminars. "Delegating became natural to me."

"You can't generate new business while you're up to your eyeballs running the business you currently have," says Ken Jacobs (jacobscomm.com) of Jacobs Communications Consulting. Delegating requires practice and is hard to do, he notes. "Since you can't create more hours in the day, your only possible choice is effective delegation."

When Bill was coaching his children in various sports, it didn't take him but a couple of seasons to realize that teaching a sport was supplementary to building character.

He was able to help other children, especially those from poor families, by giving direction and a hand up, not a hand out.

A couple of teenagers he was coaching were failing in public school so Bill put them to work so they could pay their own way in a private Catholic school. And he monitored their grades.

Bill learned to schedule time with his family.

"If you think you're going to spend time with your kids and do things with your family when you find time, you'll never find time. When you make your kids and your family the priority in your schedule, it's amazing how much you work everything around it and still accomplish it."

"By and large, employees at JWF Industries get the same flexibility to be a part of their kids' lives and I set the tone that family is important." Even with a surge of business, employees will generally be allowed to leave for important functions in the middle of the day, and then return to work to finish a job.

Juggling work and family life at JWF are much easier tasks because many employees work four 10s so they can have three days off with family (Monday through Thursday). The weekend shift works three 12s and they get four days off. (They work 36 hours and get paid for 40.)

"There are several things that keep me grounded and focused," says Tim Tebow, the first home-schooled athlete to be nominated for the Heisman Trophy, which he won in 2007 as quarterback of the University of Florida Gators. He makes this humble point: "I'm no more important than anyone else, I just have a gift (quoted at idlehearts.com)."

Shari and the children did more than keep Bill grounded.

"Their love and support have given me strength and courage to tackle any problem and sustain any hit I had taken, only to come back even stronger," he acknowledges.

Courage comes in many shapes, sizes and forms, everything from Sir Edmund Hillary climbing Mount Everest to a battered woman making the decision to leave an abusive relationship. Most of all, courage comes from the strength of family.

Bill is gratified that his father gave him a trade and taught him "about integrity and what servant leadership is all about."

His mother showed him "that no obstacle was too hard to overcome if you want it bad enough."

Bill credits Shari, in particular, who has the "aura of a classy First Lady," with being the linchpin of his family and his professional success.

Lady Bird Johnson and Barbara Bush were two of history's great women behind successful men. They reminded all of us how important a supportive, confident wife is for the ongoing success of a powerful man.

Writing online (askmen.com), Carmine Gallo outlined a number of reasons *why* a great woman is behind every great man. While such a woman is not a requirement for career success, she can make life richer and more meaningful.

"I don't know about the 'great man' part," says Bill, "but without Shari there is no way I could have done any of this."

In midst of bad news, control attitude
CHAPTER 62
Find Purpose, Passion, Not Perfection

The average temperature in northern Greenland is 14 degrees Fahrenheit, but the lows have dropped to minus 67, and for four months the sun doesn't shine, not a wink.

To protect its sovereignty over 60,000 square miles of ice cold land, Denmark dispatches several Sirius Dog Patrol teams, 14 dogs and two men from the Denmark Royal Navy.

The dogs sleep just fine in the elements, the men sleep in a tricked-out tent.

Not only is it cold in Greenland, but it's lonely, and the dog patrol may be the world's most difficult job, although some businessmen might disagree.

Running a small business can be a lonely job at times, much less being at the reins of a company that must make payroll for hundreds of workers in an industry with thin margins.

With the help of his wife, Bill found purpose and passion, not perfection. These intangibles helped him simultaneously weather all the storms of family life and growing a business.

Tim Tebow was selected in the first round of the 2012 NFL Draft by Denver and spent two seasons with the Broncos. In his book, *Shaken,* which is about discovering one's true identity in the midst of life's storms, Tebow shares how he was lonely during his brief time with the New York Jets following his release from Denver.

Part of his loneliness, he says, was "self-isolation" to avoid the media, and part of it was the thought he could push through on his own. However, what he really needed during those tough times was a loving and supportive community.

Bill found such a person in Shari.

If Bill had a bad day at the office, he made certain it didn't follow him home to his wife and kids. "I mentally separated the two," he says, although he did talk to his wife about matters that were more related to human resources.

"Unless I felt it was really necessary because it really affects her, I didn't bring problems home to Shari."

However, Bill did rely on Shari as a sounding board at times, for good reason. **"There were certain things I would talk to Shari about. Most women, more than men I believe, have a very innate ability to judge people's character."**

"Shari was able to lend counsel. She always keeps me grounded and true to my values."

The plaque on the bookstore shelf seems appropriate to describe Bill's mate: Be a girl with a mind, a woman with attitude and a lady with class.

Her assessment was especially sought when Bill was making hiring decisions with management personnel.

"And I purposely went out to dinner and did social things with my executives and their wives because you really want to learn about their true character. You also want to make sure they understand the values of your organization."

Unfortunately, **some business hiring decisions fail to account for the social connection.** It's also believed that women are better judges than men in assessing emotions.

When your business is growing at such a rapid pace, there's always a fear that you could make a bad hiring decision, especially if you've already done it once.

Life inevitably will bring some disappointments, says Molly Fletcher, sports agent-turned-entrepreneur, in her book, *Fearless at Work.* "That is when fear can take hold," she says. "Even in the midst of bad news, we still can control our attitudes and reactions."

Christian comedian Steve Harvey, who is a well-known television and radio personality, says there's a lesson in every moment of adversity, but there's a caveat. In his book, *Jump,* Harvey issues a warning: "Don't make your past mistakes larger by focusing all your attention on them and neglecting to concentrate on your future successes."

"There's a reason you create a business, there's a reason the business grows, there's a reason that people follow you," says Bill. But, **many companies lose their soul.**

When Bill needs a reality check, he need only look at what he and his team have accomplished.

In his book, *Your One Word*, Evan Carmichael notes that the Fortune 500 list was first created in 1955 to identify the largest U.S. corporations, public and private, by total revenue. "Only 13 percent of the companies on that original list are still on the list today."

What happened?

Carmichael says the others faded away "because they were boring and lost relevancy."

Sometimes it happens when ownership and or leadership changes, "and the new direction is to see how much money can be made." Scripture does not say that money is evil, but it does say the "love of money" is evil. We've already mentioned this, but the repetition is to make a point.

"If you keep the soul and the character of the organization and hire the right people who have those same aspirations, you don't have to worry about making money, it'll be there because everybody is working for the same goal," says Bill.

Money is a by-product.

Don't miss a blessing. Be sure you read Robert Palmer's Epilogue near the end of this book. -- Fred Hughes

His first paragraph says: "Bill Polacek looked in the mirror one day and found a real friend. He learned to exercise the virtues that were the bedrock of his very being. The money and success that followed were merely the scoreboard. You see, money cannot buy virtue, but virtue can create money, happiness and peace of mind."

When you're only out to make money, and that's your primary driver, you lose the soul of the company, says Bill.

Think of a football team. "If everybody is worried about winning the game, they do dumb things that can cost you the game. Instead, you focus on one play at a time, working together as a team, and moving in the same direction."

Think of driving a car. "If you're always looking in the rear-view mirror, you never know what path to take."

Some people, if forced to choose, would rather be poor and happy as opposed to rich and miserable, writes Geoffrey James, a contributing editor for the monthly *Inc.* magazine (inc.com), which focuses on growing companies.

What's the point of having money if you can't enjoy it? he asks.

"You're more likely to get rich if you're happy doing whatever you're doing," James says.

How did Bill fare in the long run? As someone once said, the proof is in the pudding.

No dissatisfied customer, not a single one
CHAPTER 63
Expect To Deal With Jealousy

Have you ever had dealings with a jealous neighbor?

Neighborhood jealousy may actually be a national phenomenon, and it definitely has a place in the Johnstown, Pennsylvania area. There are always some folks that "don't like to see other people succeed."

That's the observation of Matt Hughes, a former vice president at JWF Industries.

It takes patience, strength of mind, and great vision to work your way out of a two-car garage and grow to a one million-square-feet facility, especially in Johnstown, Hughes observed.

"I wasn't around in the early days of Bill's business but I imagine there were a heck of a lot of cynics that didn't want him to succeed. I'm sure the community talked more about his setbacks than his triumphs."

As an example, Bill remembers having a welding truck sitting in his workshop driveway with the bed extending a little way out on the paved neighborhood road. There were only a few dozen homes in a nine-block area and traffic was always sparse.

However, before he could finish the welding job and move the truck, a neighbor called police.

In a separate incident, Bill says a neighbor started taking pictures of him, "so I started posing." The neighbor was going to report Bill to authorities in an effort to stop him from running a business.

Keep in mind that this was not a community with covenants controlled by a homeowners association with rules and bylaws. It was a typical Small Town America neighborhood.

Surprisingly, there's a **boat load of research about jealousy.**

Forbes magazine published a post in 2012 on the subject. "We may never admit it outright," wrote the author, Kristi Hedges, "but there's an undercurrent of envy and gossip that exists within all of us."

Hedges, a leadership coach, speaker and author (*Power of Presence: Unlock Your Potential to Influence and Engage Others*) made mention of the 1992 alternative rock song by Steven Patrick Morrissey and Alain Whyte, "We Hate It When Our Friends Become Successful."

At its core, according to a *Psychology Today* article, envy is really self-criticism. And its first cousin is gossip. "Sometimes he's a good cousin, and other times the evil twin comes out," wrote Hedges.

In Bill's world, **jealousy and gossip are commodities that you must learn to deal with.**

In other words, entrepreneurs can escape the emotion of the moment with their intellect. Matt Hughes is able to look at JWF's CEO and visualize the big picture.

Bill forged ahead with very little financial backing and experience, he says.

"He didn't come from wealth, didn't possess a business degree, didn't have a bunch of buddies throwing work his way. He used old tools and worked in a cramped space. Although he's never satisfied, I bet Bill was grateful to have what he had and maintained a positive attitude throughout the lean years."

During the unionization attempt at JWF, one particularly vocal resident, who lived in his childhood neighborhood, wrote disparaging remarks on the social media site Facebook regarding Bill's well-to-do financial status and the upscale neighborhood where he lived.

Debbie, the second eldest sibling, got in-your-face personal and blasted the neighbor with the ferocity of a mama bear protecting her cubs. She pointed to Bill and his wife Shari's generosity and many contributions to the community.

Her defense ended with, "Shame on you!" The Facebook postings stopped.

It wasn't the first time that the elder sisters got in-your-face mad to protect their family. Barbara, the oldest, found her mother crying one afternoon at home and instinctively knew that a certain neighbor was probably responsible. Sure enough, the neighbor had insulted her mother earlier in the day.

Barbara marched over and knocked on the door. "If you ever make my mom cry again, you'll have to deal with me," she said to the startled woman, pointing a finger in her face. The neighbor never said another word, at least not publicly.

And Barbara? She was 13.

Believe it or not, a Wisconsin business that specializes in sealing asphalt driveways so they look and function like new, took advantage of the neighborhood jealousy syndrome.

"At Jealous Neighbors Sealcoating we focus on the details," wrote Brent Landowski, owner, on his website.

"We offer a fair price for an exceptional job. I am present on every job, and do them as if it was my own driveway." That's how you turn the tables on neighborhood jealousy!

Bill's two older sisters became nurses rather than entrepreneurs. Bill, on the other hand, became a **motivated** entrepreneur.

Having referred to location, location and location as the three keys to purchasing real estate, Bob Nelson, PhD, a management and motivation authority, writes: "Here are the three keys to inspiring change: reinforce, reinforce, reinforce."

In his book, *Companies Don't Succeed, People Do*, Dr. Nelson says, "In times of change, many leaders grossly underestimate the need for continuous reinforcement."

Nelson quotes industrialist John H. Patterson, who founded the National Cash Register Company: "To succeed in business it is necessary to make others see things as you see them."

It was Patterson who coined a phrase for his company's service division: **"We cannot afford to have a single dissatisfied customer."**

No great person ever made history without having guilt thrown at them or suffering some backlash from those who don't like or appreciate their independence, discipline, or single-mindedness.

That's the conclusion of Brendon Burchard in his book, *The Motivation Manifesto*. **"How we handle the enemies of our own progress speaks to our character and independence."**

Hughes likens another section of lyrics from the poem *If*, by Rudyard Kipling, to Bill:

> *If you can dream -- and not make dreams your master; if you can think -- and not make thoughts your aim; if you can meet with Triumph and Disaster and treat those two impostors just the same; if you can bear to hear the truth you've spoken twisted by knaves to make a trap for fools, or watch the things you gave your life to, broken, and stoop and build 'em up with worn-out tools: You'll be a man, my son!*

Business advisor Bruce Tulgan says the "second person" you need to manage every day is everyone else; the "first person" you need to manage is yourself.

In his book, *It's Okay to be the Boss*, Tulgan compares being effective at managing to getting in good physical condition: "the hard part is getting in the habit of doing it."

Trust your customers
CHAPTER 64
That's Not How We Do It Here!

"Ever since I was a kid, Johnstown was always looking for that big business to come here, to part the clouds and let the sunshine come down. It was right below our feet the whole time," says Bill. "All it took was a little bit of hustle."

Here's how JWF Industries unearthed the oil and gas business that was right beneath their feet, so to speak.

"People don't buy visionary products. People buy solutions to their problem," says Diana Kandler in her book, *All In Startup.*

She encourages entrepreneurs to "solve problems that your customers are already experiencing rather than try to convince them that a problem exists."

For years, that has been Bill's simple and effective approach: **"Find what the customer needs, and grow and change to meet those needs."**

Gas and oil are a constantly evolving industry. They are a perfect match for a company already deeply invested in innovation and adaptation -- an ability to quickly react to a customer's changing circumstances and requirements.

Customers know what they want, and they're willing to help a supplier provide it, says Gregory Ciotti, the marketing guy at Help Scout (helpscout.com) which provides customer service software.

"There are certain things that customers are just flat out better at than you, and one of the things they can be quite good at is understanding their peers' needs."

On his Internet blog (blog.kissmetrics.com), Ciotti references Steve Jobs:

- It can be really hard to design products by focus groups.

- A lot of times, people don't know what they want until you show it to them.

"My mantra is we can build and design anything," Bill says. **"We'll build products a year from now we haven't thought of yet. We had orders for frac tanks before we built our first one. Our speed in getting products to market will set us apart."**

As far back as the late 1700s, circus owners in America were training ponies to be obedient to commands and perform tricks. It was often a rigorous undertaking to teach a pony one special trick. For many ponies, it was too much to ask for them to learn more than one trick.

As the pony became too old to perform, the animal was retired and put out to pasture. Sometimes no other pony could master the special trick, and the trick became extinct. This may be the background for a famous expression that illustrates being diversified.

Bill's team caught the vision and realized the potential of natural gas in 2010 and diversified so as "not to be a one-trick pony."

Most school kids have heard the claim that cats have nine lives. And most of us have heard that curiosity killed the cat. The "curiosity" expression has often been used when attempting to stop someone asking unwanted questions.

But curiosity also leads to discoveries and inventions.

What if Bill had not been curious about the machinery and equipment used in oil and gas exploration? What if Bill had ignored those friends and associates who thought his company was perfectly suited for this industry? What if he was not intrigued about the prospect of diversifying? What if he had ignored his own instincts?

Imagine you're in one of those boring staff meetings, and all you're thinking about is your tickets to the big game when someone pops off with a really good idea. For a moment you forget about the big game, and your tickets. Your mind goes into overdrive.

Hey, this really is a sensational idea! You can't believe you didn't think of it first.

At this moment in time, what's the worst thing you can hear?

There's a book out that answers that very important question. Indeed, the answer is a profound statement; do not underestimate its significance.

Here's the answer: That's not how we do it here! The book, by John Kotter and Holger Rathgeber, is appropriately titled, *That's Not How We Do It Here.*

Frankly, it would have been easy for Bill to pooh-pooh this particular opportunity.

Two years earlier, Bill was just beginning to hear about Marcellus Shale, a type of sedimentary rock named for a distinctive outcrop near the village of Marcellus, New York. He wondered what role, if any, his company could play in the push to bring natural gas from the deep underground shale to the surface.

After all, there were no drilling rigs in Johnstown, at least not the massive structures that are used to extract oil and gas deposits from thousands of feet under the earth's surface.

I grew up hearing that the only person who loves change is a wet baby.

Bill is a contradiction. He has never been mired down in a mindset that wasn't open to change. In fact, he was always looking for new business ideas, as well as new ways of doing business.

He considered the shale gas industry as a great, big possibility.

He visited a drilling site and noticed drill rigs and water tanks, but did not see anything right then and there that JWF could fabricate, "but I felt we could dig deeper." He sensed it might be an "evolving business."

Bill sent a key management person to visit other sites and study the industry and "find things we can build. I thought this was our opportunity to build our own product lines."

"We observed the products in the field, asked the operators what they did or didn't like about it, and we took the same products and made them better and more operator-friendly."

Bill's company was caught up in the philosophy of building a better mousetrap.

Bill had sensed the potential correctly! Seven years after he got into the oil and gas industry, Bill's company was named manufacturer of the year.

The landscapes at drilling sites are always changing. Public involvement and government regulations are typically responsible. And JWF Industries benefits. As public involvement rises and government regulations increase, so does JWF's business.

Long before the oil and gas business, JWF was advocating environmental safeguards in all of their operations.

"Drillers used to dump the frac water in the rivers and they needed three frac tanks," Bill observed. New regulations halted the river dumping and now drillers need 100 frac tanks per site. "Boom, an opportunity to build tanks I didn't have before."

"A key question that bothers every entrepreneur is, whether he or she can spot the most promising opportunity and would that be right for them or not?" It's a question posed by Abhishek Shah, in an Internet article about recognizing business opportunities (thugstart.com).

"How does one recognize the next big thing when they see it?" he asks.

Without taking a calculated risk, says Shah, who describes himself as an experimental entrepreneur, as opposed to Bill's description of himself as an accidental entrepreneur, "you would never know whether there was an opportunity or not."

Recognizing the potential opportunities associated with the Marcellus Shale gas industry, JWF formed a spin-off company to produce specialty products for the oil and gas industry.

These products, with kooky names like frac tanks, flowback/gas buster tanks, mud tanks, API tanks and impoundment systems, ultimately allow the natural gas to find its way into our daily lives to heat homes and water, dry clothes and fuel stoves for cooking food.

The unique products Bill's company builds help ensure the cleanliness and preservation of water and land while at the same time enabling the shale gas companies to comply with safety and environmental regulations. The new company also opened the door to the power generation and chemical industries.

Developing new specialty products for the Marcellus Shale gas industry required innovative thinking.

"Innovation takes confidence, boldness, and the discipline to tune out negative voices," says Carmine Gallo, in his book, *The Innovation Secrets of Steve Jobs*. "Few individuals have such courage, which is why so few can or will be able to innovate on a grand scale the way Steve Jobs did."

Jobs was the inventor and industrial designer best known as co-founder of Apple.

Environmental Tank & Container, Bill's new subsidiary company, opened in the spring of 2011 and was officially dedicated in December of that year with Pennsylvania Gov. Tom Corbett saying it was **born of the American spirit,** referring to its parent company JWF Industries.

While taking a tour in early 2012, U.S. Sen. Pat Toomey cracked, "In July, you could hear the crickets chirping in here," referring to a formerly abandoned Bethlehem Steel building.

"What they're asking for is the opportunity to grow. As long as the federal government is not in the way, they'll be just fine," said Sen. Toomey.

And grow, it did.

The plant swelled from a handful of employees to more than 80 in less than eight months.

The once mediocre Johnstown economy benefitted from the natural gas boom in more ways than one. The secondary spin-off from the energy-rich Marcellus Shale has involved banking institutions, engineers, and construction companies contracted to design and build plant expansions.

Bill was curious, listened to friends and associates who encouraged him, he wanted to diversify, and he followed his instincts.

Here's the result: Environmental Tank and Container has become one of the biggest names in portable fluid storage, oil and gas equipment, and power generation components.

Is anything possible?

It may be if you work hard, follow your passion, and are prepared to build a better mousetrap.

"We were building things and designing products so fast that within two years, we had 24 product lines. It goes back to our mantra," says Bill. **"Find out what the customer needs."**

Andre Rush was a master sergeant in the U.S. Army who was wounded in Iraq. Today the ex-soldier with bulging biceps is a freelance executive chef at many White House functions.

Known as Tiny, he may be the only chef in America that can bench-press 700 pounds. His story was published online at westernjournal.com.

Ryan Ledendecker, a freelance journalist, quoted the hulk-like Rush as saying, "Doesn't matter where you come from, you can do anything if you're willing to work."

Give people more than they expect
CHAPTER 65
Customers Help Develop New Products

In days gone by, Bethlehem Steel's big buildings were situated near busy mainline railroad tracks. The clickity-clack of passing trains could be heard day and night. In the war years, trains were loaded with military apparatus and personnel.

In 1945 the building currently housing Environmental Tank & Container (ETC) was a shell plant (as in guns and ammo) operated by Bethlehem Steel that produced eight-inch howitzer munitions for the U.S. government.

These howitzers fired 200-pound shells and had the longest distance of any U.S. Army field artillery weapon in World War II, a range up to 20 miles.

Even when the "shell plant" was used for other steel-manufacturing operations after the war, it never lost the stigma of being known as the "Shell Plant."

Bill's father and grandfather were steel workers. "After serving in World War II in the Navy, my father got his first job welding at the former Shell Plant, which is now our Environmental Tank and Container (ETC) facility."

More than a quarter-century has passed since Bethlehem Steel closed its operations in Johnstown.

Back then "Boot Scootin' Boogie" and "I Will Always Love You" were number one songs by Brooks & Dunn and Whitney Houston.

Presidents Bush and Yeltsin proclaimed a formal end to the Cold War (U.S. and Russia).

Panama dictator Manuel Noriega was sentenced to 40 years on drug charges.

Bill Clinton was elected President.

And Freddy Haddad began evolving into an entrepreneur who eventually became the COO of Coddict, a digital marketing agency.

Freddy who? I had to smile.

My mother named me Freddy and that's the name I answered to until the day after I walked down the hall and found my dorm room as a college freshman. I was Fred ever after, except to my mother and one sister. (That's a story for another time.)

I've never met Freddy Haddad, but he comes across as a unique character and a perceptive and genuinely nice guy.

I stumbled on his blog (freddyhaddad.com) where he described 15 things he learned in his first 25 years. His findings are really a short course on beginning the entrepreneurial journey.

"Search engine optimization expert" was listed under his diverse specialties, but three words really caught my eye: "I Deliver Results."

His claim to deliver results struck a chord with me. I've always admired and appreciated people who make things happen. They're willing to wade through a sea of obstacles, if necessary, to keep their promises, to reach their goals.

Freddy discovered that family is king, a person can learn anything they want to, and money should never be one's primary goal.

He also found out about adversity: Embrace obstacles that come your way, he said, "because they will always be coming."

He cites the wisdom of Henry Ford: "When everything seems to be going against you, remember that the airplane takes off against the wind, not with it."

Against numerous obstacles -- against the wind, so to speak -- look what happened to Bill's company.

In 2015, JWF Industries announced that its oil and gas subsidiary, ETC, had partnered with Comtech Industries, Inc., to establish production of a new proprietary product, DYNA Tanks.

The partnership would add jobs to the local economy by producing the segments necessary for a complete tank in less than one week. Now, these are big, heavy tanks.

This and other similar projects required some new thinking on the part of Bill's management team, and some of the new thinking was drastic.

But one conclusion became obvious: **Aspiring entrepreneurs must not shy away from innovation.**

"We decided to build our own product lines," said Bill. "My mother put that in my head and I always thought she was right."

It's no small matter that one million gallons of water can be safely contained in the 72-foot diameter by 36-foot high tanks that have a much smaller footprint on drilling well sites and effectively eliminate the risk factors and contamination associated with in-ground containment ponds and lagoons.

There's a narrative that generally refers to all or large portions of at least nine states, including all of Pennsylvania, as the 'Rust Belt' where life has deteriorated because of economic decline, population loss, and urban decay due to the shrinking of the area's once-powerful industrial sector.

Building big steel tanks in Johnstown has put a dent in that narrative. To say the least, it's a comeback story.

Building such physically imposing projects can't be done without a rolling mill, machinery that uses a metal forming process in which metal stock is passed through one or more pairs of rollers to reduce the thickness and to make the thickness uniform.

The concept is similar to the way cooks roll dough for a pie crust. But the similarity stops there. This is not your grandfather's steel mill, and it's not your grandmother's kitchen countertop, either.

If you develop an innovative product that can't be built without a rolling mill, by all means build a rolling mill. And that's what happened.

"Today, steel manufacturing is coming back to life," Bill said at the ribbon-cutting for the $8 million investment by Comtech and JWF. It's the region's first new rolling mill in over 50 years; it's state-of-the-art, and it's one of the largest of its kind.

"This rolling mill is another step toward fully recognizing the manufacturing renaissance in the Johnstown area by revitalizing an old steel mill with modern technology and creating opportunities for the future that give a nod to our region's prosperous past."

Remember the warning by Freddy Haddad to embrace obstacles because they're always coming? The rolling mill project fits the mold perfectly!

The mill was originally headed for Michigan with final processing and painting to take place in Canada.

However, Comtech and JWF collaborated on building the facility in Johnstown, and configured a straight-line system where the rolling mill will fabricate the steel panels and then move them directly into ETC's paint line.

Said Bill, "Who would have thought you'd see a rolling mill in the 'Rust Belt,' let alone in a small town?"

There's an old African proverb: If you want to go quickly, go alone. **If you want to go far, go together.**

Steve Case draws on this wisdom in his book, *The Third Wave,* where he discusses Partnership, Policy and Perseverance. The collaboration between Comtech and JWF involved a bit of all three.

And look at the specialized service the two companies were able to provide to customers.

And here's another kind of service.

In *The Simple Truths of Service*, Ken Blanchard and Barbara A. Glanz tell how a cabbie's life and business were transformed after taking to heart advice he heard on the radio from personal growth guru, Wayne Dyer (author of the book, *You'll See It When You Believe It*).

Dyer said **if you get up in the morning expecting to have a bad day, you'll rarely disappoint yourself.**

The cabbie began providing his customers with extraordinary service, and his business blossomed.

"Always give people more than they expect to get," says Nelson Boswell, an author who's well known for brainy quotes.

Going the extra mile has become engrained in JWF's culture. Giving customers more than they expect is standard operating procedure. But many companies either can't or don't provide extraordinary service. And, statistically, it shows.

U.S. companies lose more than $75 billion a year because of poor customer service, according to a report from NewVoiceMedia (newvoicemedia.com). Even more scary is that losses increased $13 billion in two years (2016 to 2018).

Even in the manufacturing business, giving customers more than they expect is a sound philosophy, and it yields many dividends.

"Our customers help us develop new products," says Bill. **It's a feather in any businessman's hat to have this kind of relationship with customers.**

Here's one practical example.

In response to changing environmental laws, JWF designed its KwikTank above ground storage systems for large-volume fresh- and produced-water storage. It's much like a heavy-duty, large-volume, above-ground swimming pool.

Its development came about after a client in West Virginia, concerned about protecting the environment, wanted an alternative to installing liners or pits or stacking frac tanks together.

Here's another practical example.

Transportation flexibility for smaller storage tanks was a costly challenge facing JWF's customers so Bill and his team members put on their thinking caps and designed their legal-load tank, a 350-barrel upright tank that can be used as a frac tank or mud tank.

Truthfully, you don't need a thinking cap to be appreciative, or to keep your ears open and your mind in gear.

Listen to your customers! Thank your customers!

"We now have a patent on the egg-shaped design which allows for easy portability. The unique shape -- fits on a trailer without overhang -- eliminates the need for wide-load permits normally associated with hauling the predecessor of these tanks," Bill explains.

Massive is a good word to describe some of JWF's products. Their 87-feet-long bullet tank, which is 12 feet in diameter and designed with 2.75-inch-thick steel walls, is a good example.

Bullet tank barely fits under bridge as it leaves Johnstown plant on multi-wheeled trailer.

Compare that to the 1.5-inch-thick steel doors in Virginia's "super-max" Red Onion State Prison. Yes, the tank is tough. And it's heavy. It weighs 145 tons.

The tank weighs as much as America's last space shuttle Atlantis, which made its final flight in 2011, "and the tanks are being built locally so customers will save money on hauling costs, which can run as high as $1 million for a mega-load like this."

Back in the day, Big John and his fellow laborers were very protective of their jobs at Bethlehem Steel and the products they made. If anyone came to work in a foreign car, it was subject to being pushed over the cliff. "Damn cheap Chinese junk," Big John would say.

This may have been as much rhetoric as a real event, but the message was the same: foreign cars and cheap foreign steel were not welcome.

"A lot of foreign competition is sucking away jobs, but oil and gas puts nearly 100 percent of their jobs in the U.S.," Bill explains.

"These are American workers doing American jobs. I'm not sure everyone appreciates what that does for our economy, and this industry is big in helping our community. I don't know of one oil or gas company that doesn't give back."

The steel mills may have vanished, but the legacy of hard work and determination hasn't.

JWF's impact is not limited to the U.S. The company is having a global impact. In 2015, Bill announced that the company was signing a memorandum of understanding to develop and manufacture green technology that will provide a new source of electricity for West Africa.

Says Bill, "I thought I was making a product, then realized I was making a difference. And this fits our core values."

It's okay to tackle a project half way around the world, but put on your thinking cap again.

Competing globally requires an entirely new set of skills, learning how to import and export, licenses, understanding language barriers, metric versus standard measurements, laws, and customs.

"It's not like in the United States, if you need something, you go to the local hardware store."

Lack of degree does not prevent success
CHAPTER 66
Finding The Right People

There have been times, JWF officials say, when it was a struggle to fill job vacancies with talent available through the existing local workforce. So they decided to give the local workforce a hand up.

Through support from the Department of Labor, JWF started an apprentice program to bring in untrained recruits and assign them to a paid, on-the-job training program where they'd work their way up the ranks over a period of up to four years. With each upgrade in skill level, an employee's pay increases, too.

Periodically, a writer comes along and captures the gist of JWF's operations including Bill Polacek's management style. Such was the case in an article written by Jayne Gest in *Smart Business Pittsburgh*. (Although Bill repeated his statements to the author for purposes of this book, Gest gets full credit for organizing some of Bill's thoughts in her story.)

Fifteen years ago when JWF Industries needed to hire welders and other employees for its subsidiaries, Bill told Gest that his company often didn't need to advertise. Just four years later, when the company needed people, they weren't there -- which was a big surprise.

But having the right people was more important than ever as the company was growing in the defense sector, and expanding into oil and gas.

So how does Bill define "the right people" for a job at JWF Industries?

"To just teach someone to weld, production weld, that's not hard to get and you can teach that fairly quickly. But we're looking for a higher-level caliber of employee," he says, "one that not only has a higher skill level from the welding side, but also the manufacturing side."

Much of the basic manufacturing for the company's various sectors is the same, but JWF Industries needs employees who can juggle the 25 percent that varies.

"If you're peaking over at power generation, that's a different certification than it is for oil and gas, and that's different from defense, which is different than commercial," Bill explains.

"You have to be willing to learn, and get different certifications or just different technologies in manufacturing based on different industries. So, that's harder to find those folks."

At the same time the search for skilled technicians was coming up dry, Bill was talking to local high schools about entrepreneurship -- which is something he says he wished he knew more about himself at that age.

He has since learned that **no one can be too young to become an entrepreneur.**

Don't believe it?

Just look at magazines and websites like Fortune, Entrepreneur, Teen Business, Investipedia, Business News Daily, and Inc. There are stories galore about crazy-rich young people who have created a product or concept.

Furthermore, there's a vast amount of guidance to be found in public libraries and on the Internet. One such group, Entrepreneurs' Organization (eonetwork.org) claims to be the "most influential community" of entrepreneurs with 12,000-plus members in 52 countries.

Even the U.S. government is getting in on the act with resources geared to Millennial entrepreneurs (sba.gov).

Statistics indicate there are 22-plus million self-employed people in America and they do not employ other workers.

"That's about 14 percent of the entire American workforce. With drive, initiative, and a quality product, it may be more attainable than you think to make it on your own," says Jeremy Anderberg, in an article posted on The Art of Manliness (artofmanliness.com).

Anderberg points out that **some of the most successful men in the last two centuries were entrepreneurs without a college degree.**

Two examples are Milton Hershey, who had no schooling after the 4th grade and founded the Hershey Chocolate Company, in Hershey, Pennsylvania, and Frank Lloyd Wright, an architect and designer of more than 1,000 structures.

Success is not measured by how many classes you took, but how much responsibility you take on, says Bill. **And all the education in the world can't prepare intestinal fortitude. "You have to dig deep into your heart and soul for that."**

Anderberg advocates that high school graduates work a year or two before making a decision about college -- starting at minimum wage, working long hours, displaying integrity, and being respectful of customers and coworkers.

There was no such thing as minimum wage in the late 1800s when Milton Hershey was apprenticed to the printer of a German-English newspaper, or when he was apprenticed to a confectioner, where he learned enough to go into the business for himself.

He was good at making candy; he became famous making chocolate.

"Everybody is telling their kids to go to college," Bill observes.

"There's a thought-process that you can't be successful unless you have a college education. And I would mostly agree with that; you probably can't be successful unless you at least get some post-secondary education."

Bill says schools are being measured by SAT scores and what college they send students to. Many students are "pushed to college," and they have no idea what they want to do with their lives.

"These kids are growing up in a technology world, not a manufacturing world, so it's very abstract to them, and it makes it difficult to attract young people" to a welding career when the process seems so nebulous to them.

"Nobody wants to send their kids to a vocational school or have them working with their hands. So we had a very hard time getting kids that were interested in this field," reflects Bill.

The challenges are not limited to Johnstown. It's an international plight.

Chicago Tribune reporter Alexia Elejalde-Ruiz wrote an article, after interviewing a German manufacturer, contending that manufacturing's big challenge is to find skilled and interested workers.

"Recruiting has been an uphill climb as an increasingly high-tech manufacturing sector battles the image of a dirty, dying industry and a mindset that idealizes a university education," she wrote.

With firsthand awareness that a large number of parents were pressuring their children to head off to college, Bill needed to adjust his thinking about finding new workers.

"One of my mantras is the best way to predict the future is to create it," he says. "So if you want to have a better predictability with getting people that you need, you have to go out there and create the plan that encourages the type of people that you're looking for."

There's a bit of tragedy in the new thinking in schools and among parents. There's so much focus on getting a degree, so little on getting a job. Only 15 percent of youngsters who go to college get a job in their field.

There's no denying that the inclination for innovation ended up in Bill's DNA, as it was in many of his relatives and ancestors.

His dad's nephew, Bob Polacek worked for Otis Elevator Company and once brought a gadget home he had retrieved from a junked elevator.

It wasn't long before the mixture of parts had a real use in the real world, even if it was a repurposed use.

No welding was allowed in boilers, the kind that Big John was hired to repair. All tubes had to be rolled and expanded. Bob sometimes worked as much as two weeks inside a boiler, typically using grinders and wire brushes because he was smaller in stature than his brothers and was the only one who would fit in the cramped space.

Who could blame Bob for trying to make his job easier? He found a magical use for a piece of junk.

Bob proceeded to make a gearbox out of the discarded elevator parts that could be used for rolling tubes in the boilers in a close place. "Boy, it worked really good," says Joe Polacek, another of Big John's nephews. "John, he liked that. We always thought up a shortcut for doing something."

Bob was gifted in making gadgets -- custom tools, if you will -- that the crew used on boilers they called "a bitch."

Finding shortcuts came natural to innovators like Big John, his father before him, and his nephews, but these make-life-easier projects never degraded the quality of their work.

There were no shortcuts on workmanship, absolutely none.

John had a well-earned reputation. His work for customers was the same quality of work he did for himself.

Said Joe: "I know, a lot of times, John would say, 'Look at the awful job somebody else did on this. I don't know how they got away with that!'"

Do nothing, and nothing is going to change
CHAPTER 67
Peers Have Big Say In New Workers

Oh, my gosh, Web searches let me down! I was unsuccessful in finding accurate data on the number of Help Wanted ads posted daily online and in newspapers across America.

Is it thousands, hundreds of thousands, or millions? I still don't know the correct answer.

But the purpose of the question is to make a point.

Finding a welder with the advanced skill set needed at JWF Industries is more complicated than hanging a Help Wanted sign in the office window or posting online or in a newspaper.

Bill had an epiphany that he could work with the community college in Johnstown to develop the first local associates program in welding technology. He put money up front for a teacher, alongside a grant that paid for equipment, and within a year the program was up and running.

"But the hardest part was getting kids interested," he says.

"We were lucky to have three kids in the program." The word did get around eventually. "Now they've had some instances where they had to turn kids away. In fact, we hired a second teacher."

The classes are on the JWF Industries' campus, and not only attract students who weren't originally thinking of going into welding, but also give the company an ability to improve its own employees' skills.

After setting up the associates program, Bill was invited to a national meeting on the future of manufacturing by the secretary of commerce.

He shared what he had done to encourage more interest in manufacturing, and spoke to others about additional ideas.

One of his takeaways from the White House gathering was to open his doors to school tours.

So, he worked to bring his company and its products to the attention of younger children, in order to spark an interest.

"Nearly every school in the area has visited our facility -- gone through and seen the technology -- and it's been an eye-opening experience," he says.

"The schools have said that's all the kids talk about. They didn't realize what this was all about." Even behavior-challenged and clueless class clowns get the message.

With robotics, lasers, automated machining, quality controls, close-tolerance welding, and computer-based technology, "it's not their grandfather's steel mill," Bill says.

Also, with additional education, employees can be involved in a lot of different fields outside of welding, such as supply chain management, engineering, accounting, or IT (Information Technology).

If an employer wants better workforce predictability, Bill recommends exposing junior high school students to exactly what your company does -- because by the time they get to high school they may have already made up their minds.

The workplace exposure can overcome their preconceived notions or even put your company on their radar screen.

In fact, one of Bill's project managers told him that when she went to the junior high, students were asked, "What do you want to be when you grow up?"

One wanted to be a professional basketball player. Another dreamed of being an astronaut. But one student said he wanted to work for JWF.

No matter what your business challenge, Bill says the best thing you can do is start by being creative. After all, ideas fuel the engines of industry.

By the way, overthinking is not required. Don't make your ideas more complex than necessary.

English historian Henry Thomas Buckle knew about ideas, having a private collection of 22,000 books. He said, "Great minds discuss ideas. Average minds discuss events. Small minds discuss people."

In order to create a culture of trust and ownership, JWF Industries shares its vision and financials quarterly, as well as utilizing a profit sharing program with its employees.

Employees have a big say in new workers, too.

Peers watch the performance of new hires and assess whether they are an asset or liability, Bill says, **so after 90 days he has the employees in that area vote whether the workers stay or go.**

"If you've got a new worker who really doesn't care, and hurts you from the standpoint of productivity or quality or delivery, longtime employees know that that affects them, so they're protecting themselves," he says.

"And who better to know about new hires than the people that are working around them?"

Over the past 20 years it hasn't happened often, but people do get voted out and eventually leave after management determines a real problem exists. "We've never had an employee stay who was voted out by longtime employees.

The process is legitimate," he says.

Bill also has gotten creative by bringing college courses to the plant on many Friday afternoons, a practice he began about five years ago. Employees who want to get a bachelor's degree can take operational management, psychology or accounting classes.

"We take away all of the excuses and make it convenient, and it works. People have lives outside of work -- they have children, they have activities," he says. "And for the two hours we have them do that, it's certainly a return on investment."

"The more sophisticated business model at JWF Industries requires a higher pedigree within the company, so more education lifts everybody up."

It would take a long time to get a degree by taking one class a week, but the program often prompts employees to get interested in earning their degree, he says.

If employees want to go on their own, JWF Industries gives up to $5,000 a year toward tuition.

"I hear a lot of companies complain about the kids today," Bill says. "The kids today aren't any different than when we were younger. It's the same thing they said when I was younger, and, you know, you have to create the opportunity for them."

"So, you can choose to do nothing, and nothing is going to change. Or you can **choose to do something, and create that change that you want.**"

Bill was named the Western Pennsylvania area's Entrepreneur of the Year in 1996 and was a finalist -- one of three companies -- in the Manufacturing portion of the national competition in Palm Springs, California, where nominees were recognized for providing the solid foundation for future economic growth by building their own business.

Each individual and company that was nominated for the national award has a story that illustrates the courage, imagination, and perseverance it takes to pursue the entrepreneurial dream.

Warning: Entrepreneurs must not be lulled into apathy when they become recipients of prestigious awards and public recognition. These things do not guarantee a successful business.

Even amid all the accolades, Bill understands who butters his bread. Employees are his most important asset.

Gotta know your customer's first name
CHAPTER 68
Focus On Fixing The Problem

What does personalized service look like in your business? Does it offer a human touch?

Jude Arijaje, entrepreneur and owner of Minuteman Press franchise in Philadelphia, gets to the core of personalized service: "Customers love it when you remember their names."

Many years ago I met a man who was a regional manager for courses being offered by the Dale Carnegie organization. One of those courses was about how to remember names.

We were introduced and spoke briefly, two minutes tops. I met the man in a totally different setting about six months later, both times in a professional capacity in my role as a community newspaper publisher.

As I approached him, he looked up and immediately called me by my first name. I was 10 feet away. Talk about making an impression! That was at least 45 years ago.

I no longer remember his name, but I've never forgotten the lesson I learned that day. After all, I'm still talking about it.

"It's tough to build relationships until you know someone by name," say Tom Rath and Donald O. Clifton in their book, *How Full Is Your Bucket?*

"At work, become the person known for noticing when others do a great job," the authors say. And recognize them by using the name they prefer to be called.

Customers, suppliers, and employees love it when you remember their names.

As big as JWF Industries has become in the manufacturing sector, the company still operates on first names.

"I'd rather be called Bill," says Bill.

I was still in grade school when I learned another important lesson from a mail carrier, a lesson about kindness.

Even as a child, I remember hearing the characterizations made about mailmen -- neither heat, cold, sleet, snow or rain will deter them from their appointed rounds. Most postal workers walked everywhere back then.

Our next door neighbor, James, delivered the mail on foot, regardless of the weather, in our small south Alabama town. Strapped over his shoulder was a huge leather pouch with a protective flap.

Much of the year James was wearing the familiar blue/gray shorts we kids associated with post office workers. But to me, he was more a neighbor than a postal employee.

Our little mailbox was as simple as life itself in the 1950s. It was stamped from lightweight sheet metal, had a hinged lid and hung on the wall next to the front door under the roof of the stoop.

It was something that Big John Polacek might have built in his garage workshop. The mailbox was our link with grandparents who lived far away and mail order purchases sent to Sears or Montgomery Ward.

I was about eight years old when James got permission from my parents to take me fishing in a nearby lake.

James backed his beat up pickup into position at a clearing on the shore and released the straps securing the boat to the trailer. The 12-foot sheet-metal craft slid gently into the water and after a few pulls on the rope, the gas kicker sputtered and then roared to life.

The first time I read Mark Sanborn's book, *The Fred Factor,* a book that describes the extraordinary personalized service provided by an individual mailman named Fred, my mind drifted back to the fishing trip with James, our mailman.

My bobber shot down under the dark murky water near a cypress stump. As the line tightened, my cane pole started to bend. James said something about pulling back and setting the hook.

The next thing I knew, the water was swirling by the side of the boat and James quickly reached out with a hand net and kept me from losing a three-meal-size widemouth bass caught with a worm.

We were on the water less than one hour. The act of catching the fish took only one minute. The fact that he was the mailman and took time out of his day, and away from his wife and two daughters, and took me fishing, created a lifetime memory.

I could have come home empty-handed and still been happy. I've never forgotten his kindness, and that was about 66 years ago.

Kindness, whether to family, close friends, casual acquaintances, co-workers, and perhaps complete strangers, pays lifelong dividends.

Even the phenomenal growth in his company has not stopped Bill from routinely performing acts of kindness. It's a key component of JWF's culture. In fact, kindness is expected.

The world is filled with quick-witted, thought-provoking billboards, signs, and sayings that contain a measure of truth about kindness.

"No act of kindness, no matter how small, is ever wasted." That's a lesson from *Aesop's Fables.*

In addition to being kind, are you generous with your time? Bill's generosity with his time and resources is at the top of a long list of his favorable traits.

"A manager who will stop what he's doing and listen to an employee will be remembered for 'taking time out,'" says Jill Lublin in her book, *The Profit of Kindness.*

"No matter how few perks you think you can offer from a business standpoint, remember that you possess the best commodity out there: your time."

Speaking of time, as businessmen we only have so much of it, whether measured in hours, days, or years. To make a positive difference, we better get busy.

Time is "one of the few certainties that everyone shares. It can also be an extraordinary motivational force," says leadership consultant Tom Rath in his book, *Are You Fully Charged?*

He says all of us are in charge of how we spend our time.

"Use this knowledge to stay focused on doing what's most important every day," Rath says.

Thor Schrock of Schrock Innovations, an entrepreneur himself, built a computer repair company. He penned a couple of Internet articles in 2009 about good service that are "must reads" for any businessman or manufacturer.

He concludes **there are only three types of service: bad, good and exceptional** (schrockinnovations.com).

Fred's passion for his job as a mail carrier in *The Fred Factor* and his genuine interest in the people he served epitomizes the excellence and quality -- exceptional service, if you will -- that should be the goals of every person in any business, profession, or leadership role.

But providing ideal service often poses a dilemma. Folks seem to want their job done yesterday, and everybody is looking for a deal.

There are 171,476 words in the Oxford dictionary in current use. I don't know how anyone managed to use a total of only 32 words -- and several words are even repeated -- and put good service in its proper place. But they did.

We offer three kinds of service: Good, cheap, fast. You can pick any two.

- Good service cheap won't be fast.

- Good service fast won't be cheap.

- Fast service cheap won't be good.

How does a company go about making 'exceptional service' a reality?

Consider this example.

JWF Industries was supposed to be the exclusive supplier of a product for a customer that made an urgent call to report "a huge quality problem." At the job site, JWF personnel found the defective product wasn't theirs.

"Wait a minute, we're supposed to be an exclusive supplier," Bill thought. The defective part was actually made in Mexico, by a competing company.

JWF fixed the problem anyway. Try to follow this exchange between the customer and the supplier. Here's what happened.

Bill: The buyer called the next day, very humbled.

Buyer: That wasn't your crane.

Bill: I know.

Buyer: But you fixed it.

Bill: You guys needed it, didn't you? My job is to make sure you're successful. And part of your being successful is getting someone's else's frame fixed because it's on your line to meet your customers' needs, and that's what we're going to do.

"That's the way we operate," Bill says, "focused on fixing the problem instead of digging our heels in and arguing about who's right."

"Make sure your business is creating a service experience so good that it demands loyalty," says Steve Maraboli, behavioral scientist, counselor, business coach, and author of the book, *The Power of One.*

Bill identifies some of his customers as planners, others as impulsive or reactionary. "We need to be able to help them either way. We figure out a way to make our customer look good, whether they're a buyer or a project manager."

Flexibility is required; a single script won't do.

"Managers sometimes react to our customers and the manager gets too focused on getting the product out the door rather than getting it right. It was a culture we had to change," says Bill.

"The culture we're trying to create is that you're not a victim, so if you had to get it out quick and you sacrificed processes and quality, you're not a victim, you simply didn't plan well enough so you were not put in that predicament."

Bill uses a hospital analogy: "If a customer wants you to do something because it's an emergency, well it's no different than a hospital. When you go to the hospital, you either go to the Emergency Room if you need it right away, or you go to a scheduled operation.

"But in the emergency room, they don't *not* sterilize everything, they don't *not* take care of you. It's a different set of processes to get the same result.

"When a customer has a high demand, that's triage.

"We have customers that plan things out, that's your normal operating room where things are planned and organized.

"When an emergency comes in the ER, you have to have a different set of processes that has very quick checks and balances -- and it costs more money -- but you can still get the same result."

As an automobile executive, Lee Iacocca helped spearhead the development of the Ford Mustang and Pinto cars, and later revived Chrysler Corporation. "I hire people brighter than me and get out of their way," he once said.

Eric Spett is CEO of the marketing performance management company Allocadia. In a brief YouTube video promoting his company, he says he finds people "smarter than me because I'm not that smart."

Spett has a big grin on his face as the video fades. Think about it. Read between the lines.

Iacocca, Spett and Bill are not advocating surrender of their leadership positions; they're simply looking for people who can help them execute their own visions.

It's okay to make mistakes
CHAPTER 69
Dumb Young Kid Got The Last Laugh

If someone in your household cooks, they've probably used at least one recipe from Pinterest (pinterest.com). The hugely successful social media platform prefers to reference itself as "a catalog of ideas."

And there's something else it did well: the company built its headquarters in an abandoned industrial warehouse in San Francisco.

The brand and communications firm id29 did the same thing in Troy, New York where their headquarters was established in an abandoned collar factory.

Visionaries, innovators and dreamers like Bill Polacek have created some amazing workspaces by using ugly, ungainly monstrosities that sat abandoned, often for years, becoming nothing more than eyesores.

Resurrecting an abandoned industrial site in Johnstown wasn't without its problems, however, namely a protracted battle with the Department of Environmental Resources over who would pay for the environmental cleanup of metal shavings and lead paint left behind by Bethlehem Steel.

But Bill had a dream. And even though it started as a dream, Bill was quickly getting glimpses of the finished project in his head.

Walt Disney said: **"If you can dream it, you can do it."**

In his book, *Living Proof,* Adam Von Gootkin says to always remember that Disney's empire was started with a dream, and a mouse.

Bill's dream started in a two-car garage and was soon upgraded to a 40x90 structure. He had little equipment at the time so he bought a brake press with 400 tons of bending power. For perspective, 400 tons is the total weight of 160

Ford F-150 pickup trucks. Then he bought a shear that sliced through half-inch metal. The two pieces of equipment were critical to Bill's competitiveness.

He sought a redevelopment loan and was told a Phase One Test for hazardous waste was required. Seventy percent of the floor was dirt, dirty dirt. It seemed like a routine procedure.

As it turned out, the hazardous waste test was anything but routine. Metal and paint residues and water soluble oils were discovered in the soil, and all were declared to be hazardous.

Bill then experienced the aftershock. It wasn't electrical but it was a stunner. He was relying on his bank. "So now I'm sitting there, with equipment bought, and they wouldn't give me the loan."

If Bill cancelled his equipment order, he'd lose a pile of money, a loss that could cripple his operation.

On the other hand, completing the purchase before the environmental issue was resolved would have made Bill or anyone linked to the purchase, such as his bank, liable for resolving a problem that JWF did not cause.

It was a "running joke with my competitors" as they laughed at "this dumb young kid" who acquired this dilapidated building fraught with nightmarish defects. The competition referred to Bill's building as a "real shit hole" and didn't take him seriously.

Even if Bill had failed at this acquisition, he would have learned some valuable lessons.

In other words, failure could have become a positive thing with beneficial consequences.

In their book, *100 Ways to Motivate Others,* authors Steve Chandler and Scott Richardson quote George Bernard Shaw, the Irish playwright who penned more than 60 plays and received the Nobel Prize in literature: **"A life spent making mistakes is not only more honorable but more useful than a life spent in doing nothing."**

The oxygen wasn't gone from Bill's business yet, but he was in a pickle, and not the kind being bottled at the nearby H.J. Heinz Company in Pittsburgh.

Had he stopped to think about it, he was, however, already following in the footsteps of Henry Heinz, whose favorite saying was, "Make all you can honestly; save all you can prudently; give all you can wisely."

Heinz placed inspirational mottos throughout his factory and was careful to live by them himself.

For a moment, Bill's business career looked doomed. His access to money to fund his growing pains vaporized.

"I have no line of credit, the bank actually pulled their line of credit, I have no bank value, I have nowhere to go, the building is filled with hazardous waste, I'm screwed."

He engaged the services of an environmental lawyer who suggested documenting everything so Bill could utilize the building and later prove he did not add to the existing environmental hazard.

He weighed all the risks.

Bill had everything riding on the deal -- loans for the factory, new equipment, jobs already on the books and employee pay checks to cut.

Hunkering down with his lawyer, he scuttled the purchase transaction in favor of a lease agreement with the property owner, who was in bankruptcy, and used the $100,000 from the sale of his old shop to buy more machinery.

"I moved into the building. I stayed in the concrete areas. And he gave me a lease for a dollar a year," a move that had favorable tax consequences.

The tables had turned. Bill's competition was stunned; he got the last laugh.

After bagging a brownfield grant, Bill learned that the environmental plan included a proposal to "entomb" the hazardous waste by pouring a new concrete floor over all the hazardous dirt. He was soon able to take title to the place. "And then they paved the [the new facility's] driveway."

Bill was successful in getting a line of credit at another bank. **He found out later the bank president took a chance on him, "and had he not done that, I wouldn't have been able to grow the business."**

It was a critical time in JWF's history.

Subsequently, JWF's struggles with the environmental issues helped bring about state legislation that makes it easier to get abandoned buildings back into use.

In the big scheme of things, it was one of many times that Bill would be in the middle of something good coming out of something bad.

For a moment, to use a boxing analogy, Bill was on the mat and the ref was counting to ten. His opponent, an environmentally contaminated dirt floor, had the upper hand, until Bill refused to give up.

Some people are knocked down in life and never get up. Bill refused to become a victim. "Getting knocked down in life is a given," says Zig Ziglar, in his book, *Embrace the Struggle*. "Getting up and moving forward is a choice."

When Bill took over his father's welding business, the year was 1987. Twelve short years later he purchased a complex of a third-mile long building and two adjacent buildings, and then pumped $4.5 million into the structures and another $7 million into equipment.

"Entrepreneurship is not a destination; it's a journey," says writer, consultant and entrepreneur Kimanzi Constable, an Entrepreneur contributor (entrepreneur.com). Things that must be done, he says, "require you stretching yourself."

There's a theme here: Successful entrepreneurs don't have a finish line.

From the moment Bill made his decision to become an entrepreneur, he has been overcoming obstacles. That's what entrepreneurs do.

Focusing on others will serve leaders well
CHAPTER 70
Marine Corps Hero Led By Example

Bill's father and one of his dad's two brothers were among the 16.1 million Americans who served in World War II. They were not among the 292,000 U.S. soldiers, sailors, airmen, and marines killed in battle.

Johnstown sent many of its favorite sons and daughters off to war, and many were among the 672,000 Americans wounded, and some were killed, but none was more famous than Sgt. Michael Strank, who was born in Czechoslovakia (now Slovakia) in 1919 where his parents and other relatives lived in a one-room house with a dirt floor.

Like Bill's grandfather Martin Polacek, Strank's father emigrated to America in search of a better life, and then brought his family to join him near Johnstown where he had employment in a coal mine.

Michael Strank was a studious kid who played the French horn. He graduated from high school in 1937 and enlisted in the Marine Corps two years later, never expecting to become a World War II hero, much less a cultural icon.

Sgt. Strank was one of five young Marines and a Navy corpsman immortalized in Associated Press photographer Joe Rosenthal's famous photograph on February 23, 1945, of the historic flag raising on Mount Suribachi, Iwo Jima, 11 days after the Pacific island was retaken.

Perhaps the most famous Marine photograph in history, it was published all over the world as an excited nation was anxious to see the brutal war with Japan coming to an end.

Strank was fatally wounded on March 1, 1945, on the same island where he helped raise the Stars and Stripes, very likely by friendly artillery fire from an American ship.

He was 25 years old.

Sergeant Michael Strank
WORLD WAR II PATRIOT

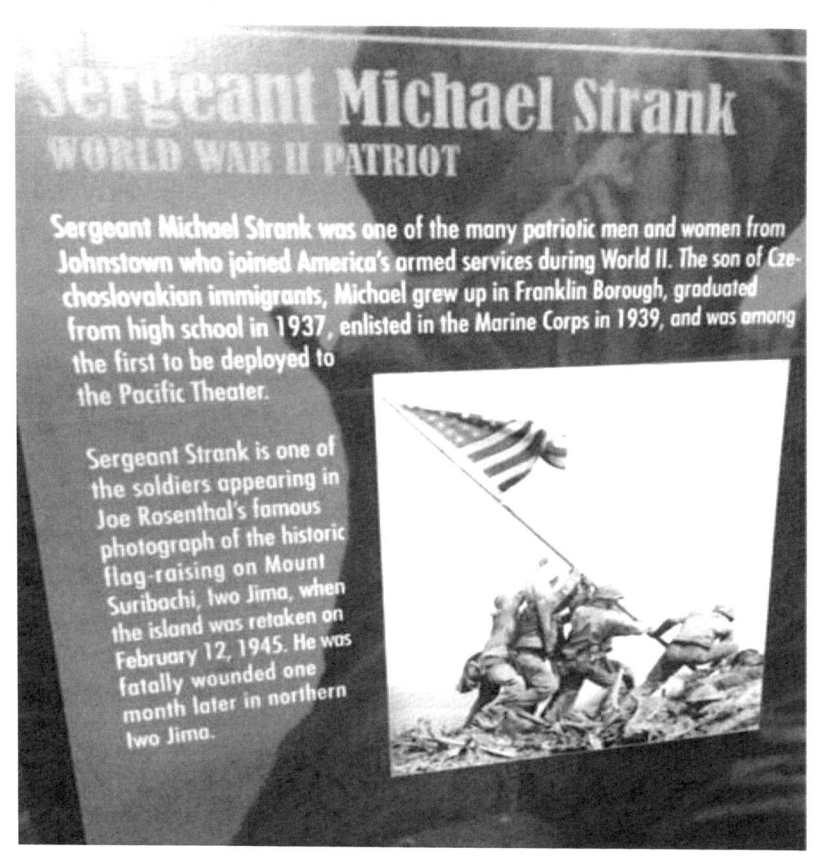

Sergeant Michael Strank was one of the many patriotic men and women from Johnstown who joined America's armed services during World II. The son of Czechoslovakian immigrants, Michael grew up in Franklin Borough, graduated from high school in 1937, enlisted in the Marine Corps in 1939, and was among the first to be deployed to the Pacific Theater.

Sergeant Strank is one of the soldiers appearing in Joe Rosenthal's famous photograph of the historic flag-raising on Mount Suribachi, Iwo Jima, when the island was retaken on February 12, 1945. He was fatally wounded one month later in northern Iwo Jima.

U.S. Marine Corps Sgt. Michael Strank is the most famous of Johnstown's war heroes. He was immortalized in the historic flag raising on Iwo Jima by photographer Joe Rosenthal. The famous photo can be seen in the city's Heritage Discovery Center as part of a permanent display.

Strank was buried in the 5th Marine Division Cemetery on the island.

In 1949, his remains were reinterred in Arlington National Cemetery.

The sergeant's memory lives on in the non-profit, The Michael Strank Project (strank.org), which was initiated by veterans groups to honor the men and women of the 'greatest generation' who served in World War II.

Strank is referred to on the website as a "beloved leader of men who vowed to do anything in his power to bring his soldiers home."

His legacy of leading by example was portrayed in the 2006 movie, *Flags of Our Fathers*.

Early in his career, Bill was inspired by Strank's leadership skills. Later in life, Bill discovered that he rode a school bus for seven years to junior high and high school that passed by Strank's home.

Management consultant Bill Treasurer says, "The first law of leadership is this: it's not about you."

In his book, *A Leadership Kick in the Ass*, Treasurer says, **"Leadership is about the people and the organization you're leading."**

It is fitting that the people of Johnstown continue to have such an impact on preserving freedom and protecting the American way of life because of the defense-related work at JWF Industries and JWF Defense Systems.

Twice a year, Lockheed-Martin, a giant in the defense industry, honors a subcontractor that has achieved superior performance in the areas of responsiveness, competitiveness and commitment to the military's Tactical Wheeled Vehicle program.

"This award is for you, the employees," announced Bill, when accepting the recognition for JWF in 2006. "You're the ones who did it. You're the ones who made it happen."

Bill has always been candid with his employees. There is a bond of trust -- a glue, if you will -- between Bill and the workforce.

Leadership requires honesty, says James C. Hunter, who heads a leadership training and development firm, in his book, *The World's Most Powerful Leadership Principle.*

"Trust is the glue that holds relationships together," writes Hunter. "Without trust, an organization is a house of cards without the glue."

With Lockheed-Martin, two incidents tipped the scales in JWF's favor, explained Louis DeSantis, vice president of system solutions for Lockheed.

One was JWF's decision to send workers to Lockheed's plant in Owego, New York, when a vehicle-design problem was found. The normal procedure would have been for Lockheed to ship the vehicle back to the plant in Johnstown for the changes to be made.

"It's what we do. In my mind it wasn't really extraordinary; it's just who we are. They were just one of the customers that really appreciated it and understood how important the supply base is to them and recognized suppliers that go above and beyond."

There's something to be said about a company's ability to do business with customers that appreciate the company's work ethic.

"We know we're successful. We're doing business with customers we want to do business with," says Bill.

Many factors impressed Lockheed-Martin's management team, but DeSantis noted one in particular; as parts demands and designs changed, JWF reacted instantaneously to these requests by fabricating and shipping the new parts in less than 24 hours.

"This is about Bill Polacek and this company," DeSantis said.

"He came to us and told us he wanted to be a supplier. He said he will meet all of our requirements and commitments, and he hasn't missed one. It's a real credit for the people who work for him here and the fine work they do."

Bill says a big part of the reason his company has been able to make such an impact in the defense industry **is the discipline and philosophy it developed during years in private industry -- treating defense work and private customers in the same manner.**

The up-armored Humvee on this book's cover was outfitted in Johnstown by JWF's Work Fighters, and reflects Bill's attitude about protecting troops as well as his hometown. He has a vision for Johnstown, an outlook that requires planning and changing and an outcome that means going forward and not backward.

"My purpose is for people to succeed," he says.

In 2015, JWF Industries made the prestigious Smart 50 list compiled by *Smart Business Pittsburgh*. Bill Polacek was in good company.

The list included David Morehouse, president and CEO of the Pittsburgh Penguins; Barbara Baker, president and CEO of the Pittsburgh Zoo & PPG Aquarium; Serdar Bankaci, founder and owner of Commonwealth Computer Recycling, and Rick Newton, president and founder of Newton Consulting LLC.

Effective leaders like Bill have mastered how to work smarter, manage better and get things done faster.

Preachers, who may prepare as many as 6,000 sermons in a 40-year ministry, often resort to a simple structure known in divinity schools as "three points and a prayer."

They're told to make sure their sermon has one big point. Make all points brief. Use simple language. Never use a dollar word when a nickel word will do. Sounds a lot like Bill and JWF's operating principles.

John Polacek, Bill's brother, who brought his military expertise to the company, sees how Bill operates.

"He embraces everyone in the company like his own family and more importantly he has embraced this community like his own family."

John once said to those attending a meeting: "You're standing in a pavilion that was donated by Bill. That's his sense of community."

Quality and on-time delivery do matter
CHAPTER 71
Promote Culture Of No Excuses

Before coming to JWF Defense Systems as a welder 18 years ago, Rob Dudinack had been to Sniper's School and was in the U.S. Army infantry that invaded Panama "and was involved in all the stuff going on in Nicaragua" in the late 1980s.

His first two years of service were spent in South Korea driving a Humvee.

At his new job, Dudinack appreciated the patriotic atmosphere and the culture of quality, both of which originated with the company's leadership, he says.

He can't remember a time when a gigantic American flag was not hanging in JWF's welding shop. "It's been there as long as I can remember."

"They were preaching quality back then," he says. **"Bill's been preaching that"** since Day One -- faith, community, country and quality.

Pride and patriotism are infectious at JWF. A key reason is that virtually every employee either fought in wars or has someone in their family fighting now or in the past. Bill's company is a breeding ground for pride and patriotism, attributes that contribute to superior quality and unmatched customer service.

The culture is how JWF landed a contract with a major manufacturer of construction equipment in the early days.

"There was a commitment by the workforce to do whatever it takes to get the job done correctly," says Dudinack, "to high level of quality, high level workmanship, and get it out the door on time." It wasn't unheard of to work 40 days in a row to get the job done.

Ironically, the big contract opened some eyes regarding product diversity and greatly influenced JWF's future, especially its diverse expansion. "Most of our business was with this manufacturer back in the day," and Bill saw that as not necessarily an attribute but a detriment "because **we had too many of our eggs in one basket.**"

JWF was making top quality products and delivering on time for their customer, but, ironically, the customer wanted out of the contract so they could build their own plant in Mexico. They did, and it turned out badly.

Bill was quoted in a *New York Times* business article in June 2017: "We've had customers who've actually brought business back from Mexico that we haven't done in seven years."

Quality and on-time delivery do matter; the customer returned to JWF to get its quality parts manufactured correctly and delivered on time.

"Things happen during the course of manufacturing that will delay progress and it pushes everybody back," says Dudinack. That's an obstacle, not an excuse. **"We still have to get the job out the door on time. The due date never changes."**

"The only thing we really have control over is ourselves," says John G. Miller, founder of QBO, Inc., a training firm. He's a believer in personal and group accountability. People and organizations "who demonstrate accountability stand out," Miller says in his book, *Outstanding.*

"Never forget," Miller adds. "The customer does not care to hear our reasons and excuses."

Not only are the workers genuinely patriotic, but JWF's workforce isn't shy about appreciating their cutting-edge technology either.

"We do a lot of things nobody else does," says Dudinack, who's now JWF Defense System's Welding Program manager.

"That's why we get a lot of the business we do." Robotic welding is one example. "We'll build vehicles from the ground up, from welding the frames to painting, assembling, putting in all the engine components, all that stuff. You have these niche companies that can do one portion of it, but not the whole shooting match."

JWF employees also aren't shy about insisting that new hires embrace the culture and have the right work ethic.

"We still have a 90-day waiting period for everybody coming in because they have to share in our profits, they have to share in the good things that happen to us, so we vote them in after 90 days. If they have a bad attitude or a bad work ethic, they won't get in."

New hires are assigned a mentor who also has an incentive to be an effective trainer. When the new hire meets all requirements, the mentor gets a $500 bonus. The program's success has a "cascading effect on the floor," says Bill. "Now everybody wants to be a mentor."

Employee expectations at JWF are high.

Unfortunately, some of the younger applicants "don't know what it's like to work yet and they really don't want to," says Dudinack. "They'll see the work and want to get out right away."

In his self-help book on management, *You Can't Fire Everyone*, Hank Gilman says "one of the biggest mistakes people make during their careers is avoiding jobs or tasks that they feel are beneath them."

To the contrary, Gilman asserts, **"Someone who isn't hesitant about working in the trenches and taking on all sorts of tasks is a good person to bet on."**

The culture of no excuses at JWF Industries embraces a wide spectrum of emotions from pride, to confidence and humor.

Humor has been a lifeboat for Bill during times of storms, allowing him to maintain his positive outlook and confidence.

Paul Hellman, in his book, *You've Got 8 Seconds,* talks about President Ronald Reagan's brush with death in 1981.

With a bullet lodged one inch from his heart, Reagan was telling his wife about the assassination attempt. "Honey, I forgot to duck." And joking with his surgeons, Reagan said, "I hope you're all Republicans."

Confidence became a way of life with Bill, as it was with President Reagan.

Hellman describes a basic truth: "You can act confident without feeling confident, and, if you act confident enough times, eventually the feeling will show up."

Hellman's point is this: Under dire circumstances, the former president "refused to look or act distressed."

Like President Reagan, Colin O'Brady was determined and confident.

It took O'Brady, age 33, only 40 days to ski solo from the coast of Antarctica to the South Pole in 2018. The ex-financier started pursuing sports full-time more than a decade ago.

Details of his trek were regularly shared to his Instagram account via a satellite phone. Thousands of school children followed his adventure.

"One of my greatest joys is sharing my expeditions with the next generation in hopes of inspiring them to set goals, live active and healthy lives and pursue their biggest dreams," he posted on Day 38.

He added, "nothing is impossible when you set your mind to it."

That's the culture Bill embraces at JWF.

Bill also embraces the concepts of out selling, out managing, out motivating and out negotiating the competition, all ideas advocated by Harvey Mackay, businessman, author and syndicated columnist.

It's one of the reasons that JWF Industries fills manufacturing orders from all over the continental USA and all over the world, including Iraq, Argentina, Israel, France, Norway, Germany, United Arab Emirates, Canada, Mexico and several African countries.

World is full of people doing average jobs
CHAPTER 72
Are We There Yet?

In real life, Bill exhibits some characteristics of the fictional Pooh Bear from Winnie-the-Pooh® fame. He has enjoyed a tumultuous but ultimately successful adventure. He's friendly, humble, thoughtful, and steadfast.

Unlike Pooh Bear, however, Bill is not naive or slow-witted, and he's known to have many clever ideas, usually driven by common sense.

Of course, the good times, when business started booming, allowed Bill and his executive team to turn their focus to finding industrious employees rather than searching for profitable work.

All combined, **the challenges of growing a successful business often test your leadership and your emotional intelligence**, he says, "and at times your faith."

In his book, *Great Teams,* Don Yaeger, longtime associate editor of *Sports Illustrated*, tells the story of Kevin Eastman. Eastman has unique knowledge of what it takes to build a winning culture as he coached for both the Boston Celtics and the Los Angeles Clippers.

"Culture must be reminded every day," Eastman said.

Bill learned to reinforce the culture at JWF Industries at every opportunity, meaning it's an ongoing process.

Every family in America who has taken an automobile trip of any duration with children has heard the proverbial question, "Are we there yet?"

It's more like a plea as though we should be able to get there sooner. The repeated inquiries make the driver crazy, but the repeated answers help the children see the light at the end of the tunnel.

"When you believe success is inevitable, you go the distance," writes Jessica Dilullo Herrin, CEO and founder of Stella & Dot Family Brands (stelladotfamily.com), in her book, *Find Your Extraordinary.*

"You don't panic when you encounter setbacks," she says. Take one step at a time. You'll get there. "You are only a failure if you stop."

Bill is always mindful of his welder-and-pickup-truck roots.

JWF Industries now boasts sophisticated computer-controlled lasers, robotic welders, more than 50 computerized pieces of major manufacturing equipment, and one of the largest double column machines in the Northeast (a massive machining center to accommodate big parts for aerospace, military and energy customers).

As Bill sees it, **success is the result of putting together a management group and technical professionals that meld into a team capable of "navigating the most challenging of times."**

Even so, success seldom comes easy.

The late Vidal Sassoon, the British and American hairstylist, businessman and philanthropist, became famous with his innovative haircuts. Yet, he was born into extreme poverty, spent his childhood in an orphanage, and quit school at age 14.

"The only place where success comes before work is in the dictionary," he once observed.

Referring to a well known business theme made famous by Theodore Roosevelt, the 26th President of the United States, Bill cited the axiom that successful top-tier management will surround itself with good people.

After all, the world is full of average people doing an average job. "These are great people!"

Roosevelt, who was a sickly child with debilitating asthma, overcame his health problems and gained national fame with the Rough Riders in the Spanish-American War.

On managing people, Roosevelt said: **"The best executive is the one who has sense enough to pick good men to do what** he wants done, and self-restraint to keep from meddling with them while they do it."

If Roosevelt's management philosophy represents the cake, the legendary former chairman and CEO of General Electric, Jack Welch, added the icing: "If you pick the right people and give them the opportunity to spread their wings -- and put compensation as a carrier behind it -- you almost don't have to manage them."

Bill learned in the early years to acknowledge the achievements of his employees, everyone from a technician to a richly experienced manager.

Winning, he says, is not being first to cross the finish line, but about how many cross the finish line with you.

"The reason we have our 15-year-plus employees here," Bill explained at the company's 25th anniversary, is that "every employee counts, and every employee is important, but these folks know what it was like when we had nothing, when I didn't offer much because I didn't have much."

"They know what it was like to have true grit, and do what we needed to do to get the job done. They're what really built the foundation [of JWF] to make it something special. They gave us that foundation to catapult us to where we are today."

"Appreciation is a fundamental human need," says Kim Harrison, public relations consultant and principal at Cutting Edge PR (cuttingedgepr.com), especially in the workplace. "People want to be respected and valued for their contribution."

"Because if they aren't recognized," says Scott Span of Tolero Solutions (tolerosolutions.com), "then they are not likely to give the 100 percent performance to satisfy customers, increase revenues, and help the organization grow and prosper

Employees need a shout out, kudos, thank you, or pat on the back for a job well done. After all these years, Bill still makes a conscious effort daily to acknowledge and reward his employees for excellence.

"People at every level in every organization need to know their work is considered important by the higher-ups," says Robert M. Gates, in his book, *A Passion For Leadership*. "At every level, **a leader should strive to make his employees proud to be where they are and doing what they do.**"

Gates, who spent 26 years in the Central Intelligence Agency (CIA) and was U.S. Secretary of Defense from 2006 to 2011, says, "It's always about people."

Hall of Fame basketball player Bill Bradley, who is also an American politician and Rhodes Scholar, is famous for this statement: "Leadership is unlocking people's potential to become better."

Find a mentor for wise and trusted counsel
CHAPTER 73
You Must Have Leverage And Options

Musician Woody Guthrie, whose musical legacy includes "This Land is Your Land," mentored fellow singer-songwriter Bob Dylan, who became one of the best-selling artists of all time.

Many famous musicians, politicians, Hollywood stars, sports stars and businessmen and women were mentored. Benjamin Graham mentored Warren Buffet, Dr. Ed Roberts mentored Bill Gates, Gary Cooper mentored Kirk Douglas, and Madonna mentored Gwyneth Paltrow.

It's much easier to start any project or career if a wise and trusted counselor is available for consultation and guidance.

Over the years, Bill learned that nothing's hard once you learn how to do it.

The first mentor to inspire Bill was his sister, Vicki, the third eldest among the Polacek siblings.

She was a trained hairdresser with a teaching certificate in "beauty culture," and at age 19 had started her own business when her employer decided to leave town. It was an *opportunity* that fell in her lap and was too good to pass up.

Surprisingly, Vicki's father, who was not a risk-taker, thought that her entrepreneurial decision came with very little risk, even though she had no prior business training or experience.

Opportunity means little if it isn't recognized.

Vicki's older sisters sold TV Guide, GRIT, cleaned houses and did babysitting. But Vicki was the first sibling to seize a business opportunity that came with some risk, however small.

Vicki operated her business for five years, during which she learned on-the-job how to handle payroll and quarterly tax reports.

About this time, her father, Big John, found himself short on cash. Vicki suggested that her dad get a line of credit, a preset amount of money that a bank or credit union was willing to lend, and upon which he could draw when he needed it. Big John was unfamiliar with this concept.

Some 15 years later, Big John, still reluctant to take a risk, complained to Vicki: "Bill and his big ideas, he's going to put me in the poor house."

Bill was already pushing his father to grow his home business, and his father was resisting.

After Bill took over his dad's business and eventually needed guidance, Vicki was ready to share what she had learned in her own business venture about payroll and keeping up with taxes.

When Bill needed new equipment, Vicki helped him get his first line of credit. She was a steady source of ideas, including how to pay attention to details.

It was Vicki's on-the-job-training skills that led to successfully coordinating JWF's booth at the annual Showcase for Commerce in downtown Johnstown. The event attracts big-name manufacturers and results in numerous new job opportunities for the region.

In the critically formative years of Bill's business career, he became close friends with his second mentor, an elderly Jewish man who had retired from his clothing business. The man had no family in town, and he and Bill came from totally diverse cultures, but he was business savvy and wanted to help.

He was a major bank stockholder, well connected, and he had the ear of a lot of town leaders.

"We brought him into our home, he became part of our family," says Bill. The relationship helped Bill avoid many common mistakes that entrepreneurs typically make.

There was a 50-year age difference and Bill's mentor was constantly giving fatherly advice and serving as a sounding board.

"He'd always tell me, 'Bill, you gotta collect your receivables.' He really impressed that upon me."

Because of this mentorship, Bill learned how a lack of options could weaken his position as a business owner.

"When you run a business, cash is king, and the time to ask for money is when you don't need it. When you need the money, your finances are probably the weakest. When you don't need the money, that means your finances are strong and the banks are willing to do more."

Bill learned about leverage.

He became knowledgeable about Asset Based Lending where the bank takes "the value of your assets, minus the liabilities, and that's what your value is. Part of that is through your receivables, inventory, work in progress, and your finished goods."

Eventually Bill was invited to sit on a bank board where he learned "what buttons to push, and who benefits from what you do."

As Bill soaked up his mentor's advice, he decided he wanted a better interest rate at his bank, better terms on his leverage points, and a higher leverage on receivables and inventory.

"I had work in process that wasn't billed, and I needed help to support that in order to grow the business."

"The bank said, 'No, you've got the best deal you can get.'"

Bill found three other banks to bid for his business. "They were hungry. I told them what I wanted, and two out of the three agreed. I told the other bank it was nice knowing them, but I was moving my business elsewhere."

"Why?" a bank official asked.

"I told you what I wanted you to do," Bill replied. **"You said you couldn't do it. I took your word for it, so I got a bank that would."**

Less than 24 hours later, the original bank had a change of heart and said they'd agree to his terms. "I told them it's too late. You should have told me that the first time."

When it comes to negotiating anything, you must have options, Bill learned. "You have to know who's benefiting from what on the other side, and have options to be able to walk away."

"If I did not have the options, I would not have had the leverage to do what I wanted to do. Part of the way to negotiate is, you have to have options. If you go into negotiations with only one option, any shark smells blood real quick, and they'll know, and you have no negotiating power."

Bill thought he was helping his elderly friend by giving him a purpose for living in his golden years, but in the end, his mentor **ended up helping Bill avoid mistakes and choose strategies with a much better chance of success.**

Ideas must create real value for customers
CHAPTER 74
Lessons Of Digging Well With A Shovel

Nothing says self-reliance like digging a well with a shovel. Although it's dangerous, back-breaking work, having cool, clean water can be worth the risk, especially if you don't have another option.

As Bill's relatively newlywed parents completed their little kit-built house and moved in with their first child, getting access to their own water supply became a priority.

No city water was available. The price tag for a commercially-drilled well was out of the question. With no savings to dip into, they were already appropriating every cost-saving strategy they could find just to survive.

A spot was marked in the backyard for a well early one summer when school wasn't in session, and a team of relatives led by Bill's grandfather, Martin Polacek, began the arduous task of digging a 13-foot diameter hole in the earth with picks and shovels.

Martin was retired. Big John had his day job at Bethlehem Steel, and he helped after his shift along with his nephews, Joe and Bob, sons of his oldest brother Joe.

The workers descended into the hole while standing in a bucket and holding the rope, lowered by a hand-crank (windless) with a foot brake that Martin fashioned from scraps of metal. Dirt was lifted out of the hole with the same bucket and windless.

"We dug down until we hit the water. It was coming in faster than we could take the dirt out, so we had to quit [at 28 feet]. We had a hand pump up on top," Joe recalled.

But it was Martin who laid the stone.

"He wouldn't let us lay it. He went down and laid the stone. It was dry-stacked -- no mortar -- so the water could seep into the well. We went in the woods and picked up rocks to stone-line that thing -- 18 inches thick," said Joe.

"We had no shoring in that hole. If that would have caved in, they'd never got us out of there. We never even gave that a thought, we just did it. Boy, that's an endless job!"

The successful well was the result of teamwork, men looking after each other's back, and the pure satisfaction of accomplishment.

If you desire to be an entrepreneur, you better be part of and encourage teamwork. You better be watching someone else's back, just as you expect them to watch yours.

And if you do not enjoy the satisfaction of accomplishment, don't even start an entrepreneurial journey. You're just wasting your time.

"People who survived the Great Depression embedded habits into their lives that they found hard to change, such as refusing to part with anything that might come in handy at any future point in their life," writes Jacki Andre on an Internet site (askaprepper.com).

Depression Era folks would not waste the ends of a loaf of bread, and they would carefully scrape the wrapper of a block of cheese, he says.

That's how it was at the Polacek home. Nothing was wasted. **Bill and his siblings learned smart budgeting by doing more with less.**

When it came to clothes, "mend and make do" was the motto of the day, at least until the threads were down to tatters. When clothing couldn't be fixed, the scraps were saved for other sewing projects. Mastering sewing skills, growing their own food, and cooking from scratch became strategies adopted by nearly all Depression Era and pre- and post-war families to save money.

Home haircuts and perms were the norm, provided by Sally and her Aunt Rose. They might have been frizzy, but the girls had curls. John used the buzz technique on the boys.

No food could be left on a plate at mealtime. Bacon grease was saved for cooking vegetables and eggs. John cut beef costs by buying half a cow. Lights were always turned off when leaving a room.

The two older girls, who were both in nursing school, fed nursing home patients after their classes to pay for their meal tickets.

Going to the drive-in picture show was a rare happening, but the kids did see Walt Disney's musical-fantasy "Mary Poppins" starring Julie Andrews, and Sally brought food in the car because there was no extra cash for snacks from the concession stand.

Why were all these home skills important to Bill and his siblings?

To create the future, we must understand the past, says independent blogger Tim Kastelle (timkastelle.org), who also contributes to the Harvard Business Review Blogs. "One common mistake that innovators make is to focus only on the future, without regard to the present or the past."

"Innovation," he says, "is about making ideas real to create value for people." And to make a revolutionary idea real requires understanding the present and the past.

Bill eventually understood that his new welding company had to work in the real world, and create real value. It was a lesson that served him well.

"Creativity is thinking up new things. Innovation is doing new things," said Theodore Levitt, American economist.

He's the same guy who proposed a definition for *corporate purpose* in 1983: Rather than merely making money, it is to create and keep a customer.

The home-dug water well, which featured **creativity and innovation**, survived years of baking temperatures, frigid winters, floods and droughts; it was one of many hand-dug wells in Daisytown drawing water from the same underground aquifer and often went dry, especially in the summer months.

It was eventually closed when John hooked up to city water in the 1960s. But the concrete lid that sealed the well did not remove the lessons learned.

So, how does a family of 11 people handle a dry summertime well?

Every evening the nine kids, babies first, bathed in the same tub of water. If the well had gone dry, the older girls carried a galvanized pail in each hand, full of water from a nearby neighbor's home, which their mother heated on the stove.

Following her pattern for bathing the children, Sally got multiple uses out of one tub of water in the ringer washer, whites first, carpets last. They were hung on a line outside, including cloth diapers, where they'd freeze stiff in the wintertime. Bill's mother often said, "Learn to do without."

Many people don't know how to live within their means; they run themselves ragged buying things they don't need, with money they don't have, for people they don't even like.

Businesses do that, too, says Bill. They sometimes spend more than they make.

Bill gleaned a lot from Patrick M. Morley's self-help book, *The Man In The Mirror*. The author asked readers if they know anyone who has won the rat race. Probably not.

Bill was too young to personally experience John and Sally's entrepreneurial training program in the early years, but he heard the true stories from his parents, and he applied the lessons as he built his business.

Martin Polacek walked to the mill carrying his lunch pail, hot or cold, rain, sleet or snow.

Will your business survive you?
CHAPTER 75
We Hire A Family, Not A Person

First, the tragedy.

Shanksville, Pennsylvania, population 237, according to the 2010 Census, was settled by Christian Shank in 1798, a German immigrant who built a log cabin, grist mill and two sawmills.

Nothing earthshaking happened here for 203 years. Then suddenly the entire world knew about Shanksville.

Johnstown, Pennsylvania, population 20,184 in 2014, is less than 30 miles the way the crow flies from Shanksville, where United Airlines Flight 93 crashed on September 11, 2001, as brave passengers attempted to overpower four al-Qaida hijackers, regain control of the airliner and prevent the Boeing 757-222 from crashing into its target, the U.S. Capitol.

On that fateful day, the nation was blindsided. Airline security protocols were forever changed. Life in America was forever changed.

The U.S. didn't expect such an attack that took the lives of twice as many Americans as were killed by the air attack at Pearl Harbor. **We were reminded, once again, that suffering and pain are real.**

Disasters can be big or small, and can affect one or many. Their impact can affect a single family, or an entire nation. Jeffrey E. Miller wrote about "When Tragedy Strikes" on an Internet blog (bible.org).

He says the Bible "does not teach that Christians are exempt from tragedies, only that the Christians can face tribulation, crisis, calamity, and personal suffering with a supernatural power that is not available to the person outside Christ."

Before JWF Industries began experiencing growing pains, Bill and his siblings came face to face with tragedy and learned to stand on their faith and deal with the death of their father.

Then they needed to plan for the future. Most of us plan our weekend projects, our vacations, as well as plan for retirement with 401(k)s, pensions, stocks and bonds, and Social Security, says Derek Hill.

He has a blog (whatchristianswanttoknow.com).

Projects and retirement are one thing, but what about the future of your business?

You started it. You grew it. You run it. But will your business survive *you*? It will if you have a well thought-out, comprehensive, written business succession plan!

In their book, *Entrepreneurs In Every Generation,* authors Allan Cohen and Pramodita Sharma explore how successful family businesses develop their next leaders.

"One barrier to long-term survival is the failure of the current leadership to develop, instill, and select entrepreneurial leadership in the next (and succeeding) generations involved in the business."

Yes, there is a plan for the future of JWF and its hundreds of employees.

For the children of Bill and Shari Polacek, the rule is they have to get a post-secondary education, work their way up the ladder, and preferably work for somebody else, and only then can they join the family business.

"The expectation is higher with family members than with the average employee," says Bill. "I want to make sure it is earned. That affects the morale of all employees."

A unique distinction needs to be drawn here when discussing *family*.

At JWF Industries, *family* extends beyond blood relatives; the company's leadership considers everyone that works there to be family.

"My father worked in the mill and got laid off. I saw the devastating effect that had on our family. Today, we don't hire a person, we hire a *family*. We don't lay a person off, we lay a *family* off," says Bill.

When a layoff is necessary, Bill considers it a personal reflection on him. "I look at it as failure on my part," he says. "The layoff is taking away their job."

Bill's vision is larger than his job, and larger than his company, for that matter.

"***Family*** **is more than the people you are related to. It's everyone that works in your organization. We are one community.**"

Bill does everything in his power to protect jobs so the extended *family* remains intact.

In her book, *Money Rules,* Jean Chatzky, financial editor for NBC's *Today* show, lists page after page of money rules -- 94 in all. She maintains that one's job, not home, is their most important investment.

By the way, there is another way to help your children, long-term, says Chatzky. "Spend more time building a legacy than an inheritance." What's more valuable, she asks, leaving $20,000 to your kids, or instilling a work ethic that lets them earn an extra $20,000 a year?

Is project well thought out and practical?
CHAPTER 76
Evaluate Complaints, Create Solutions

Solutions. Solutions. Solutions.

Motivational speaker Karla Brandau describes a lesson she learned from Douglas Ivester, former CEO of The Coca-Cola Company. On her blog at Workplace Power Institute, she wrote that Ivester stood in front of a group of executives and said, "Bring me solutions, not excuses."

Bill is always looking for solutions to problems. When he first started in business, he was asked about the company's philosophy. On the spot he replied, "We'll find out what customers need and grow and change to meet those needs. I thought that was pretty smart for a kid."

Bill became aware that one of his early customers, Sanitary Dairy, was spending a lot of money securing a company to come in and perform a specialized welding process called TIG (Tungsten Inert Gas) on stainless steel.

The stainless steel pipes were required to be hermetically sealed -- airtight from oxygen and other gases -- inside and out so that no imperfection existed in the pipe; imperfections could cause hidden bacterial growth.

Bill also heard them complaining about the costs.

New job opportunity, Bill thought to himself. And it was an opportunity without much competition! In order to create an advantage, Bill taught himself how to do it.

As he grew his business, he decided to teach one of his employees how to do the specialized welding process, and his employee eventually took over the Sanitary Dairy account and had a couple of guys working under him.

JWF's unique journey happened just that way, one project, one opportunity at a time.

"That is what we did and what we do -- we fill the voids," says Bill.

"We look at an industry, find out what the common complaints are within that industry and find solutions that we can provide."

In the steel industry, there's an operational area referred to as soaking pit beams where ingots had to be heated and rolled, repeatedly, until the process produced a strand of wire.

"Ironically, one job I got was going to be beams, right where my dad worked," says Bill. "I'll never forget, I bid on the contract. It was $35,000. That was as much sales as we had the entire year before."

Every business has its own unique way of designing and printing internal paperwork, everything from company letterhead, invoices, and even purchase orders.

"A purchase order from Bethlehem Steel looked like a check. You felt like you were cashing a check by getting a purchase order," remembers Bill.

But he was being a comic when he showed his mother the purchase order. "Mom, look what I got, $35,000." Sally didn't make that much money in a year.

His mother's reaction wasn't what Bill expected. After all, his new business was becoming more than his mother could ever imagine.

That's when she asked, "You sure you know what you're doing?"

Bill believes that was her way of saying, "Make sure you're doing the project right so you don't fail, because it is a risk."

Her comment made Bill "step back and be sure the project was well thought out and practical."

What works for one business might not necessarily work for another. But there may be one universal tenet, or attitude, that will work for virtually every start-up business, or every businessman who is struggling to find their niche.

I discovered this particular attitude by pure accident.

It appeared in a most unlikely place -- an action-adventure TV series about a resourceful secret agent, Angus MacGyver, and his sidekick, Jack Dalton, who work as troubleshooters for the fictional Phoenix Foundation.

MacGyver possesses encyclopedic knowledge of physical sciences and, with his ever-present Swiss Army knife, makes extraordinary things out of ordinary objects.

A series by the same name *MacGyver* aired in the 1980s and 1990s and returned to television in 2016 with a different cast. In one of the newer episodes, MacGyver and his cohorts are sent to Hawaii after an earthquake caused massive damage on one of the islands.

They found rescue personnel overwhelmed.

Jack says to the rescue facilitator: **"Just point to the problem, we'll make it go away."**

That is, in a nutshell, the entrepreneurial philosophy of Bill Polacek, CEO of the *big* company -- JWF Industries -- that started in a *little* garage.

This thinking is what eventually led JWF Industries to spin off JWF Defense Systems and aggressively enter into the government contracting sector, and it led to the creation of Environmental Tank and Container (ETC).

In July 2018, this same thinking led to JWF's acquisition of PCI Solutions, headquartered in Texas, which has been renamed ETC Texas, thereby expanding the Pennsylvania company's footprint in the Southwest oil and gas regions.

Rooting for the local boy
CHAPTER 77
Hometown Hero

The dictionary definition of a hero is a real, live person who is admired or idealized for courage, outstanding achievements, or noble qualities. Defining fictional heroes is a bit more complicated.

Superman. Sherlock Holmes. Batman. GI Joe. Spider-man. Indiana Jones. Wonder Woman. Captain America. Luke Skywalker. Teenage Mutant Ninja Turtles. These characters are from a long list of our fictional childhood heroes.

In the article "Growing Up With Heroes" posted online (lucknowbookclub.com), Divyanshu Tripath shared the intensity of his undying love for and never-ending knowledge of comic book characters.

"I know the name of the street where Bruce Wayne's parents were killed and I know the name of Clark Kent's first love interest (not Lois Lane)," he wrote.

On May 16, 2007, the daily newspaper in Johnstown, Pennsylvania -- *The Tribune-Democrat* -- published an editorial with the heading, "A hometown hero," and the report isn't fiction. (Sections of the editorial appear in italics.)

You can't help but root for local native Bill Polacek. Good things continue to happen for his JWF Industries and its now-handful of subsidiaries.

It's not just that Polacek has grown his trade -- welding -- from a small shop in his dad's garage to a multimillion-dollar business. But it's also that he has made his family a part of his huge success and has helped many of his friends, neighbors and others in securing family-sustaining jobs.

It probably wouldn't be too corny to call him a hometown hero.

Bill's corporation has had as many as 600 employees and is showing signs of getting much larger.

Certainly, it could -- and probably should -- be pointed out that the successes of JWFI and its subsidiaries are attributable in no small way to U.S. Rep. John Murtha, one of Congress' defense heavyweights.

He has helped lure plenty of defense work to Johnstown-area businesses.

Nevertheless, Bill Polacek could have taken his welding and leadership talents, along with his entrepreneurial desires, elsewhere. He didn't, and a lot of folks in these parts are glad of it.

Bill Polacek stands on a staircase that he built years before acquiring the former Bethlehem Steel building where the stairs were installed.

Don't forget to be grateful
CHAPTER 78
As An Entrepreneur, Have Bold Dreams

In the early years Bill dreamed of having a larger manufacturing space and eyed what he thought was a suitable building. It's a good thing that purchase didn't happen.

Today that "dream building" of yesteryear could fit a hundred times into JWF's current manufacturing footprint.

Call it dreaming, visions, or imagination. Whatever it was, Bill was infected with it at an early age. He knew his parents lived on a shoestring and practically lived in a shoebox, so he never asked for money, but he did sell chances to earn prizes.

Going door-to-door and learning the art of salesmanship on his own, he managed to earn a holiday gift basket for his mom and dad.

"There's nothing quite like the adrenaline rush of closing a sale," wrote Carol Luong in an Internet blog (saleshacker.com). "For me, it's like winning a poker hand," the marketing, sales and business development guru added.

Bill's salesmanship steadily improved, but he also learned to handle being turned down. Luong points out that dealing with a sales rejection can be gut-wrenching for some salespeople. Losing a sale did not hamper Bill.

With his early success, "I started doing more of that because I wanted to get something for my sisters." He earned a jewelry box, and he also learned a life lesson.

"When I lost a sale, I learned from it. And when I got a sale I learned from that as well. A lot of people miss learning from their successes."

"It helped me get out of my comfort zone so that I could later on realize the entrepreneurial spirit, and control my own destiny. Through my whole life, I would constantly push myself out of

my comfort zone, because if I didn't get out of my comfort zone I never grew."

He became a lector at church, forcing himself to get in front of people. "So it tied in nicely, the values of my faith and being able to get out of my comfort zone all at the same time."

Over time he embraced one of Dale Carnegie's principles: Be prepared but speak from the heart.

"When I started going into business, people wanted me to give speeches and talk, or give presentations. Well, I was not comfortable with that. They say the number one fear in anyone's life isn't death, it's getting in front of a group of people."

So where did Bill end up? In front of people, of course!

"Imagine, I want you to just dream a little bit," he told a Vision 2025 hometown crowd in 2015. "We really want to be bold."

"These aren't little dreams. These are big, bold dreams we're all going to be a part of. You can have a share in that stock in this community by getting involved today. I'm going to tell you, we're not going to accept this town going backwards. We're going to work together. We're going to go shoulder-to-shoulder, arm-in-arm and turn this community around," declared Bill.

In many ways, Bill was preparing for his "dreams" speech most of his adult life, especially when he and Shari were living in the cramped quarters of a single-wide, two-bedroom mobile home that was parked in a Daisytown neighborhood near his father's well-known two-car garage welding shop.

It seemed that space was so tight, merely turning around would put you in another room, and Bill managed to cram an office in a bedroom and a secretary actually worked there. Bill sensed that he and Shari could do better, and so could Johnstown.

"We call this Vision 2025," explained Robin L. Quillon, the former publisher of *The Tribune-Democrat,* as he was quoted in his own newspaper, "because we have a lot of good work to do, and it's going to take some time."

"There are projects already underway," noted Quillon, "some that will be started and completed quickly and many that will surface as part of our efforts. That said, we wanted to emphasize that this is a long-term commitment for our community and for all of us."

Good communication has the power to inspire and motivate.

Being an effective communicator is vital for business as well as political success. In fact, it's vital for virtually every successful endeavor in life.

President Donald Trump's skill in this area is frequently reinforced by his associates. KellyAnne Conway, a counselor to the president, has referred to her boss as "the master communicator."

Carmine Gallo is a media training and communications coach who penned an article for *Forbes* in 2011, about five specific media skills you can learn from Donald Trump, a public figure that Gallo considers a "one-man media training course."

Gallo observes that Trump is always reinforcing his brand, and doing so while wearing passion on his sleeves. "Trump once said that without passion, you have no energy and without energy, you have nothing."

Sounds a lot like Bill Polacek!

In his book *Leadership Jazz*, author Max DePree writes, "If you're a leader and you're not sick and tired of communicating, you probably are not doing a good enough job."

Bill has learned that it requires a lot of energy to be an effective communicator.

Like John Kelly, the former Marine general who served briefly as President Trump's chief of staff, **Bill embraces the idea that there's a right and wrong way to lead people.**

The *Wall Street Journal* reported in August 2017 that Kelly, after assuming his new role, picked up C.S. Forester's 1936 novel, *The General,* and read it again as a reminder of what to avoid as a leader.

The business, community service and citizenship awards "most valuable to me," Bill says, "are the ones that really personify who I am, and that is someone who feels servant leadership is the right style of leadership."

Blogger Skip Prichard, a CEO, businessman, avid reader and Eagle Scout (skipprichard.com), says one of the hallmarks of a servant leader is encouragement. According to Prichard, a true servant leader says, "*Let's* go do it," not, "*You* go do it."

According to a list of songs about dreams and dreaming published on an Internet website (spinditty.com), Steven Tyler took six years to write his 1973 rock anthem, "Dream On," and it became Aerosmith's first major hit and a classic rock radio staple.

Also known as "the Bad Boys from Boston," Aerosmith's song is about the process of growing more mature and the internal quest to become somebody. Named one of *Rolling Stone's* 500 Greatest Songs of All Time, it motivates the listener to keep striving until dreams are realized.

"A dream doesn't become a reality through magic," says Colin Powell, retired four-star general and former secretary of state. **"It takes sweat, determination and hard work."**

In contrast, during his journey, Bill has learned that it takes no effort to be kind.

There's an interesting book called *Pay It Forward Day*, where author Catherine Ryan Hyde offers suggestions that include thanking the little people -- the mail guy, the girl who orders supplies, or the door person. "Everyone's part is essential and no one's job is purposeless."

Hyde contends, "Any random act of kindness can cause a positive ripple effect restoring our faith in the love and compassion of the human spirit."

Years ago Bill noticed two young boys in the neighborhood eyeing the trampoline in his back yard. Bill knew the boys came from a home where money was tight, so he invited them to bounce, and they did so on multiple occasions.

Time passed. The boys are in their 30s now, and they still talk about the trampoline. The mother said to Bill, "You taught my boys to give back."

- Random acts of kindness.
- The ripple effect.
- Changed lives.
- Ask questions.
- Be curious.
- Solve problems.

But don't forget to be grateful; it's part of being a servant leader.

Bill gives thanks and is grateful every day for his countless blessings.

Never be willing to accept defeat
CHAPTER 79
That's My Suit, And My Car

Before Bill acquired his father's welding business, he and his brother, Marty, both found jobs in Florida.

Marty was an accountant with a large construction company that specialized in custom-built homes; Bill got a job at a metals manufacturing company where his skills led to rapid advancement.

Marty didn't have a car, so he dropped Bill at work at 7 AM and took Bill's vehicle to his accounting job starting at 8 AM. Marty worked until 5 PM but Bill was off at 3:30 and had 90 minutes with nothing to do.

One day Bill clocked out but continued welding. As luck would have it, his boss spotted him and shouted, "I'm not paying you overtime."

Well, the boss was impressed when he learned that Bill was not on the clock. But the boss had more to learn.

Marty sometimes chatted with Bill's boss, and the boss asked Bill one day, "Why aren't you more like your older brother, Marty? He's got a bachelor's degree, he makes good money, he's got a nice car, he dresses in nice clothes."

Bill replied: "First of all, that's my car. Second of all, I make more money than him. Third of all, that's my suit."

Soon after, Bill and Marty returned to Johnstown for their parents' 35th wedding anniversary. Bill asked his dad to find him a couple of jobs and he'd work on them during his home visit.

The second day back in Johnstown, Bill's sister, Vicki, who owned a beauty salon, was cutting his hair. The gal who worked with Vicki was a neighbor of a girl that Bill took to the high school prom and dated casually.

"She said to me, 'Did you know Shari's father died?'"

364

Shari's father was 42 and passed away suddenly.

"When I heard that, I just felt bad that she lost her father and how terrible that was," Bill reflected. "I sent a small bouquet of flowers and a note saying I was sorry." Shari called Bill to say thank you. And this led to several dates.

Less than three weeks later, it dawned on Bill: "She's the one."

It was a God-thing.

He abruptly told Marty, "I'm not going back [to Florida]." And for good reason. He was a victim of Cupid's arrow, something akin to the "perfect heart shot" bow hunters seek when hunting deer.

Bill was love-struck, and he was overwhelmed with the urge to follow his heart.

Acting on the urge, however, wasn't that simple for him. Bill was already developing a good career in the metals business, and he was building a resume of experience.

If he did not return to Florida, he might be giving up more than a job. The owner he worked for, who didn't have children, had already spoken to Bill about taking over the business some day.

Bill faced a dilemma. "I struggled with it."

If he stayed in Johnstown, he had to find work in a place he was being told there were no jobs to be found. But Bill wasn't going to give up easily. He had a personality and willpower that is best characterized by Wild West folklore of conquest, survival and persistence.

And let's not forget that romance had kicked in.

It was Mae West, the frequently-censored singer, actress and comedian, who said: "Love conquers all things except poverty and toothache."

For several years, Bill's frugal courtship with Shari was reminiscent of Sylvester Stallone's film masterpiece, *Rocky*, where the movie characters Rocky Balboa and Adrian eventually found themselves at the altar.

Bill suspected he would never be satisfied working for his father in the home welding business, or anyone else, for that matter. There was an obstacle. Big John Polacek did not want to grow his business; Bill did. Bill had dreams, and they were big dreams.

But he never dreamed that his father would be diagnosed with incurable lung cancer early in 1986, months before he and Shari would exchange wedding vows. And then came his father's death in February the next year.

Just like the settlers who led the American expansion west of the Mississippi, Bill was forced to consider something he knew very little about. He was headed for unknown territory.

To provide for a family, Bill needed a better paycheck, even if he had to start his own business. **"Why not create my own job?"** he kept wondering. He found no good reason not to.

However corny, the rest is history.

In their early marriage, Bill and Shari enjoyed the disparaging perception of a stereotype redneck couple. He had a pickup truck, welder, garage, and Shari was a hairdresser. All that was missing was a gun rack inside the cab and a dog that rode on the roof.

Shari had to be money-conscious in those early, lean years. She stretched a penny with the best of them, and used every coupon she could get her hands on.

Bill and Shari lived in a compact trailer parked on a small residential lot a stone's throw from the garage known as Johnny's Welding.

It was an historic moment when Bill hired his first part-time secretary. Renee showed up for work the next day.

Bill said to her, "Well, Renee, you went home and you told your husband you got the job. What did he think?"

Renee replied: "Well, he was okay with it until he found out I interviewed in one of your bedrooms (Bill's makeshift office)."

The cramped trailer bedroom became the administrative headquarters of a future manufacturing conglomerate, but not before hundreds of 18-hour days passed and at least a half dozen brushes with closure were resolved.

One day Bill was in the garage welding under a car frame, and Marty, the accountant, was inside talking to Shari. "We had been married about a year and Shari and I had been talking about having kids,"

Bill recalls. "Marty goes home and calls our brother, John, and says, 'John, we have a problem.'"

Marty proceeded to explain the problem: "I just visited Bill and Shari. You know they're talking about having kids? You know we're going to be supporting them the rest of their life!"

Marty and John both have four-year college degrees. Bill does not.

But he soon found out what Paula Nelson had come to understand. A professional singer with the Paula Nelson Band and daughter of country music icon Willie Nelson, she was once quoted as saying, "Going into business for yourself, becoming an entrepreneur, is the modern-day equivalent of pioneering on the old frontier."

Bill was ready, but not with a branding iron, barbed wire, plow, or forge and anvil. He wielded unshakable optimism, a deep faith, and a welding torch, and he knew how to use them. He had skill, and a sense of invincibility, on his side. And prayer.

"Every time I faced a tough decision, I prayed. The answer would come if I prayed enough."

He began welding leaky boilers, cracked car frames and repairing anything from lawnmowers to thawing frozen water lines, things his father had done before him.

Unlike many aspiring entrepreneurs, **Bill was determined to overcome the obstacles that stood in his way, including fear of the unknown.**

In hindsight, it's a good thing he wasn't well read yet on matters of business, management, and finance, never mind managing employees, or else he may have become discouraged.

One school of thought says ignorance is bliss. Bill didn't know enough about running a business to really be scared of creating his own job. As evolution proponent Charles Darwin observed, "ignorance more frequently begets confidence than does knowledge."

A contrary view by American novelist Herman Melville, author of the whaling story *Moby-Dick*, says ignorance is the parent of fear.

Two opposite opinions, but only one Bill Polacek.

Anyone starting a new business should be aware of the history of business failures. Bill didn't have a clue.

Author Lisa M. Amos reported a scary finding that was quoted on famousquotesandauthors.com.

"Entrepreneurs average 3.8 failures before final success. What sets the successful ones apart is their amazing persistence. There are a lot of people out there with good and marketable ideas, but pure entrepreneurial types almost never accept defeat."

Bill did not have a physical challenge affecting all four limbs like tennis player and motivational speaker Roger Crawford, author of *Playing From The Heart,* but he nurtured the same idea about defeat.

Crawford was born with a birth anomaly. He's missing his left leg below the knee and two toes on the right foot. He only has two fingers on his left hand and one on the right.

Sports Illustrated recognized Crawford as one of the most accomplished physically challenged athletes in the world. Crawford uses his life story to provide inspiration and motivation to break through self-imposed obstacles and limitations.

"Challenges are inevitable," Crawford says, **"defeat optional!"**

Show up, always give more than 100 percent
Chapter 80
Put Employees In Jobs That Suit them

I doubt there's a family in America that hasn't waited around its home, at least once, for a plumber, electrician, repairman, or contractor to show up to fix something, and they never came. And even worse, they never called to say they weren't coming or would be late!

James M. Kerr, of N2Growth, a leadership development firm, published an online article (Inc.com), titled "10 simple hacks to climbing the corporate ladder." In this usage, he's referring to a hack as a trick or shortcut to advancing one's career.

One of his hacks, to show up, is most obvious.

"Getting to your job on-time, prepared for the day ahead and ready to start goes a long way to earning a reputation as someone who can be counted on," said Kerr.

Kerr mentioned the quote Woody Allen made famous in his film, *Love and Death*: **"80 percent of success is showing up."**

In addition to showing up, there's pulling up, that is pulling one's self up by your own boot straps, a phrase that was widely used by the mid-1800s.

It refers to the imaginary and impossible feat of lifting oneself off the ground by pulling on one's boot laces. It's supposed to exemplify the achievement of getting out of a difficult situation by one's own efforts.

If you're an entrepreneur, all four of the following ideas are asking for trouble if that's all you're depending on for your success. It would be a "crapshoot," which The Free Dictionary defines as a risky and uncertain venture.

1. Fail your way to success.
2. It's who you know.

3. Show up.
4. Pull yourself up by your own boot straps.

Scratch the first one! Failing one's way to success doesn't represent Bill because he succeeded by trying hard, working hard and learning to work smart, a simple recipe that requires dedication and commitment.

Okay, there's some merit to the second point: It's who you know.

Over time, Bill learned to network and some people he met did become important contacts for his future success. **Connections often can weigh more heavily than raw talent, just as one's knowledge and skills can be less useful and less important than one's network of personal contacts.**

However, never sell yourself short by not capitalizing on contacts.

Even if you show up and claim 80 percent success by doing so, it's still only 80 percent. You need 100 percent effort for success. Actually, successful entrepreneurs give more than 100 percent. Always.

The fourth idea is also a crapshoot: The bootstrap theory. **If Bill had relied totally on his own ability to succeed, he would have been a miserable failure.** Instead, he had enough sense to look to other people for help in areas where he needed help.

The importance of cultivating mutually beneficial relationships when building a team can't be over-stressed. In his book, *The 10% Entrepreneur,* Patrick J. McGinnis says entrepreneurs must bring in the right people, people that will work with you and work with other people.

Explained another way, define the job and find the right person to do it. Then delegate jobs to the right people. **Some workers and managers are better suited for certain jobs than others. Nearly all workers do their best work when they're utilizing their best skills.**

And there's another factor to consider.

Do workers perform better when they're comfortable with the people they're working with? Described another way, how important is the psychology of relationships to entrepreneurial success?

The Harvard Men study describes the longest-running psychological studies ever done. There are "70 years of evidence that our relationships with other people matter, and matter more than anything else in the world," writes Shawn Achor in his book, *The Happiness Advantage.*

Is it any surprise that positive, reinforcing relationships are important to finding happiness? "The happier you are, the more advantages you accrue in nearly every domain of life," says Achor.

In addition to placing hundreds of employees in positions that suit them, JWF Industries is the source of many secondary economic benefits, also known as down-line activity and spin-off jobs.

A good example of a down-line job is one that's created when a major motion picture is being filmed in your hometown. The stars in the movie are being paid by a Hollywood Studio.

But the movie can't be produced without tremendous logistical support locally. The actors must eat, sleep and have transportation. Local residents are often hired as "extras."

Johnstown and most American communities boast businesses that exist solely because of one or more major employers, such as the school system, hospital system, or a manufacturer. Someone has to provide services to the employees of these major employers, plus clean and repair their facilities.

Spin-off jobs can be a big deal!

When you manufacture products, you create spin-off businesses. "They say it's a 4-to-1 ratio, which puts JWF's impact to this region at 2,000 jobs," Bill says.

Spin-offs come in various shapes and sizes. Often they're divisions of companies or organizations that then become independent businesses with assets, employees, intellectual property, technology, or existing products that are taken from the parent company.

And many times the spin-off is a totally unrelated existing or start-up enterprise that moves to meet a need that a growing company or project suddenly has.

For example, the Keystone pipeline project has tremendous job-creation potential to the tune of tens of thousands of jobs in the supply chain -- jobs for the manufacturers that make the steel pipe and the thousands of fittings, valves, pumps and control and safety devices required for a major pipeline, not to mention all the equipment needed to build it, or maintain it, plus all the food, lodging and transportation logistics for workers and materials.

If you really want to appreciate down-line activity, don't rush out of the movie theater the next time the last scene in the show fades off the silver screen.

Every movie production creates spin-off jobs. Sit for three minutes at the end of a feature film, and you'll see the names of literally hundreds of people and organizations -- the credits -- that had a role in the movie's production, people other than the big-named stars.

Not convinced?

Stephen Follows is an award-winning writer and producer who also researches data and statistics in the film industry. In his blog (stephenfollows.com), he says the average number of crew credits in his list of top 1,000 films between 1994 and 2013 was 588 people supporting the film's production.

The movie Avatar had 2,984 crew credits while Iron Man listed 3,310.

EPILOGUE
Becoming a truth seeker
Success Can Hinge On Fortitude

Bill Polacek looked in the mirror one day and found a real friend. He learned to exercise the virtues that were the bedrock of his very being. The money and success that followed were merely the scoreboard.

You see, money cannot buy virtue, but virtue can create money, happiness and peace of mind.

These are the thoughts of a friend whose talents include teaching tennis, renovating and renting dilapidated houses, and using his body as a mule. Yes, a mule, the revered four-legged work animal.

Since this book is, in large part, about entrepreneurship, obstacles and leadership, is there a best way to build a successful business? If so, what is it? Maybe this true tale will shed some light on these questions.

My trusted friend and mentor, Robert Palmer, knows a thing or two about obstacles and a lot about honor, and he weaves these stories into his book, *In Search of Honor,* the fictitious Huckleberry Finn and Tom Sawyer-type adventure of two childhood friends, Clint and Ezekiel, who grew up in the mid-1800s on a Charleston, South Carolina plantation.

Can you imagine wearing tennis shoes and carrying, on your back, every piece of a mountain cabin, including its furnishings, a third of a mile up a steep, winding and somewhat slippery mountain pathway, so you could have an off-grid remote wilderness getaway?

My friend did just that. This project was done in the early 1990s. Keep in mind, he had the physical stamina and iron will to pull it off.

A lifelong tennis instructor, who grew up in Louisiana and was educated at LSU, Robert has used the sport he loves to teach thousands of young people how to play tennis and face the challenges in the game of life.

His mountain odyssey was but one step in practicing what he preached: Never give up. Each 10-hour day proved his determination.

Some stuff he carried in his arms, some on his back. He strapped on a worn out hiking backpack and rested lumber over his shoulder on its metal frame. Some materials he simply dragged.

When done he had carried everything, including the kitchen sink, pressure treated lumber, hardwood flooring, insulated windows, water barrels to create a gravity-fed water system, bolts and nails, felt paper, plywood sheathing, metal roofing, a bulky propane water heater, and the toilet.

Over the years Robert mastered the art of associating and communicating the core principles found in the Declaration of Independence and the Constitution of the United States to daily living. And hundreds of young people were the beneficiaries.

Although the words "truth and honor" were not part of everyday conversation as I was growing up, they were principles that my grandparents and parents lived by.

As a longtime encourager, Robert managed to inspire and challenge me as I followed my own journey in life. By his example, he never let me forget where I came from.

Throughout his journey, my brother-in-law, Bill Polacek, remained undaunted in his determination to overcome the obstacles he faced. Fear, doubt, criticism, rejection, insecurity, and having to leave his own comfort zone were at the top of the list.

While we're likely to disagree on the details, **it's difficult to argue with a man's personal testimony, whether in regard to his relationship with God or how he built his business.**

Nearly everyone has heard of the spiritual virtues of faith, hope and charity. The next of The Seven Virtues is fortitude. To never give up, one may have to overcome some pain and adversity.

I saw Robert's endurance increase as the days wore on, but the important points are that he had the *backbone* to start the mountain cabin project and the *will* to finish it.

I'm honored to have Robert write the Epilogue and tell one of his own true stories that lead to his conclusions about my brother-in-law.

Read between the lines and you will understand that Bill's ultimate success was deeply rooted in two points -- a living God and his perception of leadership -- and, by extension, the concepts of truth, honor, faith and ethics.

Robert's Summation

In 1947, my father presented me with a silver dime.
"Here, son, I want you to have this."
Wow! Thanks Dad!
"It's the last dime you will ever receive from me for the rest of your life. Tomorrow we're going to Montgomery Ward's to buy you a lawnmower. I will lend you $10 for the down payment and you will make the payments monthly."

So it was with great excitement I entered the world of business as a 10-year-old. Since I was doing chores as long as I could remember, I had developed a pretty good work ethic.

It wasn't long before I had a thriving business, cutting six lawns a day, netting $15 per day, six days a week. At $90 a week, I was the John D. Rockefeller of the neighborhood.

I had mastered salesmanship and productivity, but I didn't know squat about handling the money. The laws of limitation and accountability had not entered my consciousness, so I treated all my friends to sodas and ice cream sundaes at the local drug store. I had quite a following in the neighborhood.

As my fame for generosity grew, so did my entourage. Kids poured in from other neighborhoods. I was a celebrity, a little big shot!

After several months of making the lawnmower payments and squandering my newly found fortune, I was sitting at the dinner table when my father said, "Son, I want to see you in the living room for a man to man talk." His tone was serious. He always made me nervous. None of our previous man-to-man talks were pleasant.

"Son, looks like your business is doing well. I'm proud of the way you have worked so hard and also made the payments every month."

Thanks Dad. I was relieved.

"Tell me, son, how much money have you saved?"

Ugh, I haven't saved any, Dad.

"Well, I'm curious how you're going to make the payments when the grass quits growing? You can be assured, if you don't make them on time, I'm going to tan your hide. But that's nothing compared to letting Montgomery Ward down by not keeping your word."

His riveting lecture began.

"When you assume debt, you are honor-bound to keep your word."

My father got more specific.

"Suppose that 100 of Montgomery Ward's customers broke their word by not making their payments. Suppose the revenue not received by Montgomery Ward makes it so the business could not pay its own debt. Would the company go out of business? Would its employees lose their jobs? How would they support their families? Would they lose their homes?"

My father looked at me sternly.

"You can see the rippling effect that would impact other people in a negative way, all because you didn't keep your word. You see we are all connected. We are all one big family. You pay your debt because you care about others even more than you care about yourself."

I was spellbound by my father's passion. I knew I would never be able to look in the mirror again if I broke my word. Then and there, I resolved to save my money and get the debt paid off before the grass quit growing for the winter.

My misguided altruism came to an end, and, with it, the loss of my entourage and the destruction of my Rockefeller image.

As my friends disappeared, I found a real friend. He was the guy staring back from the mirror!

Bill Polacek became a truth-seeker. In his quest, **he was helpful, patient, self-sacrificing, determined, and persistent,** and he learned to fully appreciate all the characteristics of a "successful" businessman, husband, parent and leader:

- The value of time.
- The success of perseverance.
- The pleasure of working.
- The dignity of simplicity.
- The worth of character.
- The power of kindness.
- The influence of example.
- The obligation of duty.
- The wisdom of economy.
- The virtue of patience.
- The improvement of talent.
- The nobility of loyalty.
- The joy of doing and originating.
- The warmth of being loved and loving others.
- The exhilaration of being free.
- The knowledge of his divinity.
- The reverence of his soul and of other souls.

Hire the best people, let them do their jobs
CHAPTER 81
Leaders Believe In Making Difference

During his career, three short quotes by famous people quietly resonated with Bill and captured his imagination. **They allude to visionary and creative attributes, hard work, and intestinal fortitude.** Bill relies on them as a personal and business compass:

> Some men see things as they are and say why. Others dream things that never were and ask why not.
> -- Often quoted by John F. Kennedy, but typically attributed to George Bernard Shaw or Pablo Picasso.

> Things may come to those who wait, but only the things left by those who hustle.
> -- Often attributed to Abraham Lincoln.

> One man can make a difference.
> -- Congressman John P. (Jack) Murtha.

The late Congressman John Murtha also used a variation of the "one man" quote: "*You* were put on this earth to make a difference."

Mahatma Gandhi, the non-violent leader of India's independence movement, also believed that one person can make a difference. "In a gentle way, you can shake the world."

Saint Catherine of Siena believed it, too. "Be who God meant for you to be and you will set the world on fire."

Steve Tobak, a management consultant commenting on CBS MoneyWatch, used eight words to describe **the single most common characteristic among successful leaders: "They truly believe they can make a difference."**

Tobak went on to say: "You have no idea how many people you can influence and help just by sharing your experiences and insights. It's a far more generous thing than any material gift you can ever give."

Dr. Martin Luther King, Jr. made a difference in America, and so did Nelson Mandela in South Africa, Mother Theresa in India, and King David in Israel.

Ralph Waldo Emerson, American poet and philosopher, expanded on the thought by using 33 words: "The purpose of life is not to be happy. It is to be useful, to be honorable, to be compassionate, to have it make some difference that you have lived and lived well."

According to various media reports, Arthur Blank's dismissal in the 1970s from a corporate executive position was the impetus he needed to co-found The Home Depot and establish his personal fortune.

He then bought the Atlanta Falcons in 2002 when the football franchise was anything but a Super Bowl contender, and proceeded to change the culture, hire the right people, and build the NFL team into a respectable brand.

"I hire the best people and let them do their jobs," Blank told Tim Rohan, who was writing for *Sports Illustrated* in January 2017. Blank gives his people the resources and emotional support to do their job, Rohan wrote, and the NFL owner makes certain his people "fit into the culture" and get "all the support they need from others."

Blank, who is known for his philanthropy, utilized the same business principles with the Falcons that led to Home Depot's success. His action after Atlanta rolled over the Packers and Seahawks in the playoffs spoke loudly about his core values and servant leadership.

Blank took more than 500 associates -- members of his leadership team -- to the 2017 Super Bowl in Houston, an expensive gesture in that he bought game tickets and paid for flights and lodging. In Blank's mind, "team" goes beyond players and coaches.

Like most successful people, Bill's life is an accumulation of experiences. He once had a job at a welding company where an apparently insecure foreman was given to yelling at and humiliating employees.

"He couldn't intimidate me. I think that bothered him. I learned from that company how *not* to treat people."

Notice the leadership concepts that are common to most successful entrepreneurs: changing the culture, making the right hiring decisions, developing a leadership team, and supporting and appreciating employees.

For several years in the 1950s my father was the Scoutmaster of a Troop in south Alabama. I was a Cub Scout, a couple of years too young to officially join the Boy Scouts.

So it was fitting that I inherited my dad's Handbook for Scoutmasters, copyright 1947. It's a wealth of knowledge about leading young boys to take their place as intelligent citizens in a democracy.

The handbook asserts that the relationship between a Scoutmaster and his boy leaders "is the biggest single factor" in a Troop's success, and that means making the Patrol Method work. (In scouting Patrols are small groups of scouts within a Troop working together as a team and sharing responsibility for its success.)

The test of this method is in the easy chair, a veteran Scoutmaster once told a puzzled audience.

If you can relax in a chair for the duration of a typical Boy Scout meeting and not worry about its success, then your Troop is using the Patrol Method, he explained, and "your boy leaders are actually leading."

Author and business executive F. John Reh says, the **"only way to truly learn to lead is to engage in doing so."**

Writing online (thebalance.com), he acknowledges that although "some individuals are naturally strong communicators or strategic thinkers, leaders are mostly made and not born."

Is your dream rooted in reality?
CHAPTER 82
America's Biggest Natural Disaster

Devils Tower is an isolated, stump-shaped granite formation with vertical sides and a small, relatively flat top that stands 867 feet from summit to base and attracts thousands of climbers annually.

Devils Tower was the first declared United States National Monument in 1906. The 1977 science fiction adventure movie *Close Encounters of the Third Kind* used the butte as a plot element and as the location of its climactic scenes.

The northeastern Wyoming landmark is considered sacred ground by many American Indians.

In a way, JWF Industries in Johnstown was built on sacred ground, too, utilizing gigantic abandoned buildings from another era.

The Cambria Iron Company, founded in 1852, was part of America's Industrial Revolution.

After several name changes, the company was sold to Bethlehem Steel in 1923. Bethlehem Steel was America's second largest steel producer and largest shipbuilder.

Today, JWF makes its home at this enduring historic site.

The nearly 900-foot Johnstown Inclined Plane, billed as the "world's steepest vehicular inclined plane," is visible on a nearby hill having a grade of 71 percent.

The nearby Polacek Pavilion, a public gathering place, is surrounded by a rich history.

The nearby iconic seven-arch stone three-train-track bridge, built by the Pennsylvania Railroad, spans the Conemaugh River and serves as a reminder of the Great Flood of 1889 when 2,209 people were killed.

While the bridge survived the onslaught of floodwaters and debris, the overall devastation completely altered the future of Johnstown forever.

"It's still the biggest national disaster in American history," says Bill. "The Great Flood is a lesson in perseverance and the positive impact of the human spirit. This area's leadership, entrepreneurial spirit, and the great American Dream are alive and thriving."

The American Dream is an integral part of Bill's success story, mainly because his dream was about so much more than financial success.

For decades, the American Dream was more centered on materialistic gains. Then came change.

Kimberly Amadeo, writing for an online website (thebalance.com), reveals a different view as she quotes the Center for a New American Dream (newdream.org) which envisions "a focus on more of what really matters, such as creating a meaningful life, contributing to community and society, valuing nature, and spending time with family and friends."

Financial advisor Suze Orman writes that a new American Dream is now emerging, one that's rooted in reality. Family and responsibility have replaced the want for the biggest house on the block, she says.

"It's a dream where you actually get more pleasure out of saving than you do spending," Orman says in her book, *The Money Class*. "It's a dream where you live below your means but within your needs."

For the bulk of Americans at retirement age or older, our grandparents and great-grandparents had it figured out: Save some money, do not try to keep up with Tom, Dick or Harry, be responsible, and work hard, but not to the exclusion of a good night's sleep and pleasant interactions with family and friends.

Jayne Gest, a writer for *Smart Business Pittsburgh*, captured Bill's simple management essence when she cited three "takeaways" from a 2015 interview:

- Make your employees part of the solution.
- The best way to predict the future is to create it.
- Get creative in order to start overcoming challenges.

Cambria Iron has a proud railroad heritage.

"I feel strongly that JWF is God's company. I honor Him," says Bill. **He puts his faith into action every day with this prayer:**

Dear God. Please give me the wisdom, intelligence, and emotional intelligence to take your companies, make them successful, and use that success in order to glorify you, and help my employees and their families and this community succeed.

BONUS CHAPTER
Memories often smack of reality
Funny facts, historical insights

This is "bonus material" that won't likely shed any light on how to be a leader or start a business. But it might be a little informative and worth a laugh or two.

Weddings make grown men cry -- Debbie, the second oldest, was the first to marry. The atmosphere at the wedding was more like a funeral as her father, in tears, walked her down the aisle. "I was moving away, which didn't help."

There was one consolation: Debbie's husband, John Rheel, was fond of her little brothers and he easily accepted the role of Big Brother and often played ball with them and allowed them to visit. But he wasn't always a trusted visitor at Debbie's home!

Big John and Sally objected to their daughter being alone with John when the two were dating; after all, he was five years older. So Debbie's fiancé gladly packed the brothers, or sisters Vicki and Sally Ann, in the car and headed to the drive-in theater where he and his future bride would cozy up in the back seat with the "official chaperones" sitting up front.

The boys were told to "never look in the back seat."

John handed out money freely and sent them off to the concession stand to buy candy and popcorn. And sometimes he delayed their return by moving his car.

FUN FACT: John Rheel went on to become a Pennsylvania State Trooper and later sheriff of Washington County, Pennsylvania. AND THE LAW WON!

Johnstown's famous department store -- Rick Truscello, who is married to Bill's sister, Vicki, was already skeptical about Santa as his mother led him upstairs to sit on the jolly gentleman's knee at Glosser's in downtown Johnstown where she worked.

FUN FACT: As Rick stepped away after reciting his Wish List, the white-bearded fellow in the red suit called out to Rick's mother, "Dorothy, did those cigars I ordered come in?" BUMMER!

Cheap or thrifty -- Bill was about 21 years old and dating his future wife, Shari. The two young lovebirds spent a week with one of his sisters on the beach in Florida. The menu at a local restaurant advertised that coffee was included in the cost of the meal. Because of his humble beginnings, Bill watched every penny.

FUN FACT: Before ordering, Bill called the waiter over to verify that the menu was correct, and coffee was included. PENNY SAVED!

Washing clothes a tough chore -- In pioneer days, chores were usually scheduled according to practicality and necessity. A typical week might involve washing on Monday, ironing on Tuesday, mending on Wednesday, churning on Thursday, cleaning on Friday, baking on Saturday, worship and rest on Sunday.

But there was no baking on Saturdays at the Polacek household. The girls were required to polish 11 pairs of shoes and clean seven rooms, top to bottom. The two oldest fought constantly. Attending the Saturday night church dance was off limits if chores weren't finished.

FUN FACT: Although Big John would rather have rested his weary bones, he always stayed up past his bedtime and waited at the street corner, wearing his pajamas, for his daughters to come walking down the road after the dance. SELF-SACRIFICING FATHER!

Ironing for nine kids -- Sally washed and pressed all outfits. Yep, all of them, including handkerchiefs! She was a stickler for cleanliness.

FUN FACT: Although her washer was a wringer model and she had no dryer, the kids were not allowed to wear their clothes two days in a row. BACKBREAKING!

Visiting angels -- During the Christmas season, John, Sally and children visited family and friends every night. Every night! None of this reaching out by texting.

FUN FACT: This no longer happens. MISS THE PERSONAL TOUCH.

Crank up the radio, it's polka time -- Sunday was a day set aside for family and rest in the Polacek household. "Mom would not allow us to even yell," recalls Sally Ann. The radio dial would be turned from station to station all day for continuous songs until the humming and static drowned out the last note of polka music as the sun went down.

FUN FACT: John danced with his wife and four daughters for hours, with his arms bouncing up and down like a chicken walking on hot coals. YOU GOTTA HAVE A STRONG HEART!

Donuts by the bushel -- Grandma Eva fried a wicker clothes basket full of sugar-coated donuts every so often, and aunts, uncles and cousins would gather at her home to enjoy the treats. After they aged awhile, the donuts were like rocks (good for dunkin' in coffee though). Children learned to respect their elders, who only spoke in Slovak.

FUN FACT: Martin and Eva showed little affection for the grandkids, but demonstrated their love by providing food, essentials, and desserts. A BUSHEL, YOU'RE KIDDING!

Soft ice cream was a special treat -- Taking a family ride and getting a nickel cup every Sunday at the Tasty Freeze was a regular family outing. On the way, the kids could see the highway flying by through the rusty holes in the floorboards of the family's battered station wagon.

FUN FACT: At age 11, the kids were allowed to order a dime cone, instead of a nickel version. SORRY, NO REFILLS!

House shook when carpets were cleaned -- Carpets were shaken vigorously in Eva's home, just like in the military. White billboard paper was spread everywhere to protect the floors and rugs and keep them from getting dirty.

FUN FACT: Martin carefully spit his tobacco juice in a coal bucket (so did his friends). GOD HELP THE SPITTER THAT MISSED!

Television was a family affair -- Once they got a TV in the house, the Polacek family watched the Lawrence Welk Show on Saturday night, provided someone ventured outside and carefully adjusted the antenna for the best signal to get rid of the shadows and most of the snow on the black and white screen.

Can you hear Big John? "That's it. That's it. You got it!"

FUN FACT: Of course, the four Lennon Sisters were favorites. DON'T GIVE THE FOUR POLACEK SISTERS ANY IDEAS!

The famous neighborhood train -- Big John, whose nickname was Unk to his nephews, had a way of turning his welding skills into unique civic contributions. He crafted iron work for his church and welded steel racks for a chicken BBQ tradition that continues to this day.

Big John exhibited kindness, gentleness, and father-figure ways. He was a good judge of character, and he was the guy who built a 'train' of several four-wheel carts with seats and padding that hooked together and hauled three or four kids each around the neighborhood behind a riding lawnmower.

FUN FACT: Kids loved him. EVERYONE LOVED BIG JOHN!

It was tough working inside a boiler -- Most of the boiler work was routine, except some boilers were a tight fit for a grown man. "You could set yourself on fire inside a boiler. It was a rough job. At the end of the day you had to take three baths to get clean from that soot and stuff," remembers Joe Polacek, family historian.

Big John and Joe worked on nearly every boiler in Johnstown -- hospitals, high schools, and greenhouses. Small boilers, like those typically used in tailor shops, were brought to John's place for repairs.

In those days, there were no Occupational Safety and Health Administration (OSHA) inspections. It was a hot, sweaty job, often done while lying on one's back.

SAD FACT: John and his helpers did not protect themselves in any way, not with respirators, safety glasses or ear plugs. THEY DIDN'T KNOW ANY BETTER!

Chewing tobacco was king in the steel mills -- A few men in the mills smoked, but most chewed. John's favorite was Cutty Pipe, which advertised itself as an "old friend of many thousands of men who know good tobacco when they smoke or chew it." John knew little if anything about the dangers of chewing the Burley leaf.

When Big John was working, he kept a wad in his cheek, and he had a habit of spitting his juice on the floor of his garage, where his helpers often mopped it up on their shirts as they crawled under vehicles.

"My brothers (Bob and Charlie Polacek) would get so mad at Unk," recalled Joe. "He'd be working under a car and spitting. Next thing you know, you'd be under the car, too, and have spitting tobacco all over you."

It wasn't just the shop floor, juice flowed down the side of John's car. He spit and splattered out the window freely.

FUN FACT: Sally had no hate in her heart for any soul, but she hated John's tobacco use. GOD, GIVE ME PATIENCE.

Family was musically talented -- By the 5th grade, Bob realized he had an ear for music. He learned the accordion in three lessons. "Three times, that's it," he insisted. Bob also played the piano, tuba and trumpet.

who was single, attractive and robust, stood in the man's face, raised both arms in the air, and clenched both fists.

FUN FACT: She shook her right hand, bare knuckles tight and red, and snarled, "Which do you want? My right fist, my left fist, or both fists? Leave my cousins alone!" THE DRUNK LEFT. I WOULD, TOO!

The age of the automobile -- Big John's nephew Bob was well liked by the children. He was older and often brought ice cream and donuts to Grandma Polacek's house where the family would gather after church. Although small in stature, he was protective of the girls.

Bob once brought a wayward sailor home for the weekend, intent on giving the guy some direction in his life. The sailor quickly took a fancy to the older girls, forcing Bob to warn him to stay away from his cousins.

Bob owned a 1917 Dodge touring car. "I loved riding in that thing," said eldest daughter, Barbara. "We used to feel so special. He'd say, 'Come on Barbara and Debbie. I'll take you for a ride.'"

FUN FACT: Bob was 10 years older than Barbara. YES, YOUNG WOMEN LOVE FANCY CARS!

Bob Polacek joined the U.S. Navy.

The two eldest Polacek sisters, Barbara and Debbie, were musical, too, and they'd bring their clarinets and get together some Sunday afternoons and play polkas with Bob.

FUN FACT: Bob's father and his grandfather Martin played the tuba. WHO NEEDS A RECORD PLAYER?

Am I on time -- Bill managed to succeed in spite of himself. Punctuality is not one of his strong traits. "Believe it or not, Bill was late for a meeting." That line was heard from many close associates, friends, and family members during interviews for this book. It proves one thing; you don't have to be perfect.

FUN FACT: Any entrepreneur can come up short on a basic skill or two and still succeed by over-compensating with his or her strong points. PROOF IS IN THE PUDDING.

Longing to understand one's roots -- Four Polacek siblings -- three sisters and one brother -- landed in Budapest after a 10-hour flight over the Atlantic in 2013 by way of Washington, D.C. and Amsterdam, on their way to the town where their grandparents were married.

Accompanied by several spouses and children, the siblings were on a mission to gain some understanding of their heritage. A phone call to the town's mayor led to the discovery of three distant cousins.

Three women -- a grandmother, mother and daughter, ranging in age from mid-20s to mid-70s -- lived in Moravske Lieskove, Slovakia. This was the birthplace of Martin and Eva Polacek, parents of Big John and his brothers, Mike and Joe, Sr.

The three women were excited to greet their American relatives. The grandmother kept pouring what appeared to be a "strong home brew" for her American guests. Then the travelers from the U.S. were taken to a local pub and treated to a Coca Cola. It's not every day that American women show up in a local pub.

The town drunk wasn't too inebriated to recognize his opportunity. He fastened his eyes on one of the American women and made suggestive remarks until Lubomira Bohackova,